WHERE THE GREAT CITY STANDS

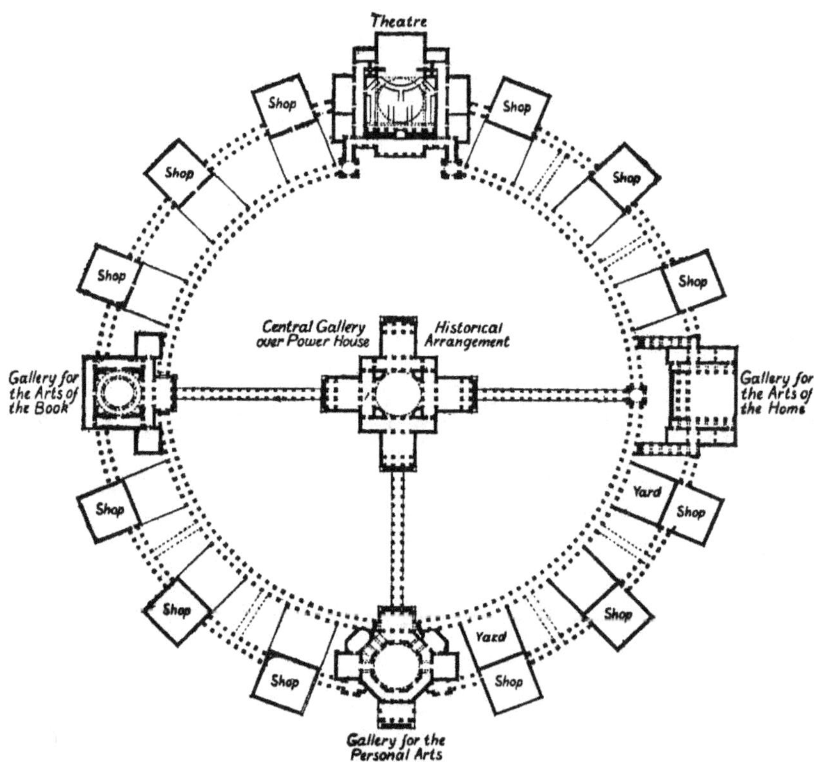

Diagrammatic representation showing how within each city the qualitative standard should be reintroduced into life by the transformation of Art Schools and Galleries into Creative Guilds.

Where the Great City Stands

A Study in the New Civics

BY

C. R. ASHBEE

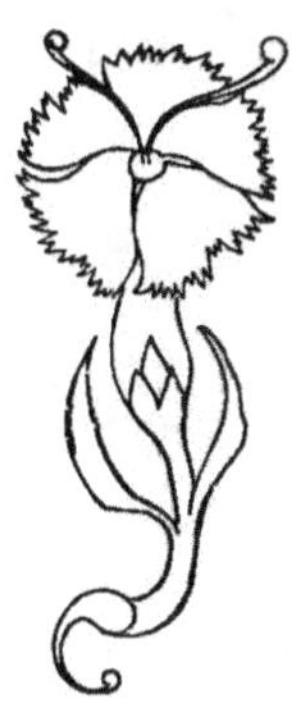

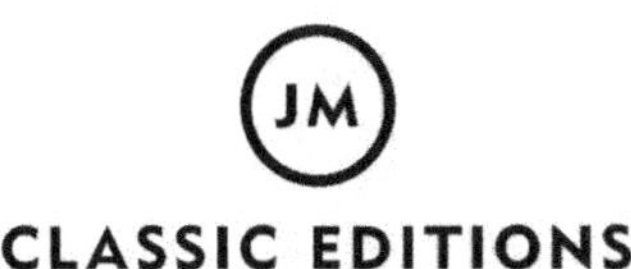

CLASSIC EDITIONS

This edition digitally re-mastered and
published by JM Classic Editions © 2008
Original text © C R Ashbee 1917

ISBN 978-1-905217-96-0

ERRATUM.

On page 149 for Diagram No. 36 read Diagram No. 38.

INTRODUCTION

HOW much of the constructive effort of the last fifty years shall we save from the wreck of the War? We cannot for many years hope to answer the question. On all sides, in Europe, certainly in England, the finer things are withering; schools and workshops closed down, great purposes laid by or definitely abandoned, and the creative enterprise of a generation to all appearance thrown away. "There will be a time for all that after the War," men say; "this is not the moment for the thoughtful, the imaginative things of life. We are at the nadir of human folly, and all must join in." Thus we buoy ourselves up with an optimism that acts as a drug.

Yet I have found that many of my soldier friends at the front have often taken a different view on these matters from those who stay at home, and it is with the young men who return that the shaping of the new state is to be. So it has seemed to me worth while, in the intervals of other work, to set down the ideals some of us had before the War came upon us.

I have tried to interpret the æsthetic movements through which we lived before the War, and to show their connexion with the catastrophe through which we have been living since 1914. Perhaps the deductions will be useful to those happier countries that may be saved from what Europe is suffering, to the young cities of America and the British Colonies destined to carry on the torch of Western civilization. My own belief—shared but by a few artists, poets, thinkers, who have little standing in a world of practical men engaged in general slaughter—is that if the æsthetic qualities, those that make for standard in life and workmanship, and that for me are the reasonable qualities in man, had been given greater scope, there would have been no War. It may be urged that Erasmus held that view at the break up of the Middle Ages, and that Plato and Thucydides said much the same.

Perhaps they did; but whatever the defeats of the idealists from time to time in human history, we must none the less keep before us the greater constructive purposes in life. The French psychologist, Le Bon, whose writings on the changing mentality of the peoples have been widely read (except perhaps in England) since the outbreak of the War, illustrates the disintegration of European society from a manifesto of the French Socialists in 1914: "This fight of ours with society," say they, "can only have one ending, the break up of society and the capitalist state itself, the seizure by the proletariat of all the instruments of production, purchase, and exchange. To bring this about, our party (the French Socialists) will employ every possible means of action—electoral, parliamentary, direct interference, the strike, or general insurrection." And then with pitiless logic, but none the less ignoring those greater needs in man which in these pages I have tried to describe, he shows how they were accomplishing this end before the War.

In England, America, and Central Europe the same disintegrating process is at work. The French Socialists do but give it a more extreme, more logical, more Latin expression. And the War, though it seems for the moment to have checked, has in reality hastened the process of disintegration.

But what is the real way of checking it? Is it by blind negation, and such resistance as we in England have shown during the last two decades to all new constructive enterprise, to all new ideas? By no means. It is by setting up, within our disintegrating society, new groups among the working people themselves, having a new creative purpose. That purpose must be *standard* and *quality* in men and things; in short, the method of the Arts. It is only by the method of the Arts that the disintegration of society can be checked, and the finer reconstruction brought about. A little of this method, and the hope that inspired it, I have tried in the following pages to set forth.

My thanks are due to those whose names are given at the head of the blocks they have kindly lent me, also to Mr. Alec Miller for his drawing of the qualitative and quantitative standard and for cutting the block on the cover.

C. R. ASHBEE.

Campden,

Gloucestershire.

September 1917.

CONTENTS

vii

ILLUSTRATIONS

ILLUSTRATIONS

ILLUSTRATIONS

WHERE THE GREAT CITY STANDS

CHAPTER I.—The Object of the Book, An Appeal to the Practical Idealist.

The object of this book is to fix public attention upon the æsthetic movements of our time, to find out what they mean and how they are interwoven or lead one into the other. It is an attempt to show what lies behind the City Life, and the obverse of this, the new life of the country, agricultural or suburban. These æsthetic movements, which we are only just beginning to regard as one great vitalizing force, are not merely English or American movements. The same causes that have made thoughtful people in England, America, or the British Colonies look for something in life better or more beautiful than the mere getting of money and the gathering together of material goods, have been at work in Germany, France, Belgium, indeed wherever we find Industrialism. I want to show the unity in all this striving, and to give hope through the understanding of this unity.

The book does not purport to be technical. It is not a book for experts. It is written by an architect who has spent most of his professional life in designing, building, planning, or, better still, in trying to feel his way through the different Arts and the social forces those Arts reflect. The architect is at best an interpreter. It is a part of his job to understand the life that goes on around him, to make it a little nobler here, a little less squalid there; to help people to live, while himself living and creating to the top of his bent. This practical poetry of life is what he has to aim at and realize in himself and others. The different movements—æsthetic, social, political, religious—through which we pass, then, are among the things he has to try to understand. His own work—it may not be much that he does—will be better by understanding the life that goes on around him, be a finer interpretation of that life and its needs.

The appeal not technical.

I

THE OBJECT OF THE BOOK

The appeal, then, is not so much to the expert, who is supposed to know, as to the practical man—the idealist, man or woman, who wants to see something of the finer life built up around him, wants to help in it and understand it. There are hundreds of such men and women, who tell you sadly that life is short, that they want to do something, to see results. It is to them I want to appeal. I hope to do this if I can convince them of the unity of my subject. And here there is a curious thing to note : these people keep on making the discovery that what they thought was a great new hope turns out to be after all but the fashion of a moment; much as the new process a clever child discovers, and then drops, having discovered it. I want to show that this is not true of life ; that each of these new movements, fashions if we like so to call them, is a part of the one finer life we are trying to build up. This finer life, for me, is the life of Industrial Democracy.

As for our own particular job, whether it be a petty craft or a large industrial concern, whether it be some betterment scheme we run as a hobby, or some educational enterprise for ourselves or our neighbours, if we are in earnest about it and handle it properly it will make its mark. Sincerity is the only thing that counts.

CHAPTER II.—Axioms.

In a previous work that had to do with the teaching of the Arts* I based my arguments upon six axioms. These have so far not been controverted, and as they lie at the root of my subject—the Arts as an integral part of Civics—I repeat them. Further, I have added four other axioms, Nos. vii, viii, ix, and x ; these seem to me necessary now that we are considering the subject of the Arts from the point of view of the citizen rather than of the teacher.

AXIOM I.—Modern civilization rests on machinery, and no system for the encouragement, or the endowment, or the teaching of the arts can be sound that does not recognize this.

AXIOM II.—The crafts cannot be learned in the school; the crafts can only be learned in the life of the workman in the workshop.

AXIOM III.—The purpose of the Arts and Crafts (understood as an æsthetic movement) is to "individualize," to set a standard of excellence in all commodities in which the element of beauty enters. The tendency of machine industry is to "standardize"—that is to say, to create as many pieces of any commodity to a given type as is economically possible.

AXIOM IV.—There is a Gresham's Law in the industrial arts as there is in coinage. In the latter the bad coin tends to drive out the good. In the former the bad product tends to drive out the good product, the unskilled workman and the machine tend to drive out the skilled craftsman.

AXIOM V.—Machinery is neither all good nor all bad. An intelligent community will distinguish which is which, and the æsthetic education of the community in our day should be directed towards this distinction between the bad and the good.

AXIOM VI.—The distinction between what should and what should not be produced by machinery has in many trades and crafts now been made. This has been the discovery of the last twenty-five years.

AXIOM VII.—The new relationship of man to life which machine industry has brought with it, finds its fullest expression in the new life of our city. This implies that through the city and its proper adjustment to mechanical conditions will man realize again those finer values which the arts bring into life. Through the city we focus civilization.

* "Should We Stop Teaching Art ?" (Batsford. 1912.)

AXIOM VIII.—*Man's control of mechanical power has yet to be made effective. The making it effective is not only a matter of inventing or exploiting new processes, it is the discovering of means whereby mechanical power shall be best used in the public service—in other words, how it shall be " socialized," and not merely used to enable men to exploit each other. As Hellenic civilization made the gentleman with the aid of the slave, so we may make the gentleman with the aid of the machine.*

AXIOM IX.—*The arts, postulating as they do the motive of joy in their creation, and the freedom of the individual to go on creating, do not flourish under conditions where men think it right to exploit them for profit.*

AXIOM X.—*In an industrial civilization, the reconstructed city cannot be stable without a corresponding reconstruction of the country. Town and country should be correlated and react upon one another. This correlation is a necessary consequence of the conditions of machine industry.*

CHAPTER III.—How the Art Influences of Our Time Have Come to Us.

These axioms we will pick up from time to time as we go on; let us now briefly review the Art influences of our time, and try to find out what they stand for. They have come to us mainly in three ways: (1) in the form of teaching and stimulus from the artists themselves; (2) as a part of the social enthusiasm—a force not primarily æsthetic—that has had so much to do with the constructive work of the beginning of our century; (3) through new ideas of a quasi-religious nature from the East.

The first is best illustrated in the principles held by the painters of the three schools that have followed each other in our time, the Pre-Raphaelites, the Impressionists, the Post-Impressionists and Futurists. With these principles I deal below.

The Art influences that have come to us as the result of a social rather than a purely æsthetic stimulus are more important and far-reaching. They touch us in the reconstruction of our cities, they are in some cases giving us new cities, they imply a new workshop life and a remodelling of our schools. With all these I shall deal later (in Chapters V, VII, VIII, XII, XIII).

The Art influences that have come through what to us are new ideas from the East are not so easy to define. They are subtle. It is not so much that they have inspired definite schools of painting, architecture, or craftsmanship, as one might take Sumner Green's building on the Pacific coast and say " There is the Orient "; or Tagore's painting and say " Here in modern form is India "; or William de Morgan's lustre ware and pottery and say " This is Persia." Rather have they from time to time by a subtle alchemy entered into the minds of our artists and our social thinkers.

The doctrine of Evolution has now become part of our thought. *Art and* No æsthetic philosophy is conceivable without it. We realize now *Evolution.* the " ascent of man towards truth, goodness, and beauty," and the tremendous hopefulness that comes from this knowledge pushes all other things on one side. We know now that if we practise an Art that is no longer in and of our own time, that Art is of little consequence. It is in that knowledge that we are cut off from our fathers—the men whom we knew and admired in the nineteenth century.

HOW THE ART INFLUENCES OF OUR TIME HAVE COME

A novel of Maria Edgworth's turns on the question whether the amenities of a great estate are to give place to a coal shaft—beauty and history versus development. Romance is in both, but the hero's choice is still a personal one. To the later Victorians, however, the forces of progress came in the form of Necessity. Personal choice was no longer possible. We had done with romance that the individual could take or leave.

This blind Necessity has now given place to another that is no longer blind. Who shall control the hidden power? Is the possession and enjoyment of Beauty a mere chance after all, and Aladdin's lamp the property of whoever picks it up and rubs it? Is Beauty itself mere enjoyment? These are the questions our generation is putting, and we are answering them in ways of our own. The difference between us and the later Victorians is that for us Necessity is not in the Mechanical power, but in the Will that is to dominate it. For us Beauty is no longer mere enjoyment. Much less is it the enjoyment of a privileged class. We do not accept the hedonistic view. For us Beauty is a spiritual force pervading all things, a heritage into which every one is born, a state to which every one can attain—more or less, according to his power or his sympathy. On this conviction the new social order is being built up, and the War has helped us to find out how best this order shall be regulated. We may have ten, twenty, fifty years of reaction; but we can never go back to the old fundamentals, to the belief that man is a fallen or pardoned outcast, to the certainty of a fixed scheme to which everything must in the end conform. On this hopefulness, this sense of the unfolding of God within ourselves, this new Humanism, the Art of the future, even as the new social order, is being formed.

Our artists do not consciously preach these new truths; but they feel them. When we talk with them individually we find this is so, and often in their work they instinctively interpret. But when the Victorians, who had not yet assimilated the doctrine of Evolution, turned from the ugliness and horror of actual things to the creation of beauty, it was as to a world outside. Through the Oxford Movement in England there were churches to make and beautify— even as Bodley made Hoar Cross (see Nos. 1, 2), or Burne-Jones in his drawings and Tennyson in his verses gave us an artificial Round Table of gentlemanly and emasculated knights, or Morris bade us " forget the piston stroke " and enter into an earthly Paradise entirely remote from life. For all our artists, whether in words or plastic

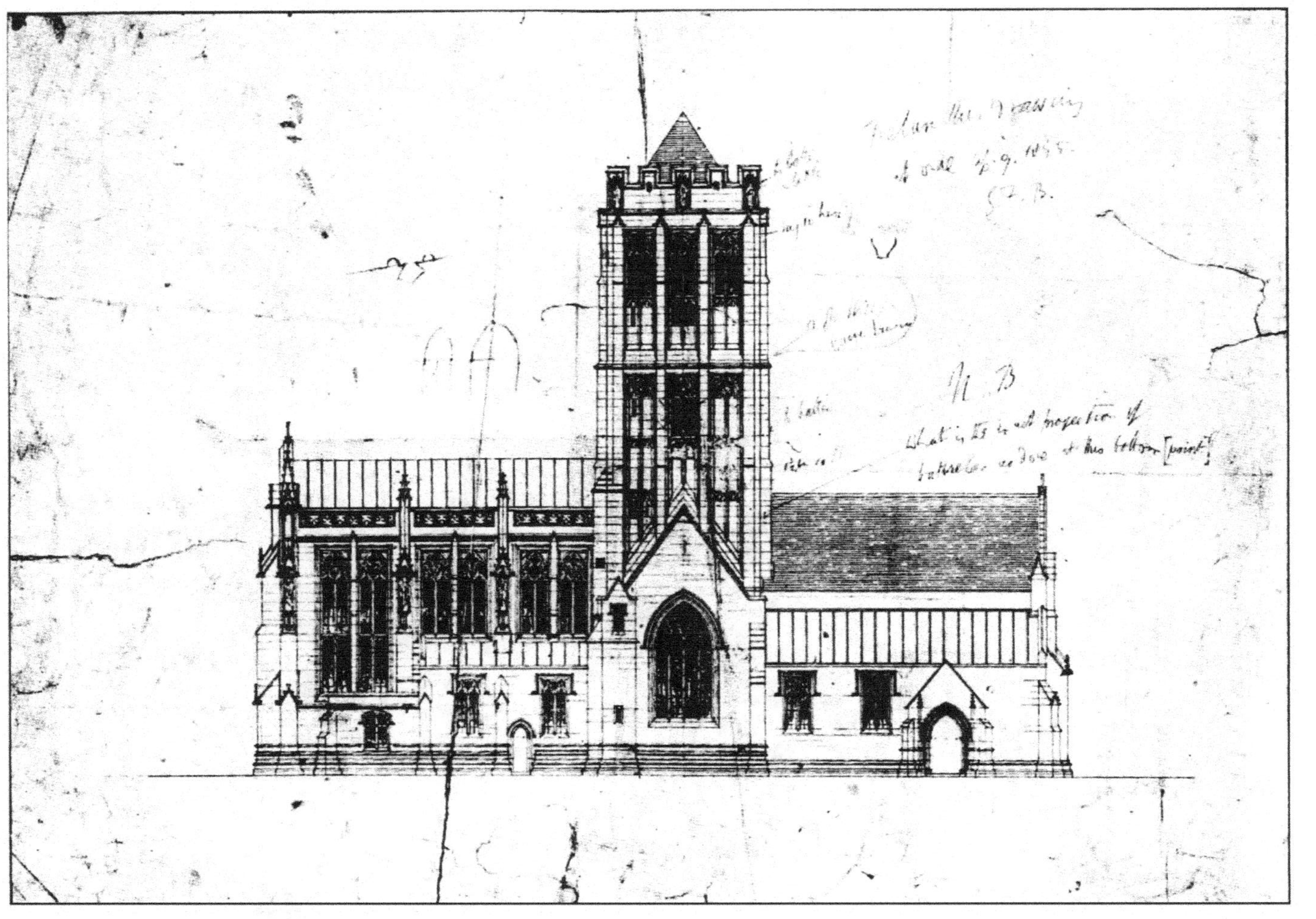

Church of the Holy Angels, Hoar Cross.
By G. F. Bodley.

One of the original working drawings.   It will be observed that the drawing has on it the master's autograph notes and instructions to the builder.

No. 1.

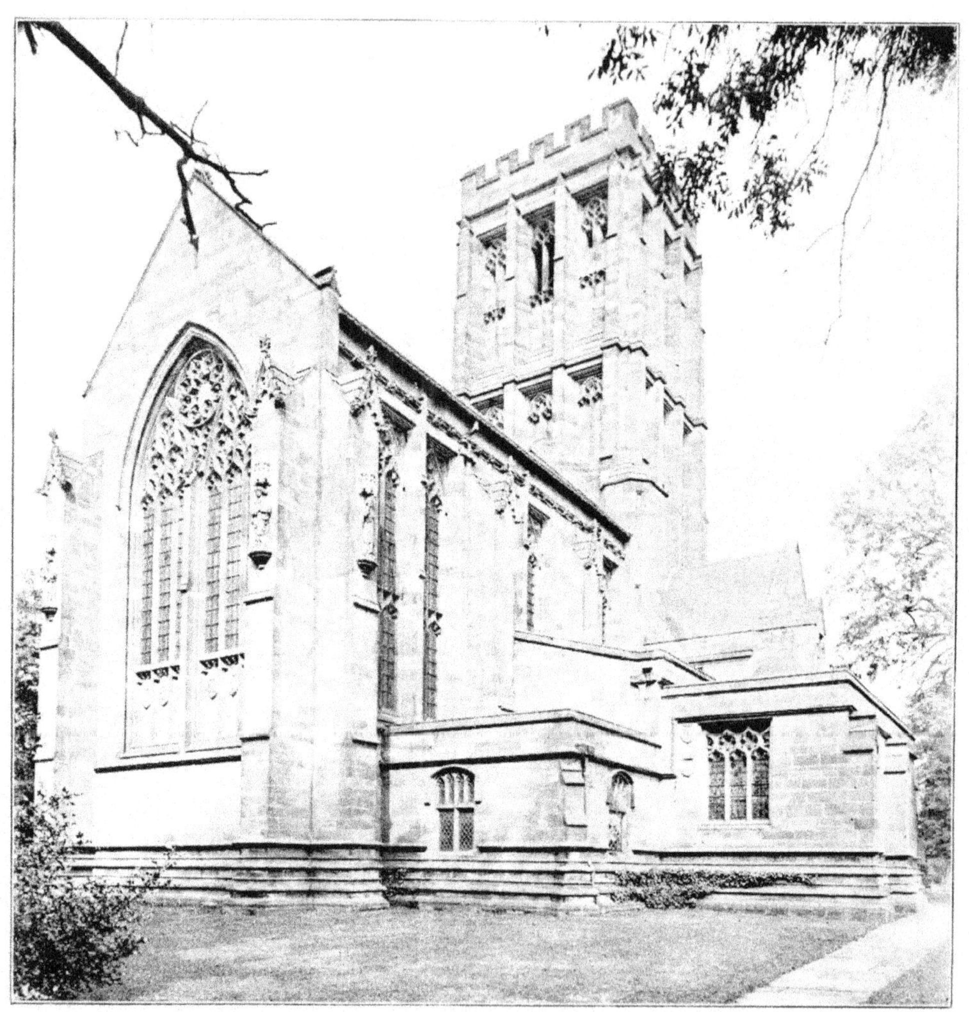

Church of the Holy Angels, Hoar Cross.
By G. F. Bodley.

No. 2.

form, Keats became the type, because he best showed how we could get away from blind Necessity and

> . . . keep
> A bower quiet for us, and a sleep
> Full of sweet dreams, and health, and quiet breathing.

But all that is over. However beautiful the things these men created, they are as remote from us now as the Rococo was from them. The red line of the War divides us. The War has somehow shown us that if the Arts henceforth are to have any validity they can no longer be outside life ; they must be within it. We could not have been fighting in the last years as we have, had it not been in the conviction of our ascent towards "Truth, Goodness, and Beauty." But this applies to our enemies just as much as to ourselves. All Art from now on can be but the mirror of this conviction.

CHAPTER IV.—THE PRE-RAPHAELITE INSPIRATION.

The great Mid-Victorian influence in æsthetics came from the Pre-Raphaelite painters in England. It was far-reaching and profound. It affected not only the painters themselves, but the architects, the makers of books and book illustration, and, indeed, all who were engaged in finer creative work with the hands.

Pre-Raphaelitism and the need for the Arts in life. It did more than this : it changed our point of view towards the Arts, made them assume a much more important and vital position in life. The Pre-Raphaelite movement made them more serious and real; it made them, for all thoughtful people, greatly worth having. All this has so often been written about that it is superfluous for me to go into it again. I want, however, to show what were the ideas behind, and this is best done by quoting W. M. Rossetti's sonnet which appeared on the title-page of "The Germ," the little paper this group of young artists used for disseminating their ideas :—

> If whoso merely hath a little thought
> > Will plainly think the thought that is in him,
> > Not imagining another's, bright or dim,
> Not mangling with new words what others taught ;
>
> If whoso speaks, from having either sought
> > Or only found, will speak not just to skim
> > A shallow surface with words made and trim,
> But in that very speech the matter brought . . .

"Let us get back to reality ; let us have something to say ; let us shirk no detail; let us be sincere," said these men ; and we see it finely set forth in such noble pictures as Holman Hunt's "Shadow of the Cross" (No. 3), or Ford Madox Brown's "Last of England" (No. 4), or Rossetti's "Annunciation" (No. 5). Earnestness and spiritual intensity was their object; or, as they themselves put it, "to express the qualities of sincerity and directness, of honesty and definite inspiration, which they discerned in the painters before Raphael."

It is difficult for us now to put ourselves into the Mid-Victorian mood, or to understand that break with the conventions of English middle-class Protestantism and propriety which the work of these men implied. A subsequent generation of painters has cast aside

By the courtesy of Messrs. Agnew.

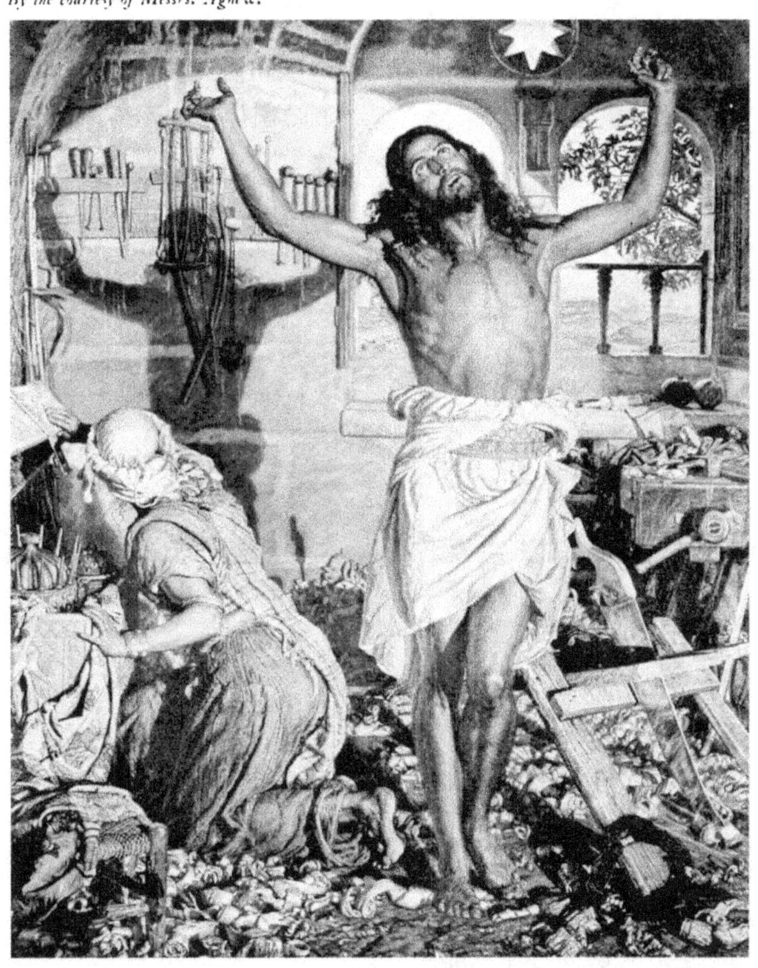

No. 3.

"The Shadow of the Cross."
By Holman Hunt.

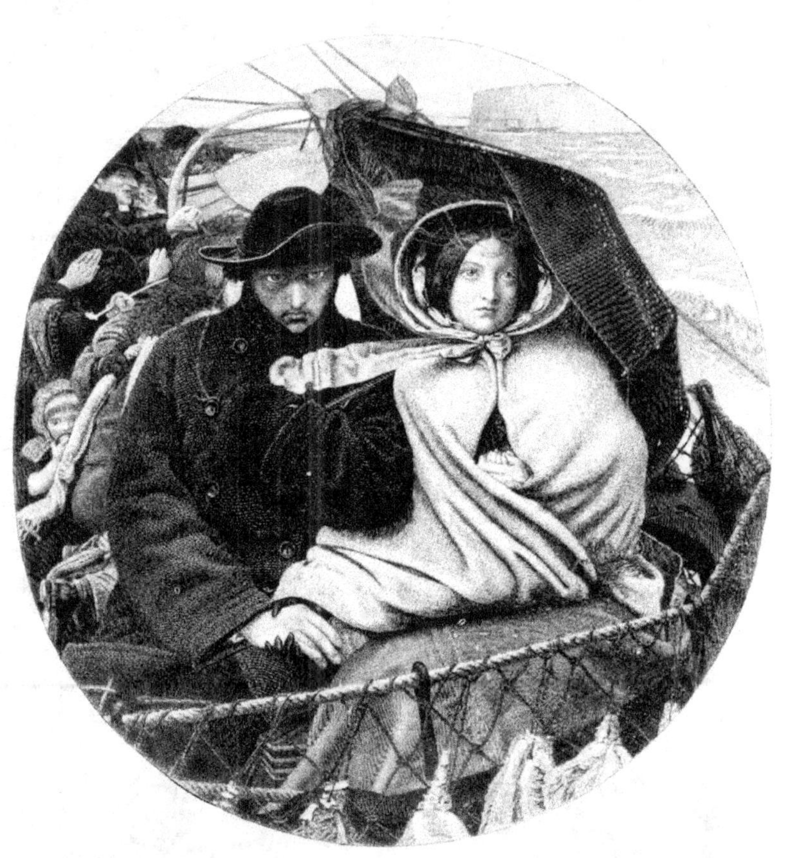

No. 4.

" The Last of England."
By Ford Madox Brown.

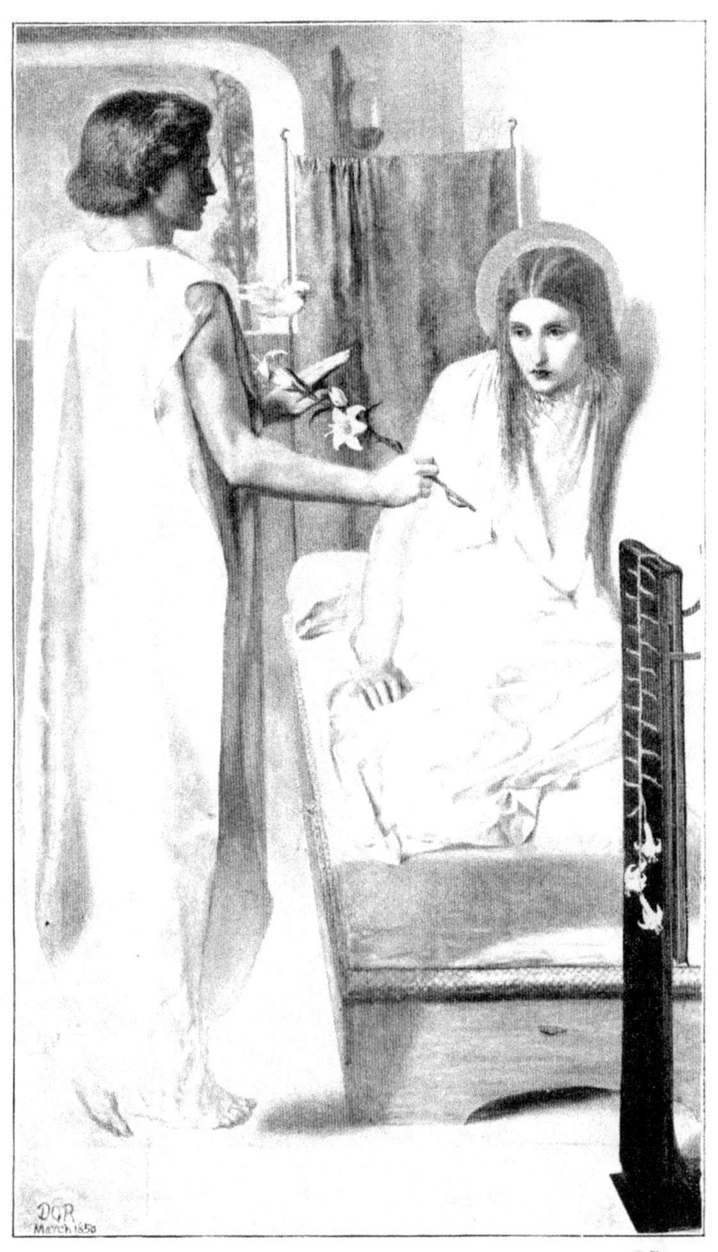

"The Annunciation." By Dante Gabriel Rossetti.   No. 5.

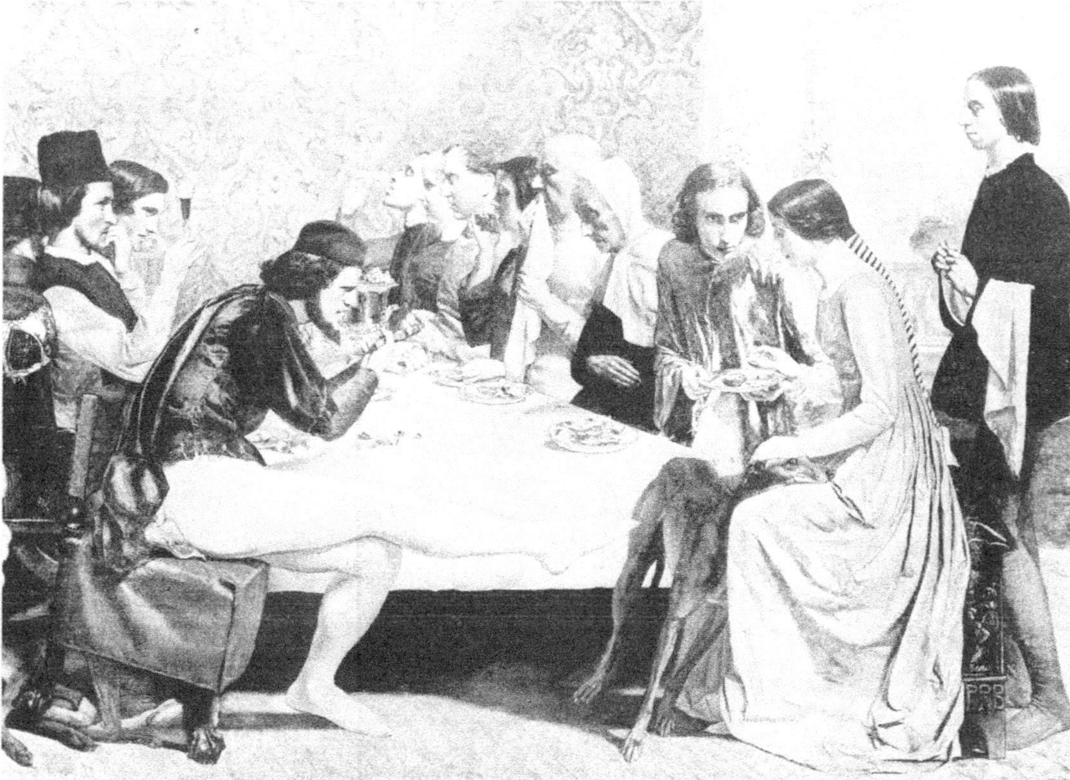

" Lorenzo and Isabella."
By John Everett Millais.

No. 6.

what it called the "anecdotic" in the choice of subject; but in the work of these men it was precisely the choice of subject and the way the subject was handled that implied reality and rebellion. We see this in their choice of Keats—they all chose Keats—and in their choice of religious subjects, especially from the life of Christ.

Keats was the artists' poet, the painter in words and epithet; to use him, explore him, develop him, as Millais did, for instance, in the "Lorenzo and Isabella" (No. 6), was a direct challenge to all conventions. As for the handling of the Christian story, or, worse still, what any young whipper-snapper of genius chose himself to put into it, this appeared to the conventional bourgeois of that age unspeakably shocking. It was flat blasphemy against a Godhead men carried within themselves, but which they no longer knew how to interpret. When those young reformers rent the temple veil, men and women who had a sympathy for beauty, and were not afraid to face the truth, suddenly saw colour and light.

"It is impossible for me to describe to you the thrill that passed through us," said an old lady to me as she recalled that generation, "when first we saw the Pre-Raphaelite pictures. You are so blunted, you don't know what it means; but we were often moved to tears."

There are two stories told of Holman Hunt and Rossetti that *The Pre-*
illustrate the earnestness, the longing for scientific truth, and also its *Raphaelite*
futility beside that other truth which is the artist's. When Holman *aim.*
Hunt painted his "Shadow of the Cross," he went to Palestine in search of "local colour," and to give the uttermost, unflinching truth. On his return he told a friend that he had tried to do this to the very curl of the shavings studied in a carpenter's shop in Nazareth.

"But," said the friend, "surely you've made some mistake. Isn't the tree from which those shavings were cut the wrong tree?"

And the story goes on to tell how the painter journeyed back to Palestine to make sure which particular type of cedar our Lord would have laboured on.

The other tale illustrates the unity of the Arts at which the Pre-Raphaelites aimed. Rossetti had a visit from Whistler, and showed him his latest picture. Whistler was delighted, and praised it. A month later Whistler visited Rossetti again, and was shown

a frame finely carved to suit the picture. Again he praised unre-
servedly. A month later he came once more, and Rossetti read
him a sonnet concerning the picture.

"Beautiful !" said Whistler ; and then added, "I say, Rossetti,
I wish you'd take the picture out of the frame and put the sonnet
into it."

The line of cleavage between the two schools — the Pre-
Raphaelite and the Impressionist—is here revealed, and to the point
of view of the latter we shall return in Chapter VI.

CHAPTER V.—THE IDEA BEHIND THE ARTS AND CRAFTS MOVEMENT.

The Pre-Raphaelite inspiration, when it touched other things than painting, led inevitably to the Arts and Crafts movement. But to make this movement, as the men of the eighties of the last century understood it, an effective movement, there was needed also a strong social impetus. Thus it had altruism as well as æsthetics behind it.

The men who preached its gospel were not less strong for the enthusiasm that inspired their work. The working craftsman, said they, the man who could make beautiful things with his hands, was down-trodden; give him a chance, he would make beautiful things again. Talent only needed to be brought to light. Let the craftsman be his own designer, let there be no more "ghost work," no more sham Art produced in factories. There was a great want for the beautiful and simple products of the hand again; and if a society, "The Arts and Crafts Society," could only be formed having this principle, it would revolutionize Modern Industry.

The society was formed—it did not revolutionize Industry. It *The Arts* was formed not in England only, but in Europe and America. One *and Crafts* of its most successful outcomes was the "Boston Arts and Crafts" *Society.* in Massachusetts. Its most logical and consistent development has been the co-ordinated workshops of Munich and Vienna. Numbers of men and women who would have been easel painters on the one hand, or absorbed into factory production on the other, turned their attention to what were discovered to be new materials—wood, stone, clay, glass, silver, iron. There was a fresh and vigorous creative outburst. Heywood Sumner's Hunting Tapestry, woven on the Merton looms, is an example of this (see No. 7), or Lawrie's delightful grotesques at West Point in Virginia (No. 8), or such works as I show in Nos. 9, 10, 14, 35, 88. They are the work of men and women who were made by the Arts and Crafts movement, or were inspired by its principles.

But the Arts and Crafts movement, though it did not revo- *The re-* lutionize Modern Industry, made a great social discovery: it redis- *discovery of* covered the small workshop. In so doing it gave us a new historical *the small* generalization. *workshop.*

We used to be taught as children that the real dividing line in history was for us in England the Norman Conquest, for the French

THE ARTS AND CRAFTS MOVEMENT

the Revolution, for the Americans the War of Independence; but the real division between the past and the future has been the nineteenth century, when the Industrial Revolution was being worked out. It was then that the social order that had been in existence for over a thousand years—the order that still exists in the Orient—was destroyed. With the coming of mechanical power and the displacement of the hand by the machine, the conditions of human life were changed—the home and woman's portion in it, man's labour, his relation to society, his conception of right and wrong. The history of every country for a thousand years has no fact so important as the change from domestic to factory industry. The disappearance of the small workshop, with the Guild system that regulated human labour and set its standard of quality in life and in the work of man's hands, is more far-reaching than any religious or dynastic change. But the Arts and Crafts movement made the discovery that it was only in the small hand workshop that those things could be had again for which that movement stood.

The early "workshop structure" of society.

It is not alone the Elizabethan translator of the Bible who points to the significance of the workshop structure of society. What the seventeenth century found as a fact had been a fact also in the age of Solomon. It is not the intellectual things only that count. The man that puts his trust in his hand is of them who maintain the fabric of the world. "So is every artificer and workmaster, that passeth his time by night as by day; they that cut gravings of signets, and his diligence is to make great variety, he will set his heart to preserve likeness in his portraiture, and will be thankful to finish his work. So is the smith standing by the anvil and considering the unwrought iron; the vapour of the fire will waste his flesh, and in the heat of the furnace will he wrestle with his work; the noise of the hammer will be ever in his ear, and his eyes are upon the pattern of his vessel; he will set his heart upon perfecting his works, and he will be thankful to adorn them perfectly. So is the potter sitting at his work, and turning his wheel about with his feet, who is always anxiously set at his work, and all his handiwork is by number; he will fashion the clay with his arms, and will bend its strength in front of his feet; he will apply his heart to finish the glazing, and he will be wakeful to make clean the furnace. All these put their trust in their hands; and each becometh wise in his own work. Without them shall no city be inhabited, and men shall not sojourn nor walk up and down therein. They shall not be sought for in the council of the people,

By the courtesy of Messrs. Morris & Co.

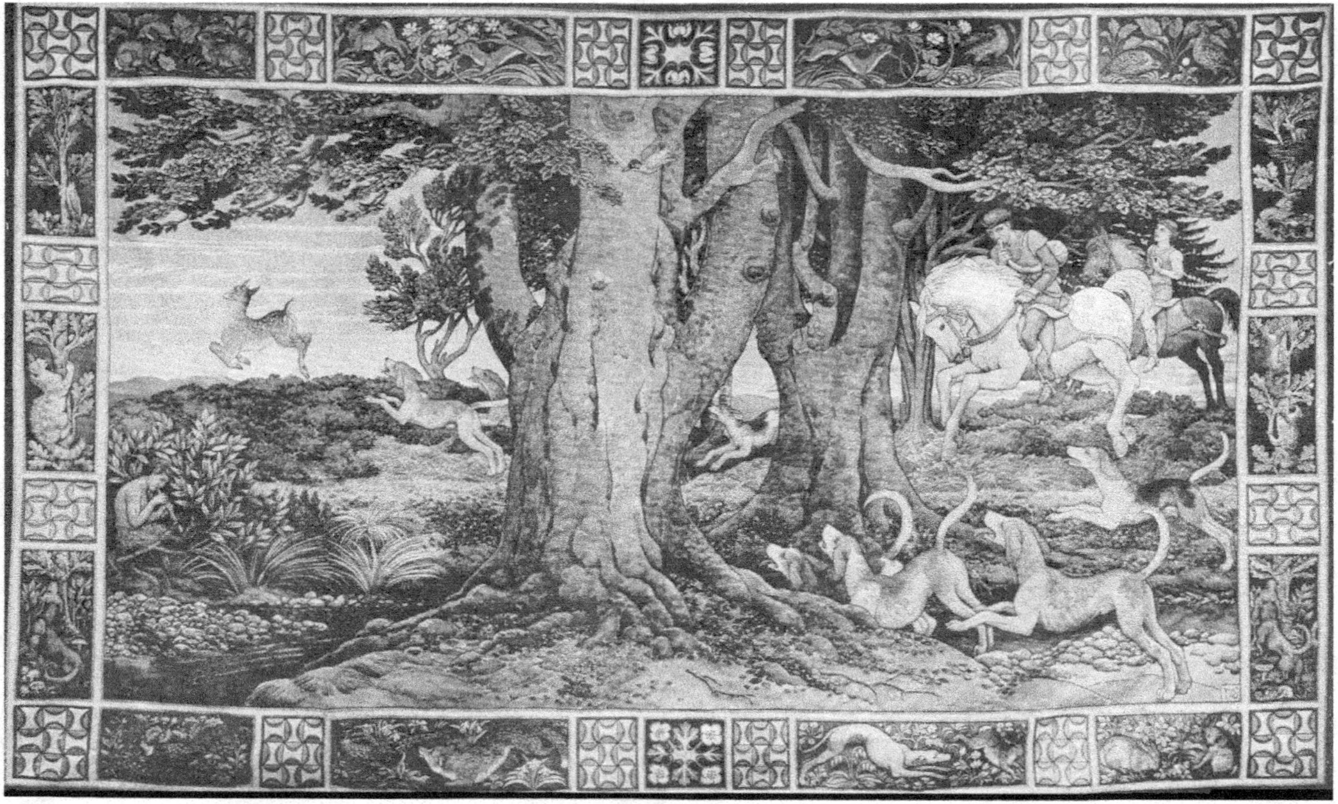

Heywood Sumner's Hunting Tapestry.

No. 7.

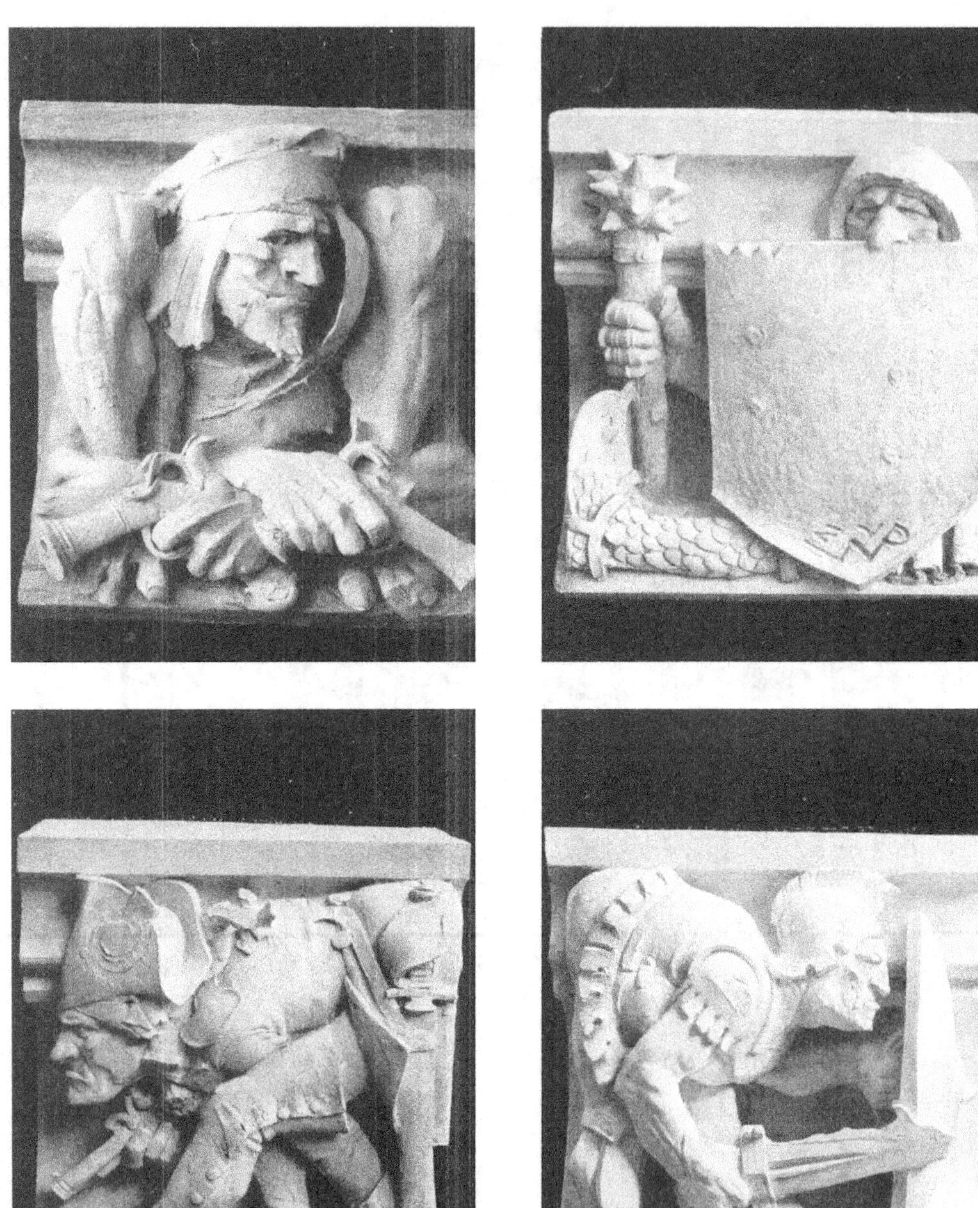

Four Grotesques at West Point, Virginia.
Modelled by Lee O. Lawrie.

(Messrs. Cram, Goodhue, and Fergusson, Architects.)

No. 8.

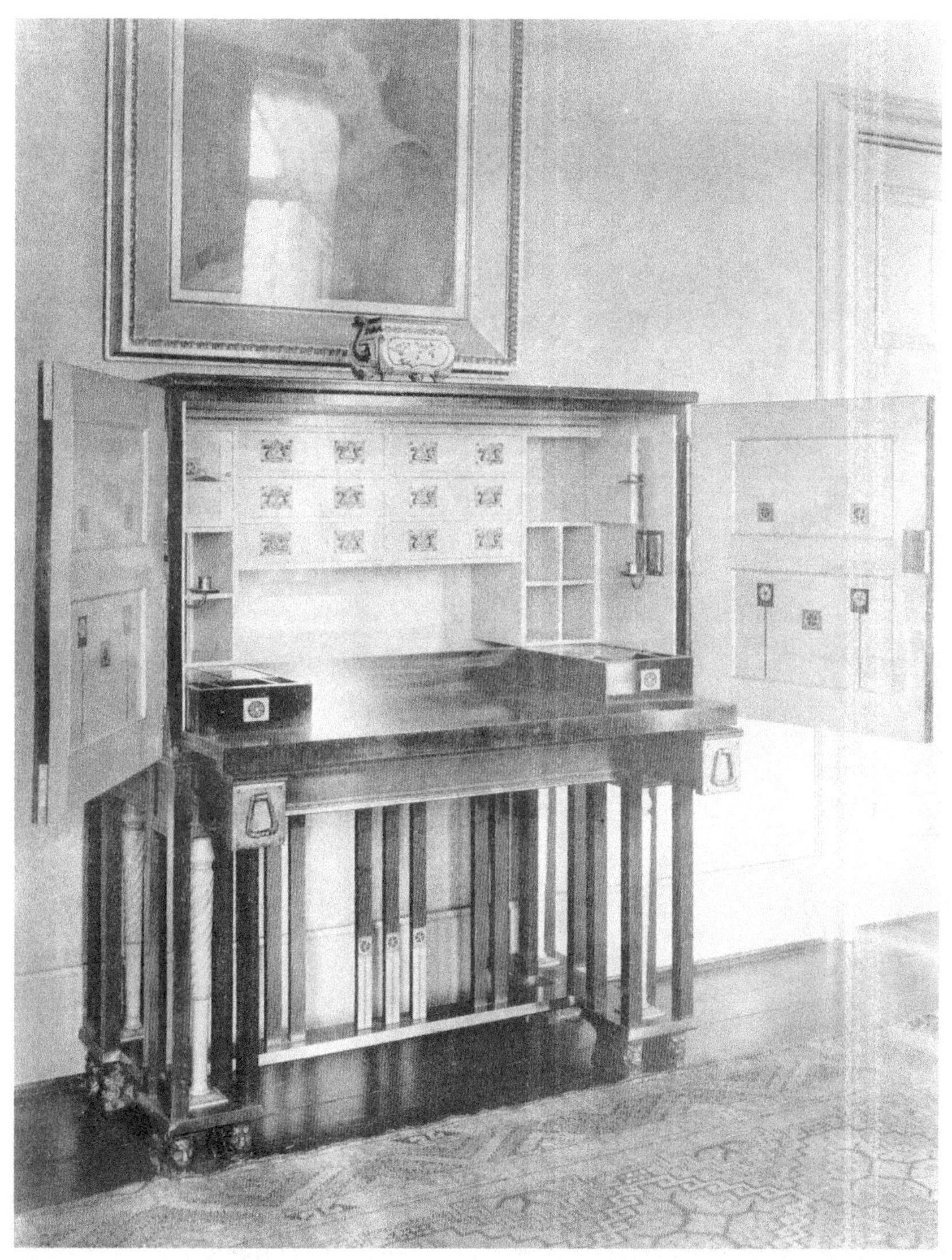

Cabinet in Ebony and Holly.   *No. 9.*
Designed by C. R. Ashbee.   Executed by J. W. Pyment of the Guild of Handicraft.

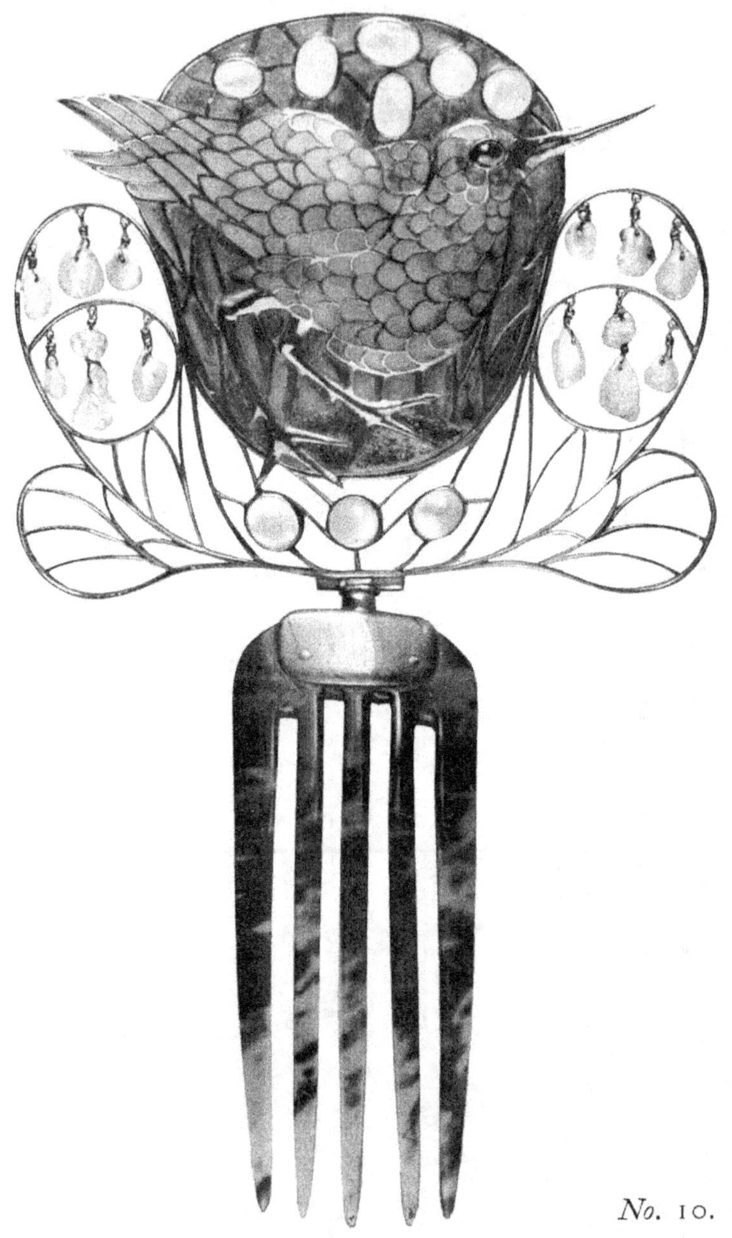

No. 10.

Jewelled Comb in gold, pearls, and plic-à-jour enamel.
Designed by C. R. Ashbee.   The enamel by W. Mark.

and in the assembly they shall not mount on high; they shall not sit in the seat of the judge, and they shall not understand the covenant of judgment; neither shall they declare instruction and judgment, and where parables are shall they not be found. But they shall maintain the fabric of the world; and in the handiwork of their craft is their prayer." *

The nineteenth century, in destroying the workshop structure of society, changed all this, and the Arts and Crafts movement set itself to undermining the work of the nineteenth century. It sought to bring back again the quality of prayer, to find out what the new fabric of the world was to be.

* Ecclesiasticus xxxviii. 27–34.

CHAPTER VI.—The Impressionists.

The Arts and Crafts movement, for reasons which we shall
examine later, failed of its great purpose, but while it was in progress
another movement had already set in among the painters. The
Impressionists, as they called themselves, reacted against the teachings
of the Pre-Raphaelites. " Let us get rid," said they, " of the didactic.
We want none of your d——d ethics in Art. Art should not
preach. Let it take the moment ; let painting have atmosphere ; let
it look at light ; let it be itself ; above all, let us have Art for Art's
sake." Led by Whistler in England and the men that looked to him
as their master in technique, much beautiful work was done. The
" Peacock Room," the portraits of Thomas Carlyle (No. 11) and
Whistler's mother, will remain for us among the classics ; also the
lithograph interpretations of the light and landscape of the Thames.
Chelsea, the artist centre of London, became more glorious than ever,
and there grew up through this younger school a sympathy with
Paris and the more logical Latin point of view in the Arts. Perhaps
the greatest thing gained was a further withdrawal of the art of
painting from realism. A good portrait or a good landscape came
to be valued for the personal interpretation rather than the reality
conveyed by the painter. "To tell the artist," said Whistler in his
"Ten o'Clock," "that he may copy Nature, is to tell the musician
he may sit upon the piano." Even greater than the influence of
Whistler was that of Monet, Dégas, and—though he is not strictly
with them—of Puvis de Chavannes in France. Like all teaching,
it was stretched by the younger men beyond its possible limits. An
Impressionist, Francis Bate, once made a portrait of me. Another
Impressionist, who some years later became a Post-Impressionist,
criticized the portrait as not being a good likeness. "That is not
the issue," said the painter; "my picture purports to be the impression of Ashbee's mood on my mood." "That's all very well,"
said the critic, "but the impression of Ashbee's mood on Bate's
mood will not alter the bone structure of Ashbee's nose."

The contribution of the Impressionists was a great one ; but the
price had to be paid, and it meant the drawing apart of the painters
from the other arts: they became a rather exclusive caste, and lost
touch with the greater social forces of life. A gospel that is for the
artist alone, and that appeals only to the painters of pictures, is hard
for the public to understand. just as it is hard for the public to under-

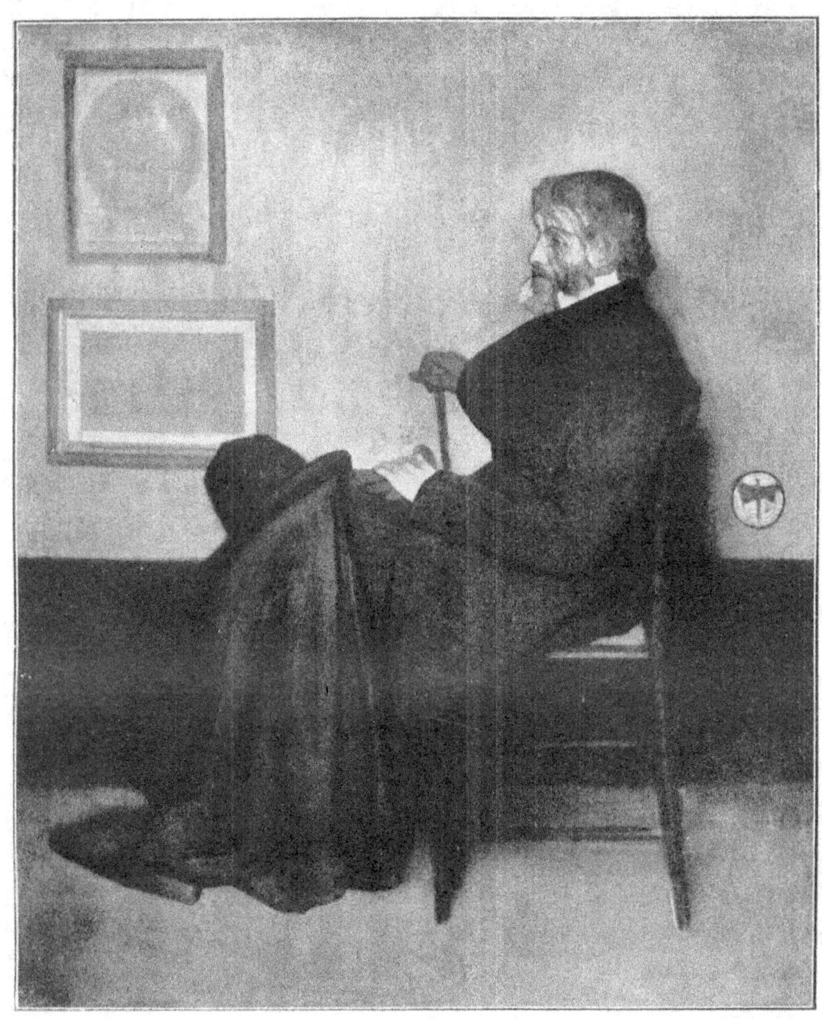

Portrait of Thomas Carlyle.
By James McNeill Whistler.

No. 11.

One of the groups before the State House, Harrisburg, Pennsylvania.
By George Gray Barnard.

No. 12.

stand a poet whose appeal is primarily to other poets. There is no doubt that this withdrawal from the actual things of life has damaged the artists themselves, weakened their power, narrowed their sympathies, impaired their solidarity, and led to that disintegration of the art of painting with which I deal below (Chapter XI).

It is possible to show the influence of Impressionism in music, in poetry, in drama. Learned Germans have done this.* In the writings of Oscar Wilde we get the Impressionist touch, in the German poet Stephen George, in Verlaine, and in the Flemings Maeterlinck and Verhaeren. There is in the writings of all these men some quality akin to the work of the painters. We get atmospheric effect in language, suggestion and subtlety rather than directness or emphasis of detail. They bring us to beauty by another road.

Within the sterner limitations of the art of sculpture Impressionism brought its own message. Rodin was the great leader here, and we have his last word in the Balzac. But the influence is far-reaching, and there is much noble modern work, e.g. that of Hildebrand, Meunier, McMonies, Saint-Gaudens, Ivan Mestrovic, or George Gray Barnard in the Harrisburg groups (No. 12), that gives us the same high exaltation of stone. The attempt, indeed, might be stated in the words of Socrates, himself the son of a sculptor, when he told men that the object of the craftsman in stone was to present the workings of the mind, not the mechanism of the limbs.

The appeal of the Arts and Crafts for a fellowship among the plastic arts, and for the emancipation of the artist from the machine; the appeal of the Impressionists for a single-minded devotion to the Art, free of social questions, was answered by the other Arts. Music also went back to the root of things, in Folk-song. In the Russian Ballet the dance became once more elemental. In its fight with the censorship English Drama took its stand on realities. Every censored passage in the play of any artist of note turns on a point of æsthetic principle. The characteristic of early twentieth-century literature, as we see it for instance in Masefield's " Everlasting Mercy," or W. W. Gibson's " Fires," or even Wells's " Mr. Britling," is the direct expression of emotion in language that is actually spoken. To this the Irish (in Shaw, and Synge, and Moore) added a wit and vision that was wanting to the more sure-footed Englishmen. These men in their work pierced for us the Celtic twilight, and for their wit we

* e.g., Richard Hamann, " Der Impressionismus in Leben und Kunst."

forgave them that perpetual wailing in the dimness that is so trying to English nerves.

The interesting thing to note—and this is the paradox to which Impressionism with its concentration upon the Art itself leads us—is how all the Arts began to speak together. In all of them we got the same appeal to first principles, the same cry for emancipation from Mechanism. "As an actress," says that gracious lady with whom ten generations of youths before and after my day were at one time or another in love, "I salute dancers with the reverence of a man for his ancestors. The dancer is certainly the parent of my own art, but he has other children. All arts of which the special attribute is movement descend from the dancer. The Greek word 'chorus' meant dance, and the Greek choruses were originally dances. It can be proved that dancing movements formed the first metres of true poetry. Why do we speak of 'feet' if not because the feet of the body used to mark the rhythm of inspired utterance?" She is telling of the Russian ballerinas, and she says: "They do not hammer out steps—it is a false notion of rhythm that there is a hammer-stroke on every strong beat—but take a collection of steps, as a singer takes a collection of notes, and calmly and gracefully phrase them, in the manner of a bird beating the air with its wings, rather than that of a blacksmith hammering on his anvil. Still, I doubt whether the Russians would have conquered Europe had they come to us merely as revivers of classical dancing before it became mechanical and ugly. They owe this revival to a great extent to Tschaikowsky." And then, with the true vision of the artist who sees the spiritual light behind, she says: "I dislike the word 'reformed,' however. Reformations are generally tiresome. *Transformations* are far better. Saint Francis transformed, Luther reformed; and the Russians are with Saint Francis rather than with Luther."*

And in this common speech of the Arts there begins to grow up a common purpose. The Arts are lonely in a world that has abused them. "The Stage Society," "The Little Theatre," the Morris Dancers at Stratford, the "Irish Players," the "Georgian Poets," the "Elizabethan Stage Society"—poets, painters, craftsmen—in whatever they do of good work, and in so far as they are not pot-boiling or working to order, are in frank revolt against Society. The demand is for a more complete life. What is this life? It is not to be found

* Ellen Terry, "The Russian Ballet."

in material goods ; these are the gauds with which the artist who creates the beautiful thing also bates the trap for wealth. This new life aims at less Materialism just because it demands more Beauty, at less conventional religion because it needs more Spirituality. Just because we have put the Oxford Movement and the Neo-Catholicism behind us, we want the great things they contain without the untruths they imply. But we need the Spirituality, here and now ; with the life hereafter we are less concerned. Above all, the new life insists, with stern English insistence, on justice—as the word is understood in Galsworthy's play—and on the freedom of the individual to live his own life, in spite of the controlling power of the machine.

In this search the last word for the moment is, perhaps, in *The new* Raemakers's or Will Dyson's War cartoons, or in the work of the *form to* younger painters, such as Nevinson, or in the sculpture of Eric Gill. *express* They are feeling for a form in which to express the mechanical *mechanical* force that has so far baffled us in war as in peace, and that now *force.* stands before our civilization in blind unreason.

An illuminating restatement of what we have many of us for the last twenty years been trying to say—Douglas Pepler's " Devil's Devices "—suggests " Service versus Control " as the way out.* Perhaps it is. Let us be ourselves, let us give ourselves. There must be some new method in life that shall enable us to do this. Better we should find it ourselves as free men than have it found for us by some Prussian State Order. Yet, may not the mechanical system imply a militarist state ? The answer is still in doubt. But the spirit of Hellas is not in doubt, nor is the Christian ethic. State Socialism is largely a German product ; it means order, discipline, grading, authority ; and it is suggestive to note how many English artists have been Socialists—Morris, Crane, Henry Wilson, Shaw, Barker, Wells, Arnold Bennett, many of the painters, even some of the architects; but when it has come to having their own wings clipped they have always dodged the machine, and they always will. There is logic in the paradox. Even Sidney Webb, who for many of us is the antithesis of that freedom we are seeking, once said to me : "After all, the individual is the trump card for which we play all the rest of the pack." To be an artist you have first to be an individual. The way out is in the new ethic by which we shall discover the *Axiom VIII* limitations of mechanism—our eighth Axiom.

* See also " The Game " for October 1916.

CHAPTER VII.—The Progress of Architecture.

The Art of Architecture rooted in mechanism.

Let us now consider how the Art of Architecture was influenced by the new ideas that came with the Pre-Raphaelite and the Impressionist inspiration, or that lay behind the Arts and Crafts movement.

Architecture, more rooted than all other arts in the varieties of human labour, has with the change of industrial life come to be more dependent on mechanism. That is the reason for its supremacy in the United States. Mechanism alone warrants or justifies so daring a conception as Hornbostel's proposed addition to Richardson's State House at Pittsburg (see No. 13). For the same reason the Art of Architecture is less directly influenced by the spiritual forces in the movements we have just been considering. Many illustrations could be given of how these movements have left their mark on Architecture. We see it in the grouping of building masses, or in the concentration of live as against the distribution of dead ornament; in the economy of detail, resulting from an understanding of the mechanical principle of the conservation of force; and in the gradual abandonment or refinement of all ornament by the more intelligent architects. To deal fully with these points would take me too far afield and into technicalities, but in illustrations Nos. 14, 15, 16, 17, 18, 20, 21, 22, I show buildings which have what I call the new influence.

Most interesting is it to notice how the Americans and the English are, each in their way, touched by the new spirit. The effort with both is the same: to escape from dead machine ornament. In the American work (see Nos. 18, 20) the artist arrives at his result by unloading all ornament except that which he can, through the machine, directly control. In the English work (see Nos. 14, 15, 16) he does it by collaboration with working craftsmen whose guiding principle is freedom from the machine incubus. The result to Architecture is the same: the art becomes alive.

The Art of Architecture indeed, much as the art of jewellery or fine metalwork (Nos. 10, 88), is more severely held within the limitations of its material, and so its appeal to us is less direct than that of the painter, the sculptor, the musician, or the dramatist. But it was not until building with concrete and steel had passed out of its experimental stage that architecture, which like most of the arts in the Industrial era had drifted from its moorings and lost its truthfulness, came back to first principles. This meant a revision of academic

18

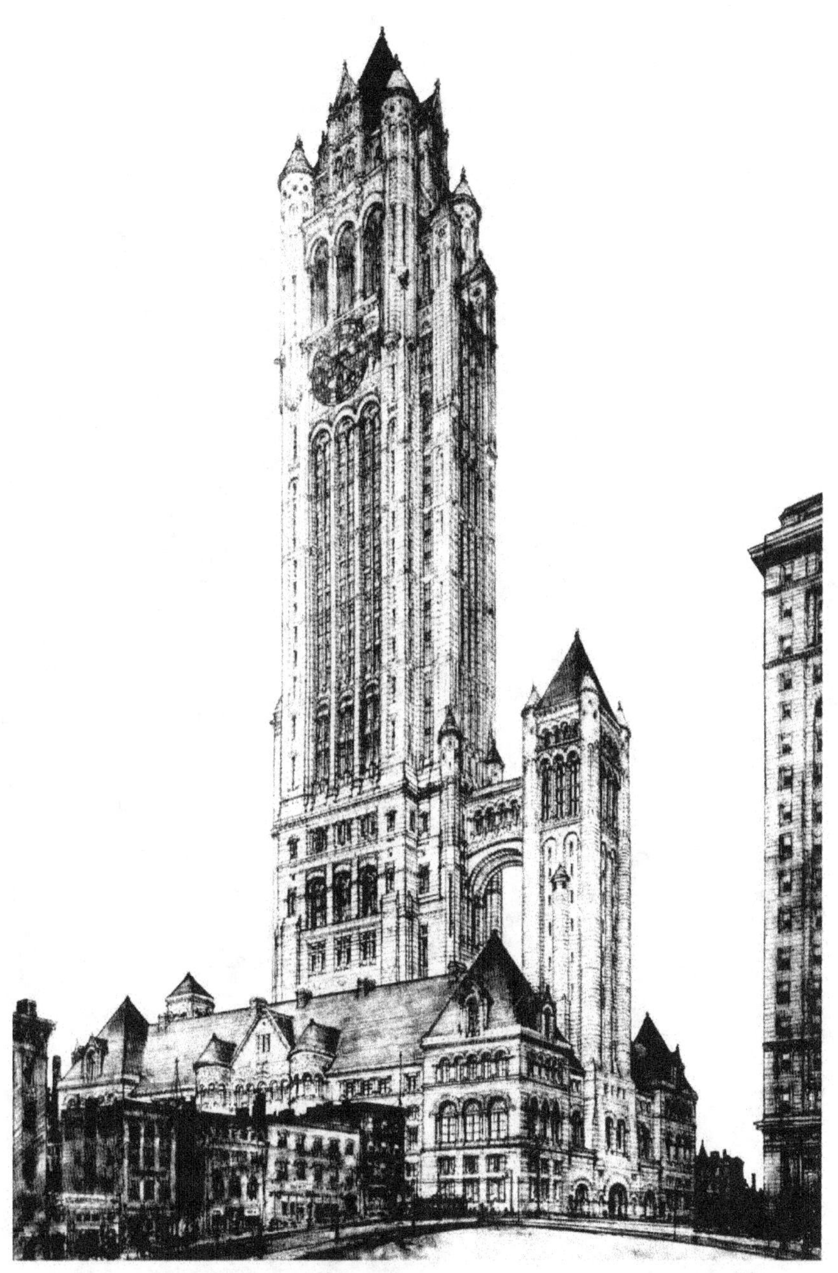

Hornbostel's proposed addition to Richardson's State House at Pittsburg, Pennsylvania. No. 13.

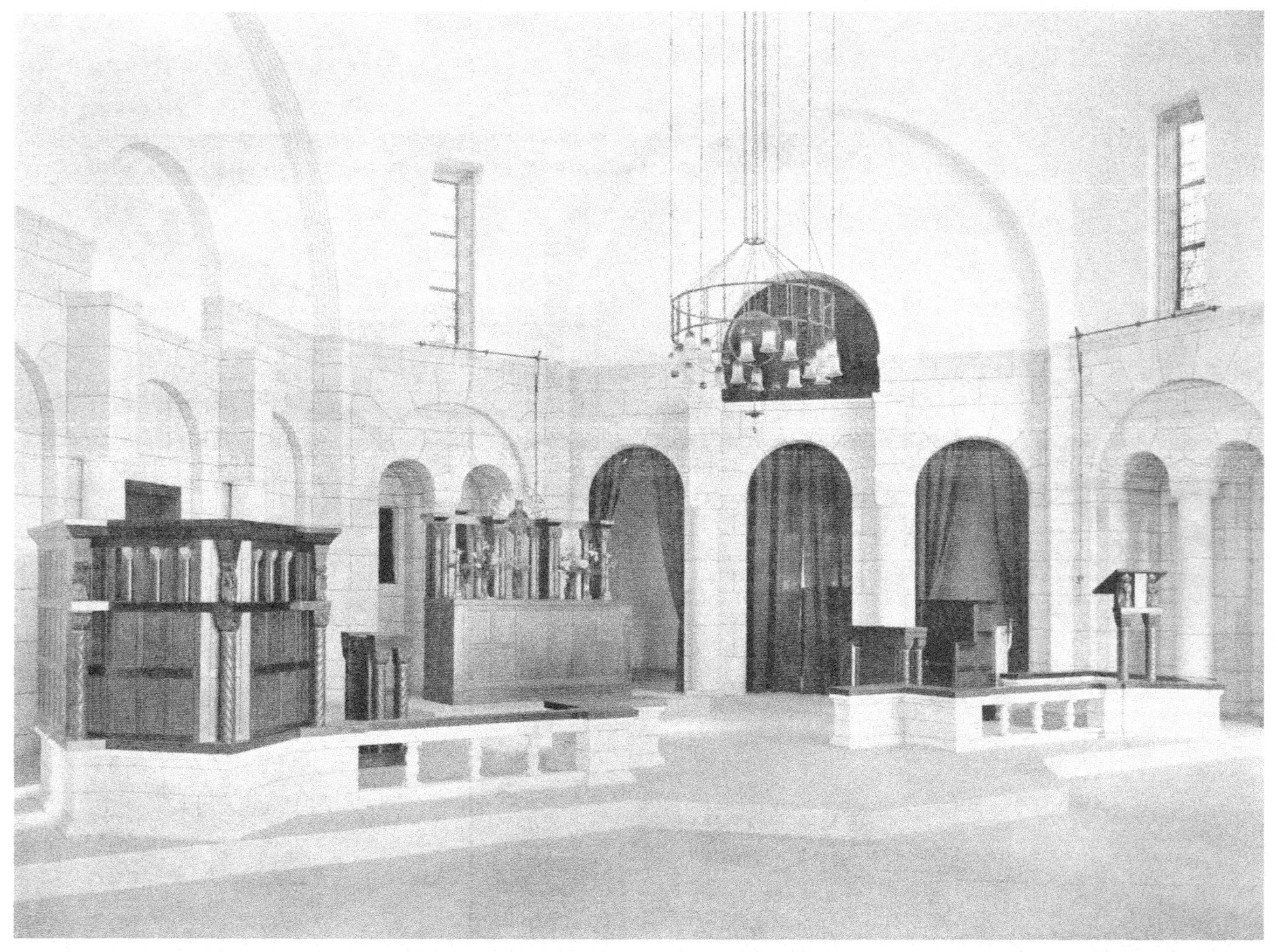

The Sanatorium of King Edward VII.
By Adams and Holden.   The carving and detail by the Guild of Handicraft, Campden, Gloucestershire.

No. 14.

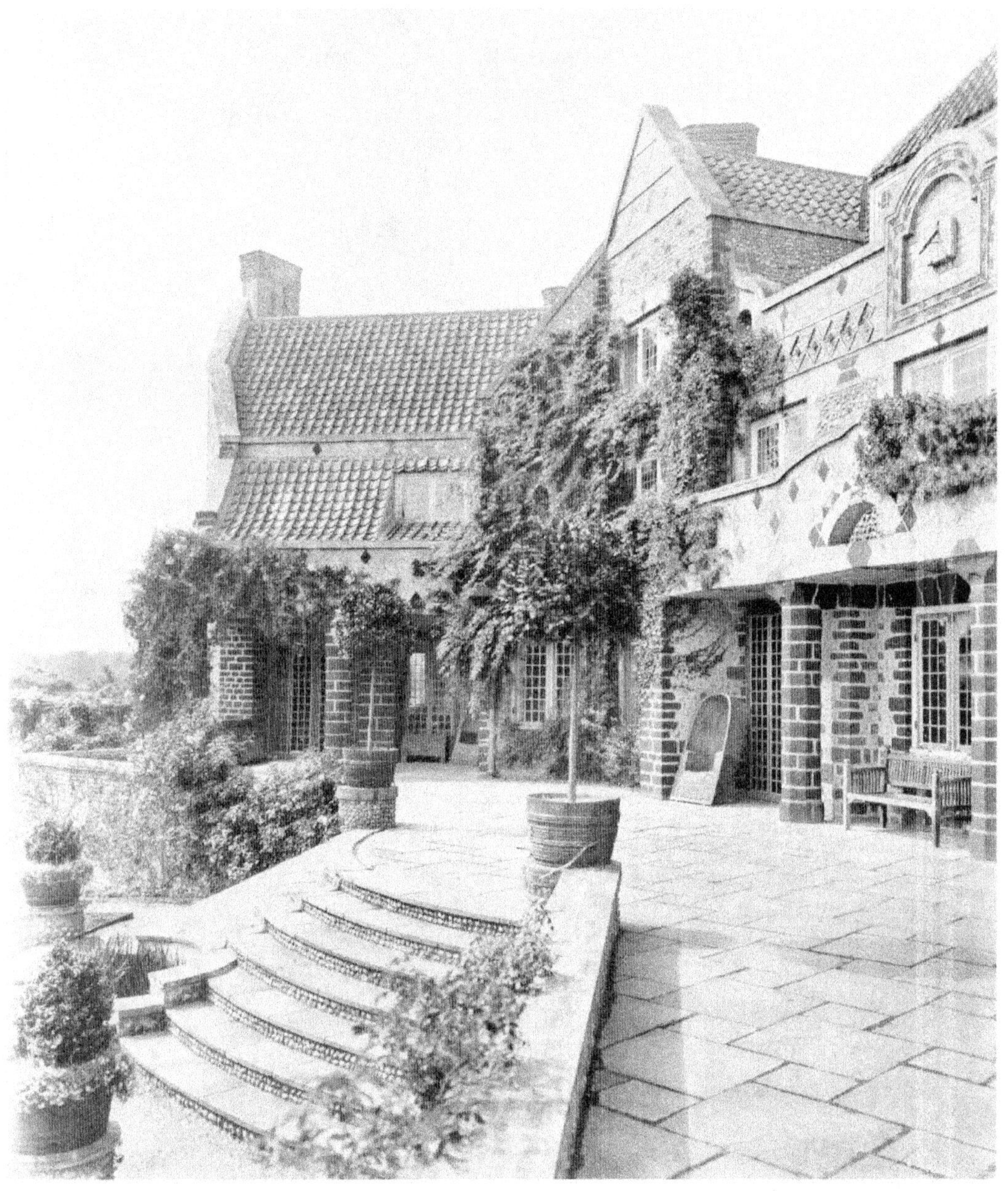

Home Place.
By E. S. Prior.

No. 15.

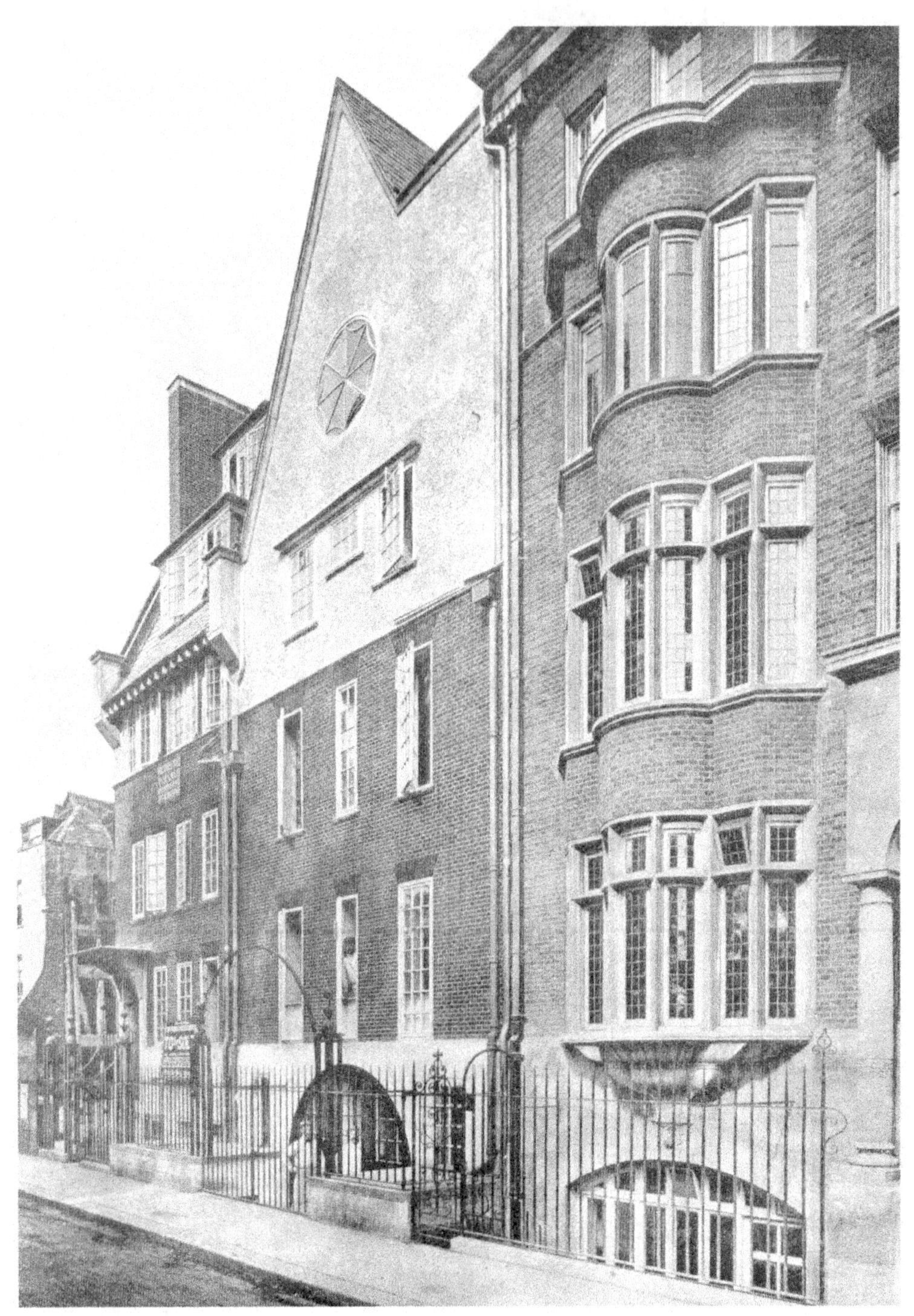

Houses on the river front, Cheyne Walk, London.
By C. R. Ashbee.

No. 16.

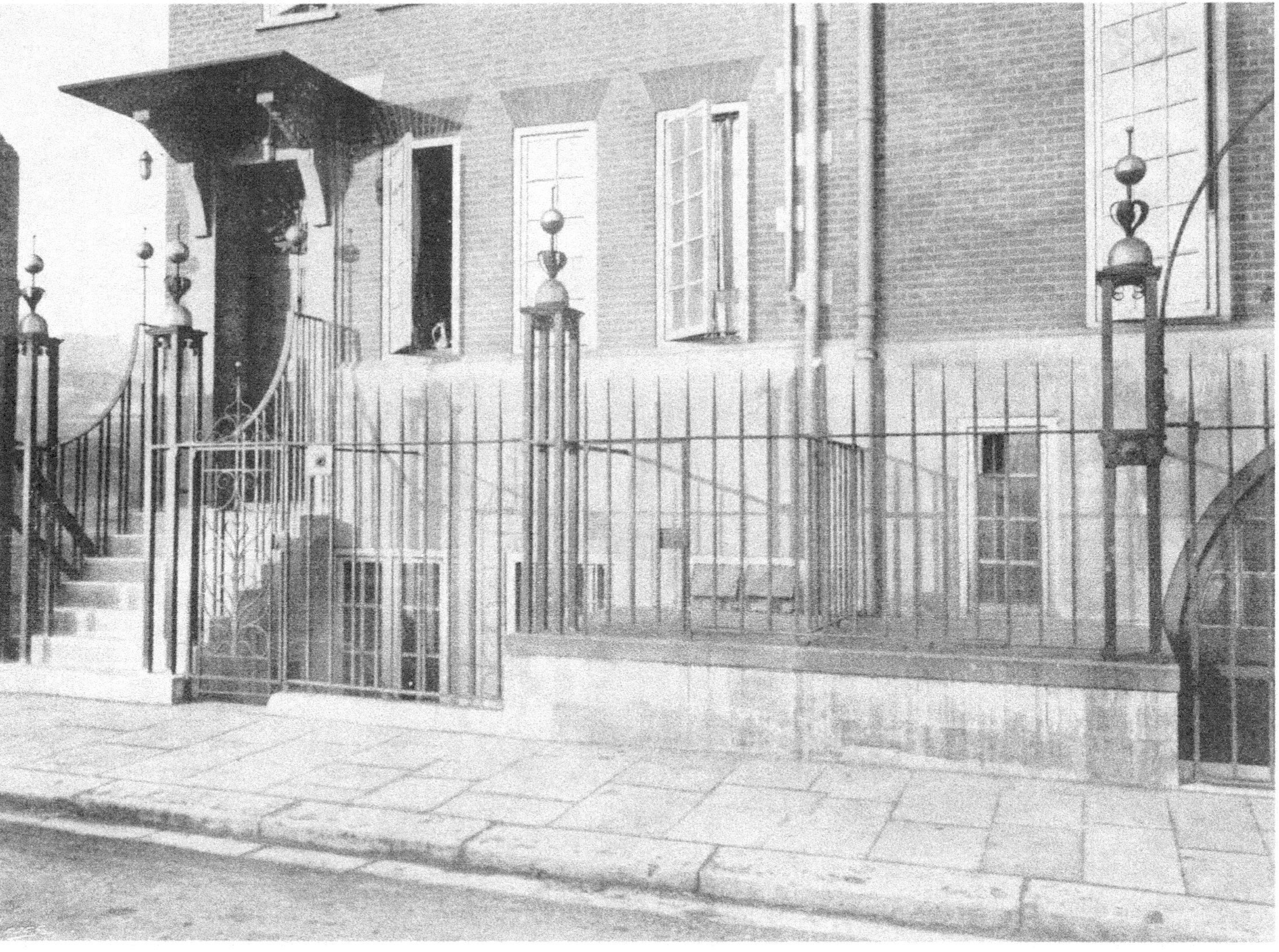

On the river front, Cheyne Walk, London, showing the lower portion of the preceding illustration. By C. R. Ashbee.

No. 17.

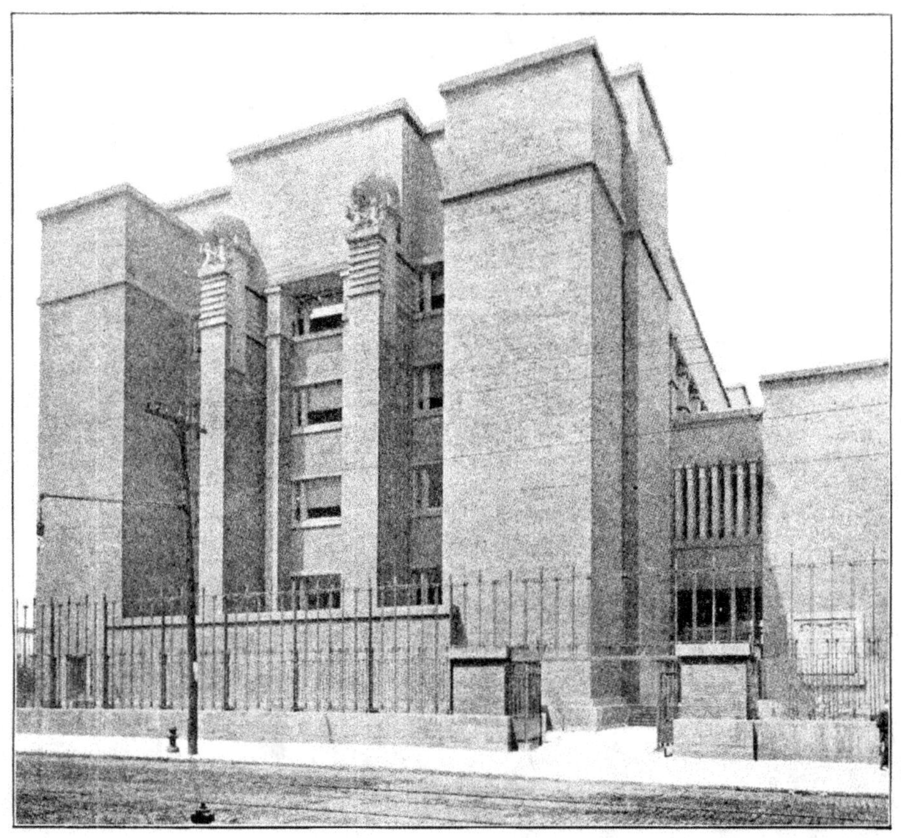

No. 18.

The Larkin Building, Buffalo, U.S.A.
By Frank Lloyd Wright.

forms; orders, columns, cornices, all flummery stuck on, was pruned *The return*
away; a real structural form, true architecture in the Greek or Medi- *to first*
æval manner, was once more evolved, as we see this in the work *principles.*
of some of the builders of the American Middle West, the Pacific
Coast, and the engineer bridge builders (see Nos. 23, 24, 25).

Perhaps it was not so much that the arts influenced each other,
as that they were moved by the same spirit. The "reality" and
"sincerity" of the Pre-Raphaelites, the "being oneself" of the
Impressionists, found its echo also in the mother art. Architecture
likewise began to look within. Through the Arts and Crafts movement it came to see the need for internal workshop reconstruction.
In England the influence of the Arts and Crafts movement on
Architecture did not go so far as in Germany or Belgium. With
us in England the movement hesitated, halted, and broke down
from want of effective organization. Still, it left a few fine examples
in a small way.* In public buildings it was never given a chance.
It is essentially great in its detail—those minor arts where the personal
touch and character of the individual tells. Arts and Crafts Architecture in England was finally swept on one side by the eighteenth-
century revival, the Neo-Georgian, which we shall consider directly.

English building, indeed, was burdened with too many difficulties. *Architec-*
It had no traditional style as in France, it had no sound organiza- *ture and*
tion as in Germany, it had few of the great opportunities given it *social*
by intelligent "big business" as in America, it was hampered by *problems.*
mechanism and pseudo-engineering methods, it had to fight the
"trade" and was itself riddled with commercialism and dishonesty,
it had lost its roots in craftsmanship and got out of touch with labour.
Before a live style could be formed these difficulties had to be faced.
The men who were ready and willing to face them had been brought
up on the old individualist tradition, they were incapable of co-
operating, they were neither trained nor organized. The difficulty
was an ethical one.

The fifteen years that ended with August 1914 were for
thoughtful architects, the men who treat their subject as an Art,
years of somewhat bitter experience—akin to humiliation. We were
not able as we would wish to utilize our art of architecture for the
expression of that intelligence and joy we knew it to contain. Every
art has its own power of interpreting life, of revealing to man his soul;

* The early work of Lutyens could be cited, or the work of Lethaby, Prior,
Detmar Blow, Ricardo, Holden, Cecil Brewer, and one or two others.

the soul that "is form and doth the body make." In the art of Architecture there lies a power that can give the city its form. But why were we, for whom our art contains a religious quality, not able to convince those for whom we laboured of this truth? Perhaps it was a want of vision in ourselves. "L'art," says Rodin,* "c'est la contemplation, c'est le plaisir de l'esprit qui pénètre la nature et qui y devine l'esprit dont elle est elle-même animée. C'est la joie de l'intelligence qui voit clair dans l'univers et qui le récrée en l'illuminant de conscience. L'art, c'est la plus sublime mission de l'homme, puisque c'est l'exercice de la pensée qui cherche à comprendre le monde et à le faire comprendre." And then he goes to the root of the matter, the subject with which I here am concerned :—

Rodin's analysis and the machine.

"Autrefois, dans le vieille France, l'art était partout. Les moindres bourgeois, les paysans même ne faisaient usage que d'objets aimables à voir. Leurs chaises, leurs tables, leurs marmites, leurs brocs étaient jolis. Ce qui est utile, dit-on, n'a pas besoin d'être beau. Tout est laid, tout est fabriqué à la hâte et sans grâce par des machines stupides. Les artistes sont les ennemies."

The influence of "concrete."

Yes, we are fighting these stupid machines because we believe that the artists are not the enemies, but have a definite constructive purpose in modern life, and that is to bend the machine to the higher will. The application to Architecture of casting, the process by which simple straightforward forms are stamped through means of a wooden mould upon the final material, has given to the art something that is not only splendid in the Roman sense, but that meets the needs of the great stadia, railway stations, libraries of the new democracy (e.g., No. 19) ; and one of the most significant of the efforts at dominating the machine through the art of Architecture is the application of the unit system to the processes of concrete in the building of small houses to interchangeable plans, as is now done in the Middle West of America.

Here in the hands of Frank Lloyd Wright the processes of standardization, of which I speak more fully below (Chapter XXVII), have been so perfected that it is possible for one creative mind to build with an almost infinite variety of mechanical parts, each of which has been in the first instance thought out in its reference to the machine that has made it or that will finally put it into its place on

* Paul Gsell, "L'Art."

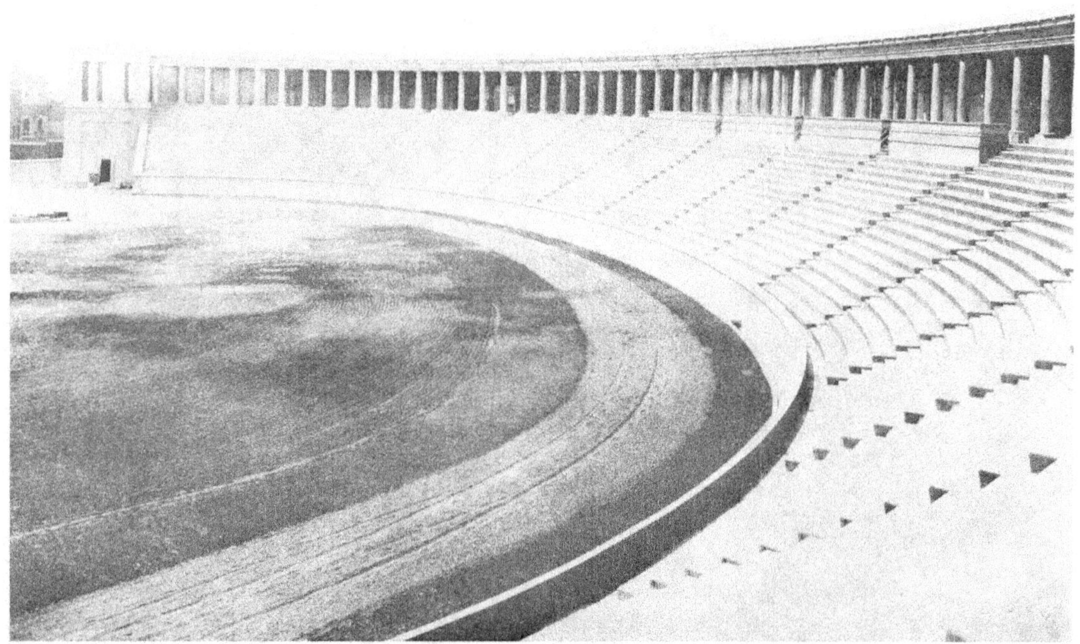

No. 19.

The Great Stadium, Columbia University, New York.

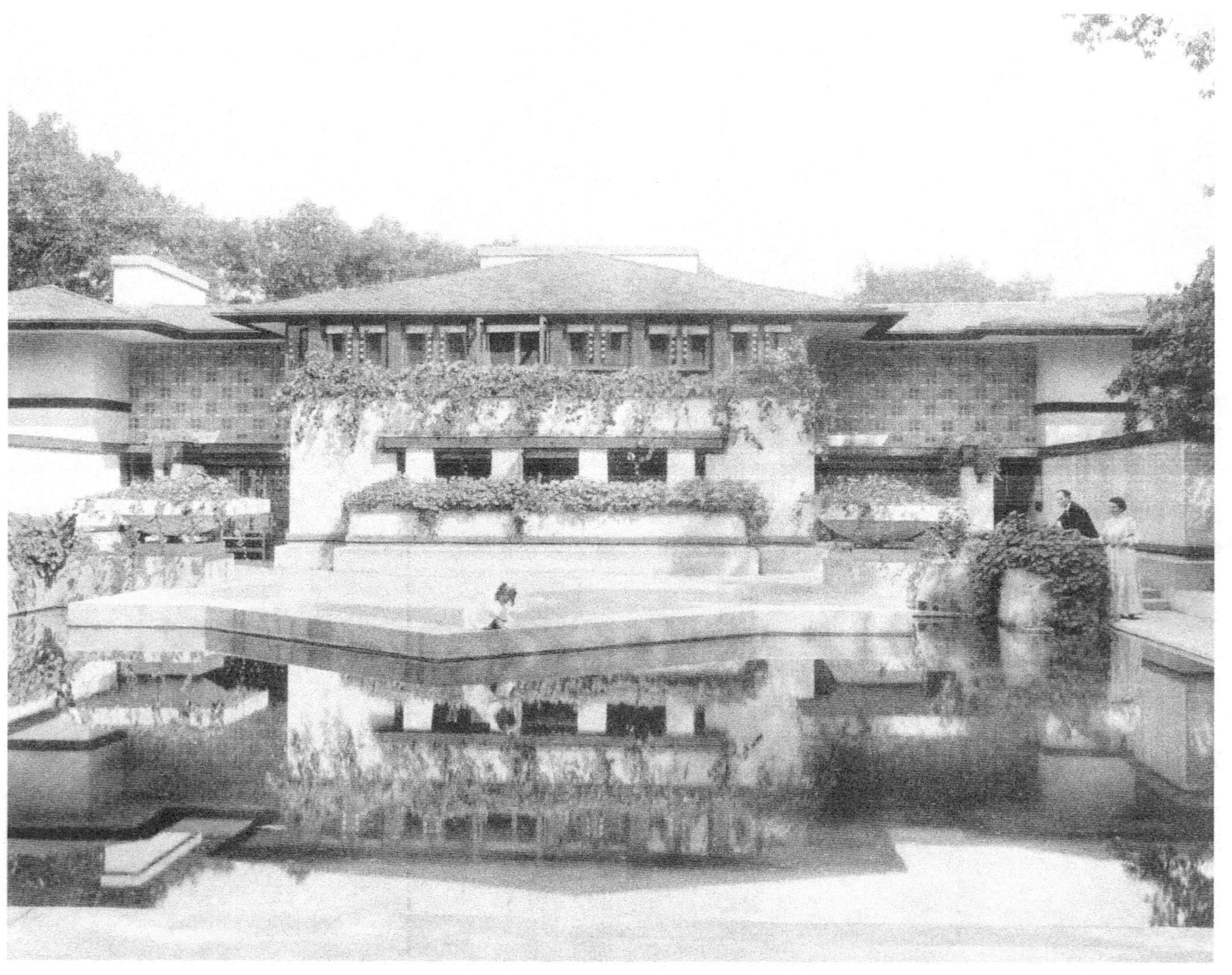

A Country House near Chicago, Illinois.
By Frank Lloyd Wright.

No. 20.

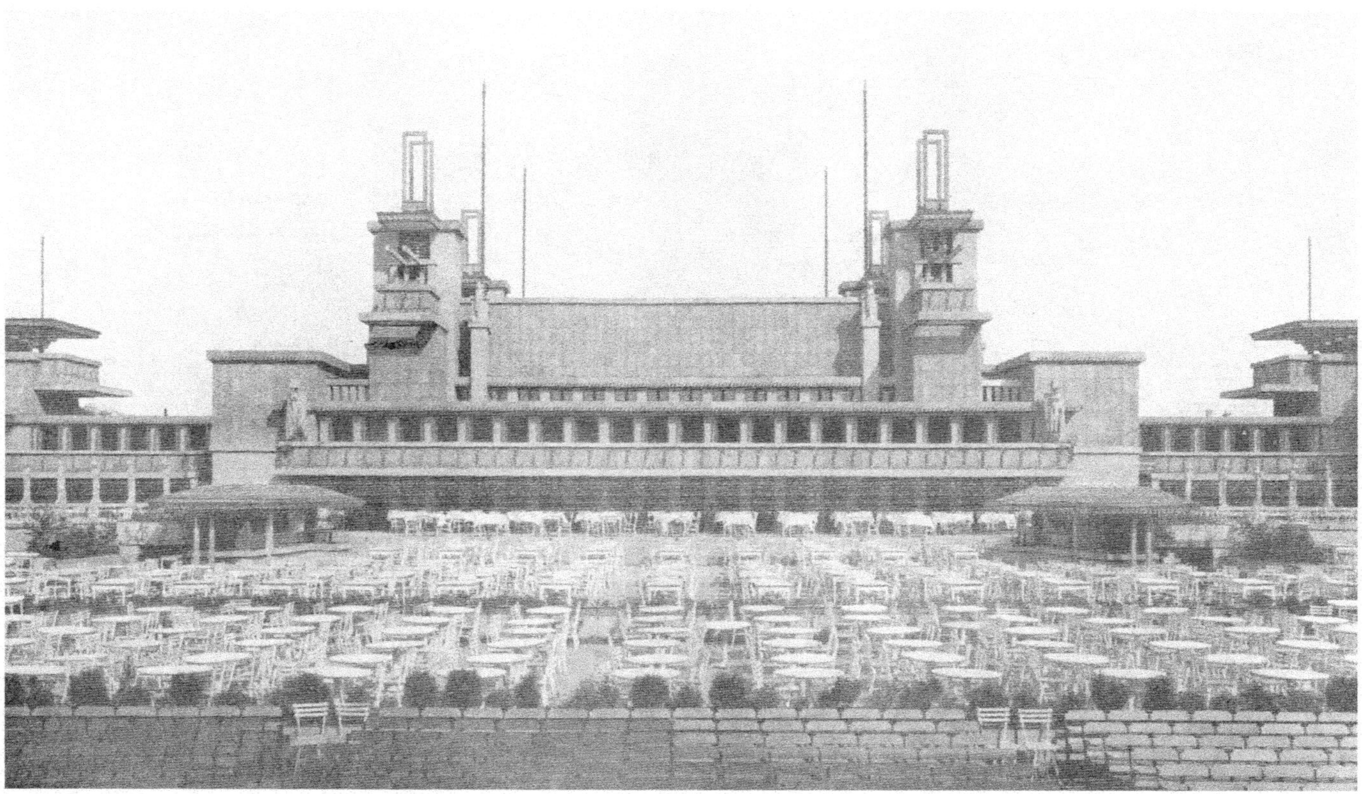

The Open-air Theatre and Garden in Chicago.
By Frank Lloyd Wright.

No. 21.

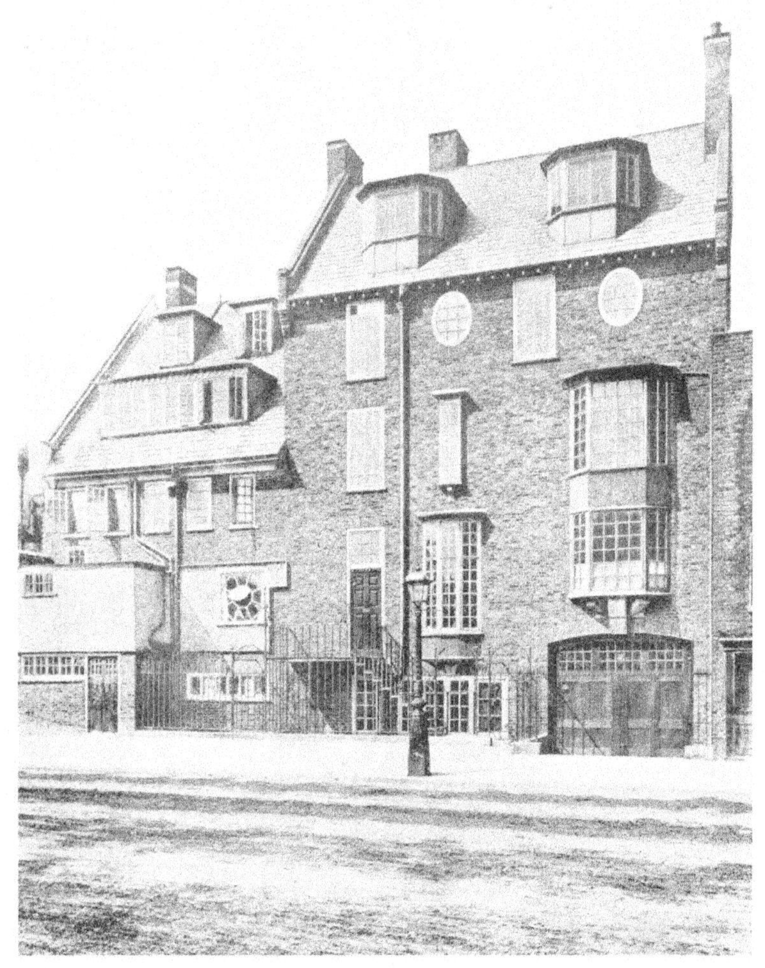

Buildings on Cheyne Walk, London.
By C. R. Ashbee.

No. 22.

the building.* There is no limit to the variations that one imaginative mind can give to houses thus set together, and I conceive that many beautiful cities are likely to grow up by these methods. The limitation will rather come through the want of sympathy of those who dwell in them, or through some desire on their part to create for themselves.

In this question of the control of power it is not merely a question of the work of art. We know (Axiom VI) that beautiful things can be made by mechanical power. It is the system as a whole we have to consider. The factory system that makes great riches, and knows not how to use them, has its heavy hand, like Watts's Mammon, on the head of the girl, while at its gilded feet is the broken body of the boy (see No. 52). We must free the human spirit again. It was freed once from the material brutality of Rome when Christ stood up to Pilate, freed a second time from the obscurantism of the Mediæval Church when Erasmus wrote "The Praise of Folly" and Luther burnt the Pope's bull. We have to free it now from the incubus of mechanism—of power misunderstood, misapplied, miscontrolled. The objective is the same, but the method is different. We have now to find a means for man to labour again with his hands—not mechanically, but inventively, imaginatively—to labour with the motive of joy. One of these ways —perhaps the greatest because it holds within it all the arts of the city—is the art of Architecture.

*As in the case of the Milwaukee Building Company's work, and Frank Lloyd Wright's designs for it.

Mechanical power in relation to the whole social structure.

Axiom VI.

CHAPTER VIII.—The Growing Regard for Amenities and the Preservation of History.

It was the war with commercial vandalism that made men turn to the past as to a citadel that had to be defended. For the artists the things most worth preserving seemed to be within. Inevitably men said, "If life is to be beautiful as a whole, as we see it in the past, what better objective can we have than to save the best things of the past?" We producers were inspired not only to create beauty, but to preserve it. For us it lay in the past as well as in the future. The historic conscience came with the æsthetic rebellion against commercialism. It was high time. The industrial utilitarianism which had begun with the greatest piece of vandalism in modern history— the destruction of "Old London Bridge, the wonder of the world"— destroyed everything that crossed its path. A factory and power plant was built actually on the chancel of Southwark Cathedral; Elizabethan palaces * were turned into doss-houses and lunatic asylums; eighteenth-century London fared no better: men suddenly discovered that the stately Haymarket colonnades "harboured immorality," and they were cleared away for commercial purposes. In England and America when the Devil wants something he lets loose the Puritan conscience. The end of the nineteenth century, thanks mainly to the writings of Ruskin, realized the folly and barrenness of all this. Men started societies for saving the London City churches, for turning the church-yards into gardens, for protecting public buildings, for preserving historic houses. In the United States innumerable organizations were formed.† In England the National Trust was founded, and became in the end something in the nature of a Government Department. As usual, we laboriously followed after where the French with clearer vision in their "Monuments Historiques" had pointed the way long before.

Much of my own professional work has been the preservation and protection of beauty. In Nos. 26, 27, 31, I give examples. Many other famous examples could be given of the fitness and wisdom of preserving the noble works of the past. The churches of St. Mary-le-Strand and St. Clement Danes in the great London Improvement Scheme, for which we artists fought desperately hard, the preservation of Washington's Mount Vernon (see No. 32), the re-setting of Alfred

* See London Survey publications. "The Old Palace of Bromley by Bow."
† See Ashbee's "Report to the National Trust, 1902."

22

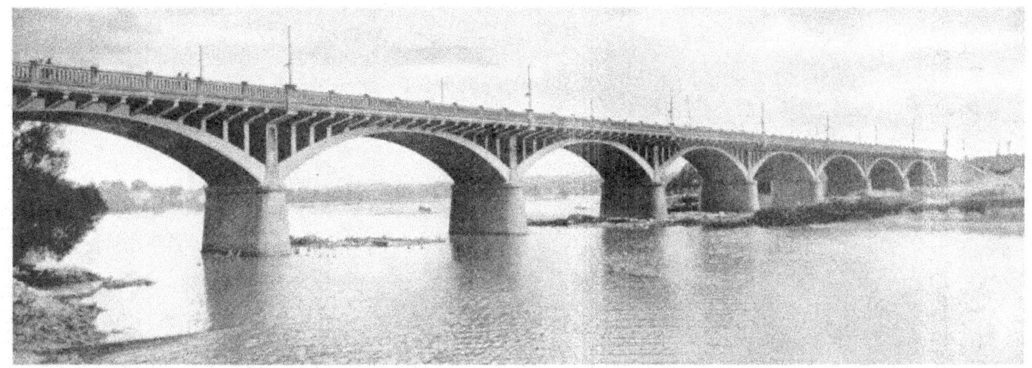

Colorado River Bridge, Austin, Texas. No. 23.

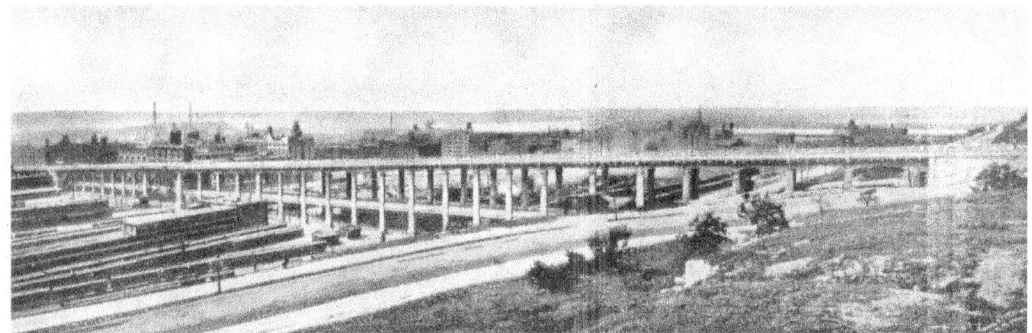

Viaduct, Kansas City, Mo. No. 24.

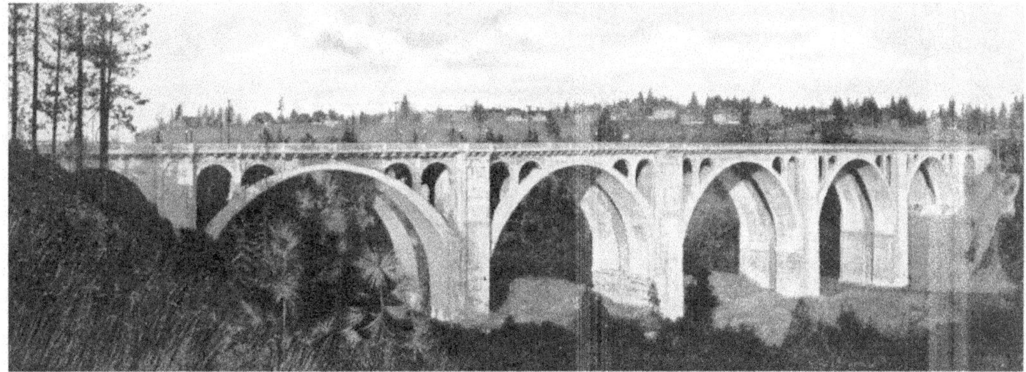

Latah Creek Bridge, Spokane, Washington. No. 25.

Three concrete bridges by Messrs. Harrington, Howard, and Ash,
Kansas City, Missouri.

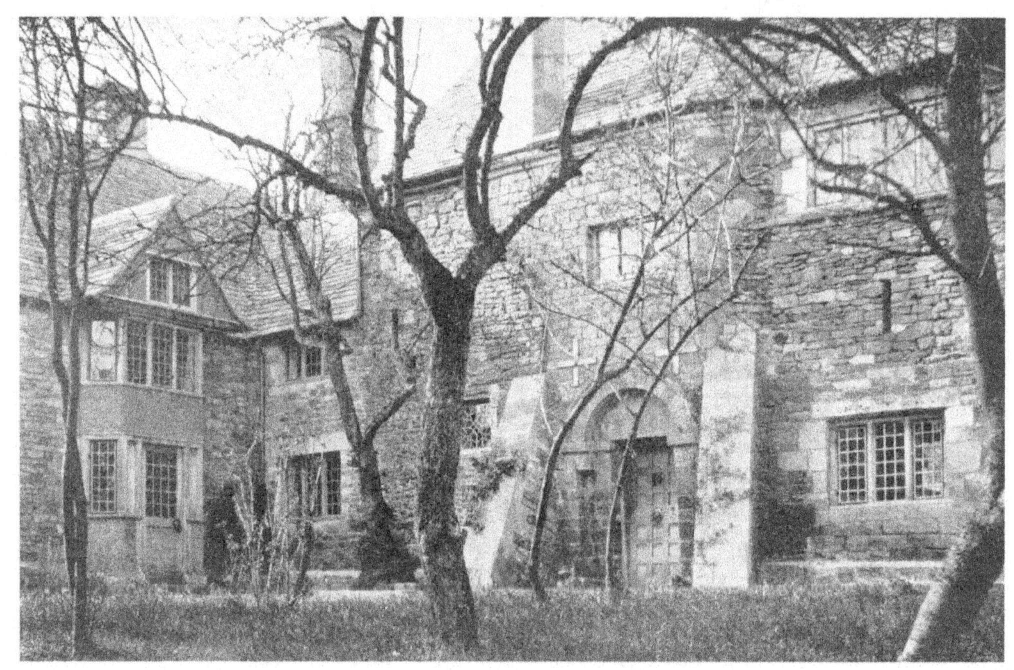

The Norman Chapel at Campden, Gloucestershire, as repaired, with additions, by C. R. Ashbee and members of the Guild of Handicraft.

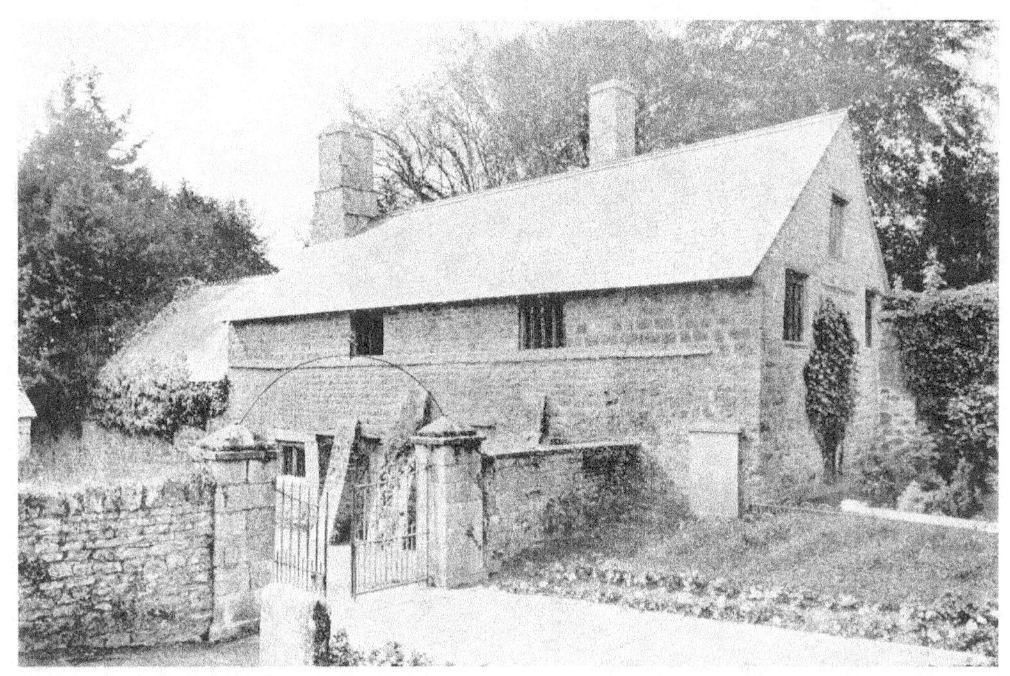

No. 27.

The Holcombe Rogus "guild" or "poor" house in Devonshire as reconstructed by C. R. Ashbee and members of the Guild of Handicraft.

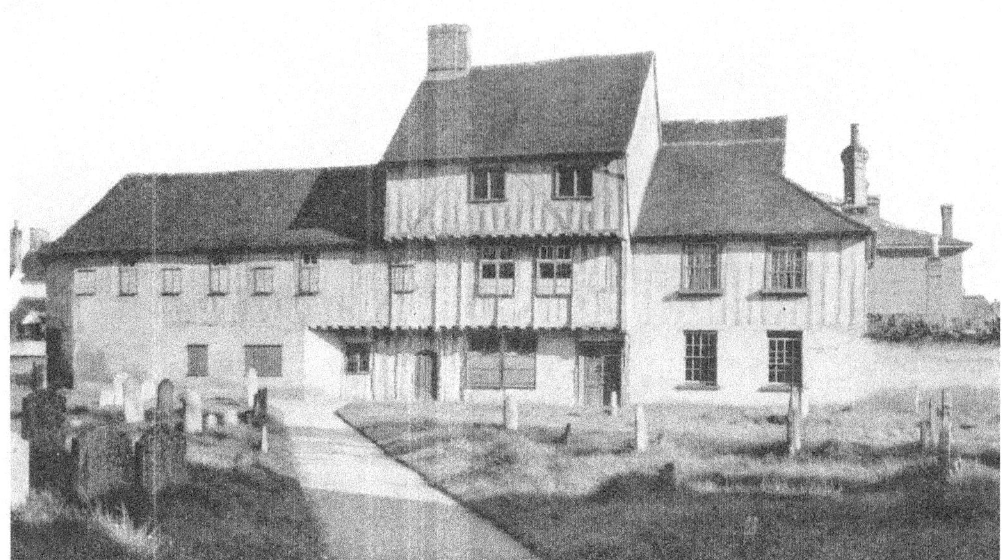

Hadleigh Guildhall, Suffolk, before repair. No. 28.

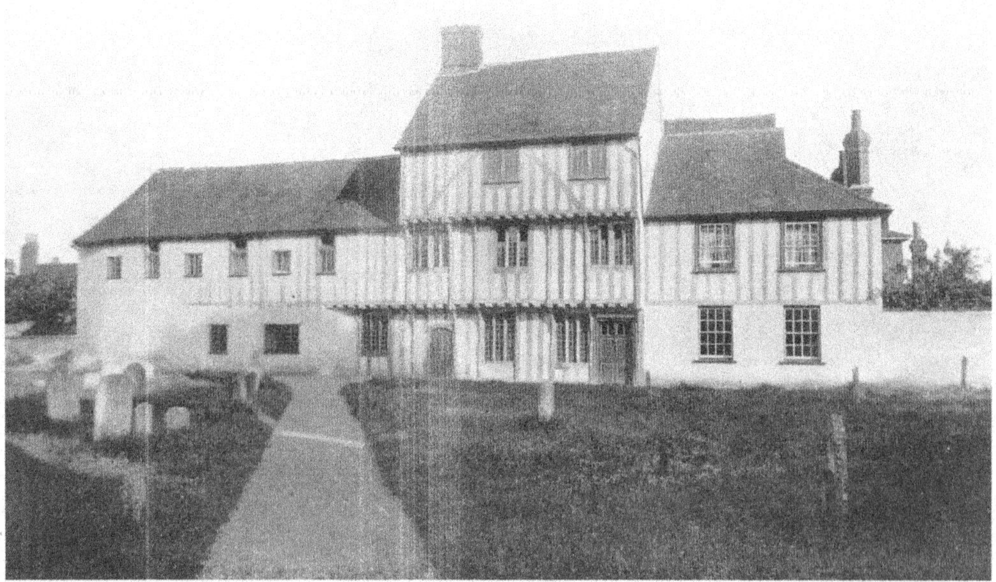

The same after repair on Society for the Protection of Ancient Buildings principles. No. 29.

Stevens's monument to Wellington (see No. 33), the house of Turner (see Nos. 30, 31) which I restored some years ago in Chelsea, the Hadleigh Guildhall in Suffolk (see Nos. 28, 29), the Jewel Tower, Cardinal Wolsey's Oratory, the Old Court House at Crendon, the Alfriston Clergy House, the Lyveden New Building (see No. 100), the Chancery of the Duchy of Lancaster—all these contain historic principle. The stone cross and dovecots I show (Nos. 89, 92, 93, 101) are but records of mediæval and Elizabethan England. Among the most gracious works of the English National Trust has been its "dedication" of historic and beautiful landscapes. The preservation of these things is a form of ancestor worship, necessary to any community that would save its soul.

The preservation of parks and open spaces, beautiful trees and avenues, when new suburbs are laid out, touched us on the side of health. The children could not get out of the great cities. The life of the race was even more important than that of the ancestors. We discovered that when the speculative builder and the estate lawyer were wrecking a potential garden city, they were destroying the lives of the children. We are only just beginning to learn that, in the Arts of the City, to create and preserve are part of one great principle, much as the General Thanksgiving puts it: "We bless thee for our creation, preservation, and all the blessings of this life." We must do more than mouth it. Whether for the individual or the community this truth applies. To put behind us the temptation of destroying some past beauty for the sake of a new creation of our own is often difficult. It taxes not only our modesty, but our sense of duty. *Preservation and creation go together.*

A man once offered me the commission to reconstruct the interior of a Wren church. There was much that was dowdy and needed cleaning, but nothing that justified reconstruction. We argued long on what should be done, and what should be left; but my client had his money, and it was burning a hole in his pocket. I could not get him to see the beauty in what he wanted me to destroy, so at last I played my trump card.

"Then you really mean," said he, "that you will resign the commission rather than do this reconstruction?"

"That is what I mean."

"Then," said he, "I suppose I must be wrong, and the old stuff beautiful after all." *

* A famous recent case is that of the Tong Chalice, where a community wanted to sell its finest heritage in order to build a new church.

THE GROWING REGARD FOR AMENITIES

Instinctive
sympathy
for beauty. Among peasants, craftsmen, and workpeople, I have often noted a sympathy for things old and beautiful. It is subtle and instinctive rather than reasoned, but it always disappears at the solvent of commercialism. We have to recognize this quality in man, and find a place for it in the new civics—save it from obliteration. Our great new commercial universities, "the imperishable cities with their arms about each others' necks," the wonderful inventions of science—all these have given the new age great ideals ; but something they have lost. Ideals are not sufficient : perception also is needed. We English and Americans have many ideals, and the generous impulses that go to their fulfilment—but it is not enough. If we lack perception we lack that finer understanding of the right moment in life—the moment that tells us when the thing is fitting. This understanding of the right moment one might call the Sense of Beauty.

"Vice" and
"sin" as
they touch
our sense of
beauty. An American sociologist * recently gave us a new definition of vice and sin. Sin was conduct that harmed others, vice the harm we did ourselves. The implication of his book was that the time had come for the community to cease wasting itself on the vices of men which only harmed them as individuals, and concentrate upon the sins which harmed the whole community. Of such is the destruction of all amenities that make for common enjoyment and health. If we developed the sense of beauty, the understanding of the right moment that tells us when the thing is fitting, we should learn more easily to discriminate between vice and sin ; further, we should learn when we were overstepping that borderland which our Puritan fathers called "temptation," and passing out of "fitness" into sin or vice. There is, as Christ so clearly taught,† no absolute right and wrong ; it is a matter of the heart and the perceptions. A sense of beauty leads us to a more logical view of the Great City, both as to what we should save of its past or create for its future.

The idolatry
of the past. This preservation of the past had its evil side. Veneration begat idolatry, and the beginning of the twentieth century, which tested every value, put this veneration to the severest test of all. The commercial mind saw money in it, dealing in old furniture became a mania, and thousands of beautiful houses, particularly in poverty-stricken Ireland, were wrecked and gutted for the sake of their ceilings, mantelpieces, and panelling. The movement ended in an orgy of bric-à-brac, in which the prices were kept up by American

---

* E. Alsworth Ross, " Sin and Society."   † St. Matthew, chap. v, verse 28.

buyers and manipulated by gangs of Jews. Productive artists meanwhile found that the curse of "dealing" helped them little in their livelihood, while the need of preserving the past in our cities remained misunderstood. To strip the frescoes from the churches, the façades from the houses, and stick them along the walls of vast museums in gloomy towns, may preserve them as stuffed birds are preserved; but it also destroys the first principle of their creation: they can sing and fly no longer. They were designed for their setting, and in the life and joy of their time; to tear them out of it is often a social sin. When, therefore, in our cities, we preserve, we should do it with two motives—historic association and intrinsic beauty. Of these the second, so little understood, is by far the more important of the two, because it implies unity in life. Shakespeare, George Washington, and Turner may be dead; but the little house at Stratford-on-Avon, Mount Vernon in Virginia, and the Riverside Cottage at Chelsea have in them a quality of their own that will not die, unless through the negligence, the blindness, the death of the race itself. Beauty, in that it is an attribute of Divinity, has in it race consciousness.

CHAPTER IX.—Neo-Georgianism.

It is claimed by some of the artists who build in English Renaissance that theirs is an essentially English tradition. There is no more justification for this than for any other form of building that has appeared in the country before.* It is, however, true to say that it represents a certain aristocratic sentiment, suitable to the country house and to the hanging of pictures. It is this that gave the eighteenth century reaction its strength in England and America. Arts and Crafts building, with its more Gothic or Pre-Raphaelite inspiration, with its cross lights and its endeavour to give the individual craftsman his chance, was thinking of other things—tapestry, for instance, as Morris and Burne-Jones understood it (see No. 34), or co-ordinated workmanship as we see it in Sedding's church of "The Holy Trinity," Sloane Square. But the painters were powerful in the last decade of the nineteenth century ; they wanted wall space for their pictures, and the individual craftsman could not free himself from factory control—he had no organization.

There was this further value in Neo-Georgianism : the plutocracy in England and America needed educating. An easy text-book of taste was essential. The conventional detail of the eighteenth century is sympathetic to the architect's scholarship rather than to the craftsman's imagination. The reduplicative power of the machine was at the architect's right hand. The swags, and urns, and pocket-handkerchiefs that John Ruskin had laughed away for an earlier generation all came back again ; and now, thanks to the hundred new devices of American machinery, five-ply panelling, plaster reproduction, "compo," electro-plating, artificial stone, "carton pierre," the carving machine, the tree-peeling machine, the drill, the punching-bear, the metal chuck, and a thousand others, it was possible to give an easy semblance of wealth and taste. Vast catalogues were compiled of stuff pilfered from country houses, English, Irish, Old Colonial, French ; doors, porches, balustrades, friezes, mouldings were measured, photographed, classified.† All the architect needed, if he had the necessary sense of proportion and scholarship, was to pick, as a tradesman, from his catalogue. To this standardization of eighteenth-century forms the contractor and the factory quickly adjusted

---

* Reginald Blomfield has made this claim. My own master in architecture, G. F. Bodley, made the same claim in an earlier generation for English Neo-Perpendicular.
† See the "Architect's Compendium" and the "Exemplar."

26

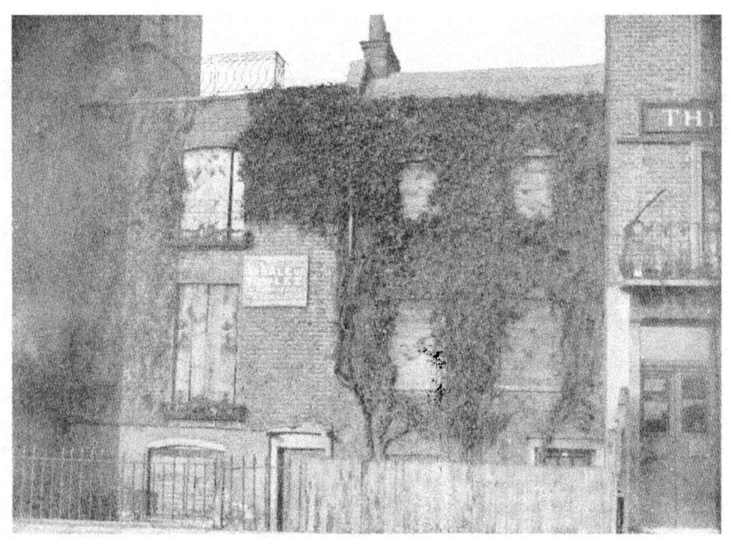

The Turner House, Chelsea, as condemned for demolition.   No. 30.

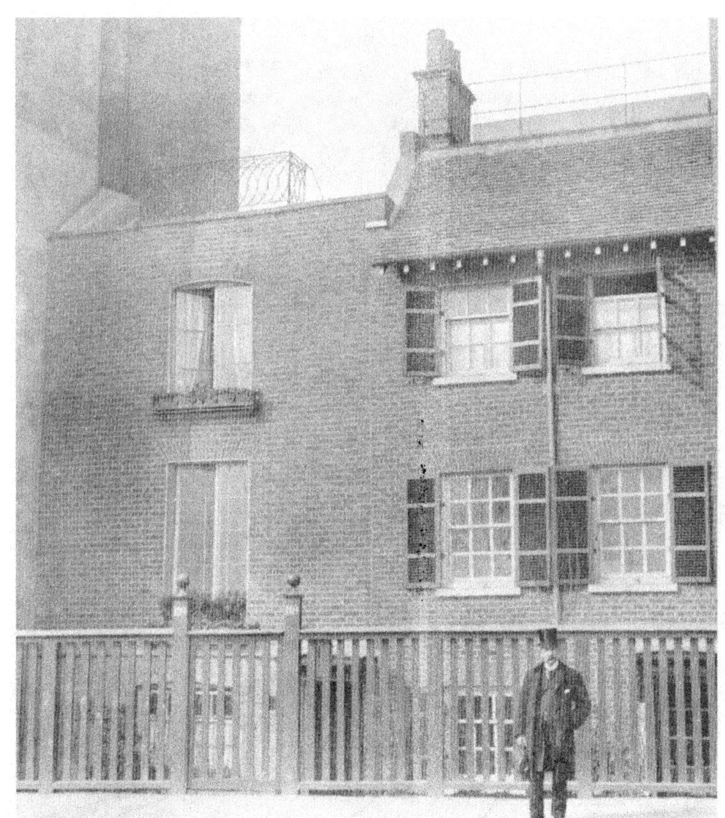

The same, after repair by C. R. Ashbee.   No. 31.

(Note the roof balcony Turner put up to paint the sunsets from.)

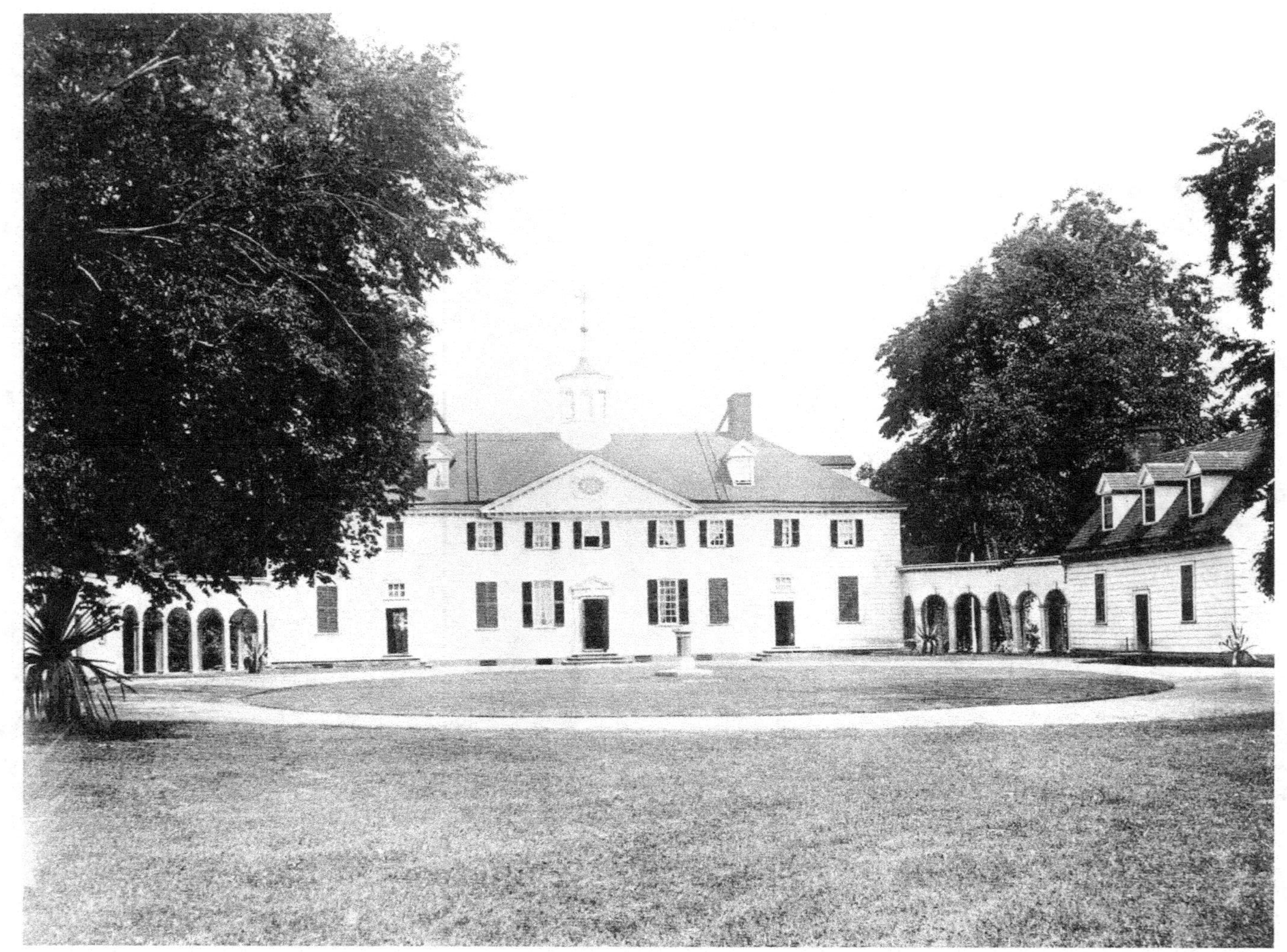

George Washington's Mount Vernon in Virginia.

No. 32.

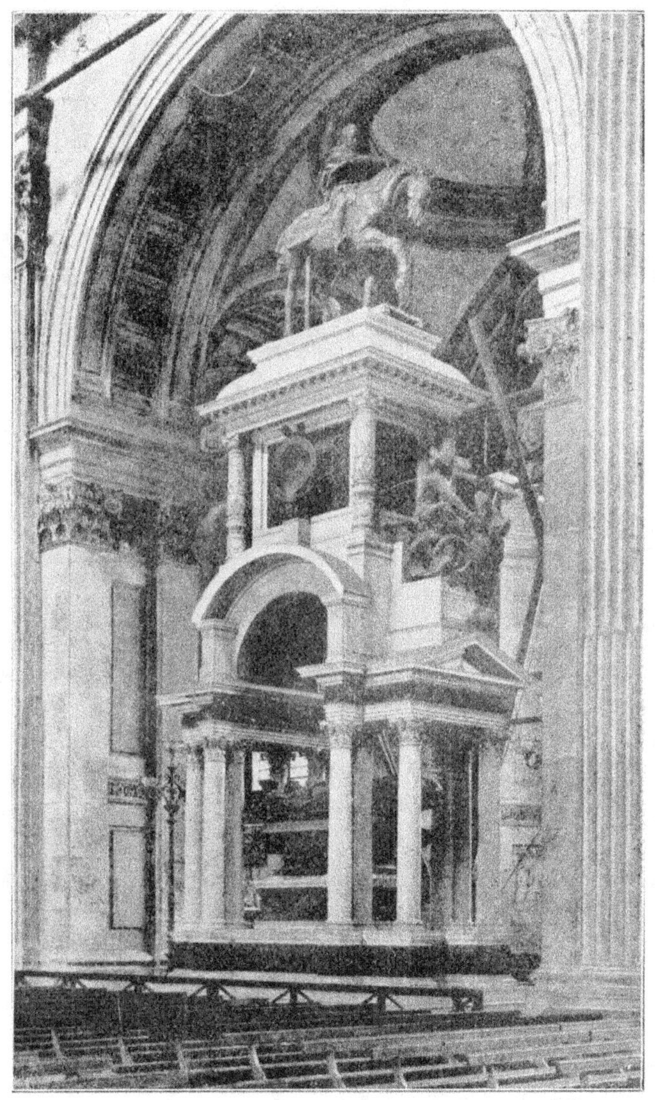

No. 33.

*Alfred Stevens's Wellington Monument
in St. Paul's, as re-erected.*

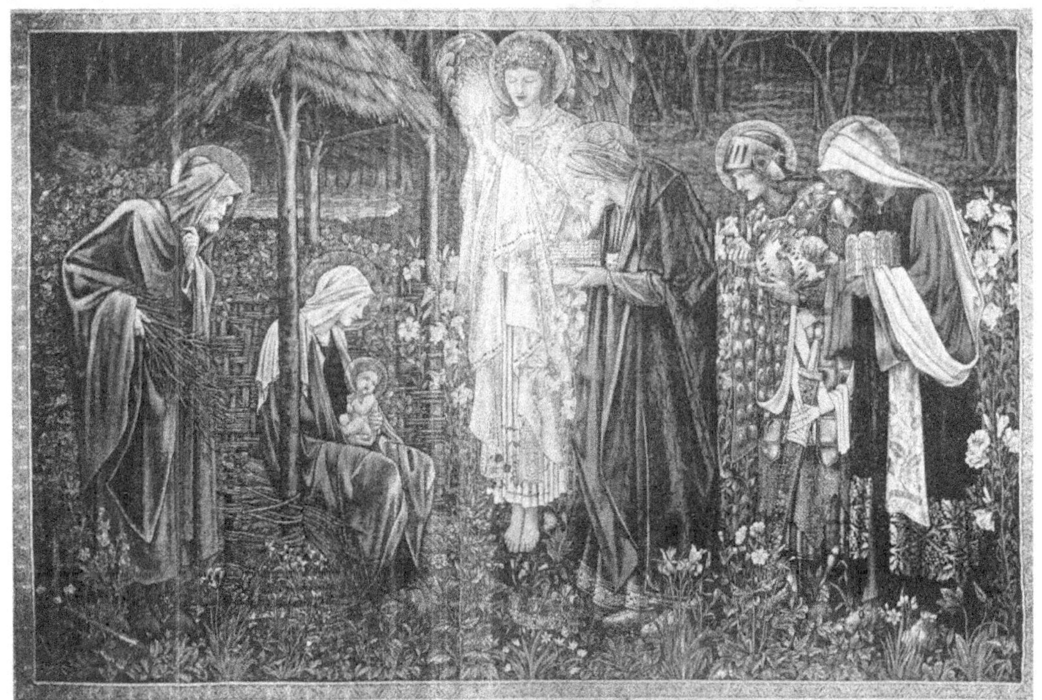

No. 34.

The Epiphany Tapestry.
By Morris and Burne-Jones.

themselves. But it did not help the artist craftsman, nor the human spirit within him. Grinling Gibbons, Robert Adam, Flaxman, did not work that way ; and it was in the way they worked that they found the sweetness and distinction of their style. There is an hotel in New York with a faultless Adam ceiling, where the rich men dine with their women-folk ; but a wit, who doubtless knew the true value of dead forms and the temptation they bring, summed it up in the phrase, " Adam above and Eve below."

Perhaps the underlying reason for all this is still obscure to us, and the princes of privilege and holders of franchises in American cities do not themselves understand why they want their houses to look like those of eighteenth-century aristocrats. There is little doubt, however, that the eighteenth-century reaction is the working out, in practical æsthetics, of that negation of the democratic spirit which led, in 1910, to the fall of the English House of Lords, and culminated in the European War, a cardinal issue of which is Democratic versus Autocratic government.

The fashionable Neo-Georgian architect is apt to forget that *The main-* the maintenance of these great houses, even with an expenditure of *tenance* £10,000 on American plumbing, depends upon cheap and willing *of great* domestic service. But our American cousins, coming home to the *houses in a* Islands of the Blest for comfort, found when they took their English *democratic* servants back with them, that these melted away into the democracy *society.* of the New World. The " perfect butler " came to have views of his own ; the cooks and housemaids were in a few years mistresses of ranches in Canada or the Middle West. I once designed one of these great houses for a wealthy man. It was a beautiful house, and he was a delightful man. He is dead now, and only a fragment of the great house came to be. Among other amenities there were to be fourteen milk-white, super-sterilized bathrooms on the American model. By one of those curious readjustments of finance involved in our credit system, the resources that were to keep this great establishment going, including the architect, suddenly disappeared, and our halls, reception-rooms, baths, gardens, and terraces became, as once to the builder in Ecclesiastes, all vanity. Perhaps his children profited by the change ; I doubtless lost much honour in the eyes of my professional colleagues. But what happened here to me may, after the War, not inconceivably happen to all of us who build or live in great houses.

It will not be the first time that architectural history has been revolutionized by Act of Parliament. Every French château is an object lesson.   In England Henry VII's statute of 1487, in regard to maintenance and the keeping of retainers in great houses, or the legislation of the Long Parliament, when Democracy fought Monopoly, could be cited.   Raby, Haddon, Whitehall are witness, or, better still, Audley End, the greater part of which was pulled down because it was too heavy a burden to maintain.

Insincerity in architecture.   When we probe Neo-Georgianism we are conscious of insincerity.   There is a want, such as we feel in a "Gothic revival" church.   A young soldier, reviewing in hospital the end of the Victorian era and the unrealities that followed it, suggests the answer:* "The Oxford Movement, which might have developed a national religion, was embittered to take refuge in the arms of Rome.   The Æsthetic Movement, which might have led to a national art, was ridiculed into preciosity and early decadence.   The Victorians laughed at their prophets."   Insincerity followed this betrayal of ideas, and men went back to the old used-up stuff, the old dead gods.   It was the same in America.   "If you want the English anti-democratic obscurantism really defended," said an American Southerner to me in 1915, "go to Boston, Massachusetts."   His people had been through the valley of the shadow, and themselves driven from a Georgian homestead in Virginia.   Adversity had brought him the real thing, taught him the meaning of Democracy.   Neo-Georgianism and all it stood for he detested.   "There is a certain type," said he, "who will never join your nobility in the trenches, but will stay at home and talk to us of the wickedness of trade unions."

Disraeli once said : "Genuine Toryism is never afraid of Democracy"; that may be true, but Neo-Georgianism and genuine Democracy are, and always will be, incompatible.

* Shane Leslie, "The End of a Chapter."

CHAPTER X.—What William Morris Stood For.

It was significant that the eighteenth-century revival began to make itself felt just at the moment of Morris's death. His life had been intransigeant; but it was also conservative, it was constructive, and it was Utopian. These paradoxes made men, in his own day, call him a Philistine. They saw him as a man wearing a great mane of hair and a blue shirt; they may have enjoyed his poetry, they did not understand his art. There are two verses in his "Message of the March Wind" that finely sum up his own attitude towards his time, have its sigh of social aspiration :

Social aspiration through the Arts.

> The singers have sung, and the builders have builded,
>   The painters have fashioned their tales of delight ;
> For what and for whom hath the world's book been gilded
>   When all is for these but the blackness of night ?
>
> . . . .
>
> Come back to the inn, love, and the lights and the fire,
>   And the fiddler's old tune, and the shuffling of feet ;
> For there in a while shall be rest and desire,
>   And there shall the morrow's uprising be sweet.

The blackness of night lay in the purposelessness of the industrial city, the great communities that knew not how to live. The old Inn was the village England. In himself Morris was the minstrel and story-teller, loving beauty, and, before all, beauty in building. He knew more of the architecture of Greece and the Middle Ages than any man living, because he knew it not bookishly, but as a creative artist, from the feel of the stone. For the painter's work he had sympathy, provided it told "tales of delight"; and whether these were in wool, as was the great Epiphany Tapestry (see No. 34), or tempera, on the loom or the wall, or in stained glass, mattered little to him. But easel-painting disturbed his scheme of decoration, as it would that of anyone who loved cross-lighting in architecture. His philosophy of art was rooted in these practical applications. If we were artists there was divine purpose for us, and our object the gilding of the book of life, even as the mediæval scribe gilded the letters of the sacred text. This was the best part of the book, and unless conceived as the life of the people best left alone.

The paradox of the revolutionary Socialist and the conservative craftsman was logical. I have heard him say, "We artists have a

WHAT WILLIAM MORRIS STOOD FOR

The para-
dox of the
revolutionary
Socialist and
the conserva-
tive artist.

duty—we are but links in the golden chain that has been handed down to us through the Middle Ages, we must hold it for the greater time than ours that is to come."

But where his art was constructive—those wonderful shops at Merton, as one remembers them in the old days—his Socialism was iconoclastic. He realized that Socialism would destroy Industrial Society. He wanted society destroyed because it was unsympathetic to the arts, to the point of view in life for which he and all artists stood. Thus viewed, Morris is the greatest force in our time, because he contains within himself, and in his life, the parable of the artist in Industrial Society. The artist says: "Either you make it possible for me to live, or I destroy you and this world you are creating. I am the soul of your city: without me the great city has no place."

Axiom IX. See Axiom IX.

There must be room made for these imaginative, creative people, or they set to and disintegrate the social order. They are doing it at present in Europe, and the cataclysm through which we are living Morris foreshadowed. He did not bother about the politics of the question, and he took no account of time. A quarter of a century more or less mattered little. The break-up of the industrial system was for him as certain as was the power of men to create, and to create a new order, through the individual motive of joy.

The motive
of joy.

It is hard for the rich man, the commercial, the peasant grown banker, the Fabian economist who has never worked with his hands, to realize the fact that this motive of joy is the point of new departure. As for machinery, the fulcrum upon whose purchase the whole fabric of economic theory as of Fabian Socialism turns, he neither believed nor disbelieved in it; he merely said that much of it was worthless. In his Utopia he assumed the existence of mechanical power as a matter of course.

Axiom VI.

In Morris's day it was not yet possible to lay down, as we can do in Axiom VI, that "*The distinction between what should and what should not be produced by machinery has in many trades and crafts now been made.*" Our workshop experience had not yet been tested. He helped to test it. But his greatest contribution to economics is summed up in the prophecy that beauty in life, the great city of the future, is possible only when, as he puts it in "News from Nowhere," "Mastery shall be changed for Fellowship." If his teaching led us to it, it was his

Axiom IX.

life that enabled us to give practical shape to our ninth axiom. Let us recall it: "*The arts, postulating as they do the motive of joy in their creation, and the freedom of the individual to go on creating, do not flourish under conditions where men think it right to exploit them for profit."*

We must free the arts from mechanical servitude. He gave us the clue to the new workshop ethics—gave it in his life and personality; and that is why not only is he so great among artists, but why he makes of all artists, despite antiquarianism or scholarship, the greatest appeal to the working classes. He has come to stand for the truth that the freedom of the arts connotes industrial freedom.

CHAPTER XI.—THE IDEA BEHIND POST-IMPRESSIONISM AND FUTURISM.

But let us return to the painters. By the close of the nineteenth century they had practically arrogated to themselves the term " Art "; all the other arts had been mechanized away. The economic debacle of the Arts and Crafts movement following upon the teachings of Whistler seemed to justify the public in its belief that nothing any longer was " Art " that was not bounded in the four sides of a frame of gold.

Plastic art and the direct expression of feeling.

There came a curious and sudden shock. Within a few years the golden frames were filled with strange and bizarre patches, lines, blotches, cubes, and stripes of colour. There were thousands of these things in gold frames in hundreds of exhibitions. The painters themselves understood them—perhaps; but for the public, what did it all mean? They rushed to the exhibition catalogues to find out and have the mystery explained, and they found: " We have ceased to ask ' What does this picture represent?' and ask instead ' What does it make us feel?' We expect a work of plastic art to have more in common with a piece of music than with a coloured photograph."* The public set to work to analyse its feelings.

The frescoes of Roger Fry and his group of decorative painters who were let loose on one of the South London technical schools created quite a little storm.

" I know nothing about Art," said a young cockney engineer, as he wandered past the much-condemned frescoes, " but this makes me want to whistle."

" That," cried the painters, triumphantly, " is precisely how we want you to feel."

Speaking of the painting of one of the younger exponents of Post-Impressionism, their herald and champion says : " His art, whatever else may be said of it, is certainly not descriptive. Hardly at all does it depend for its effect on association or suggestion. There is no reason why a mind sensitive to form and colour, though it inhabit another solar system, and a body altogether unlike our own, should fail to appreciate it."

* Clive Bell, "Second Post-Impressionist Exhibition Catalogue" 1912. See also " Art," 1914.

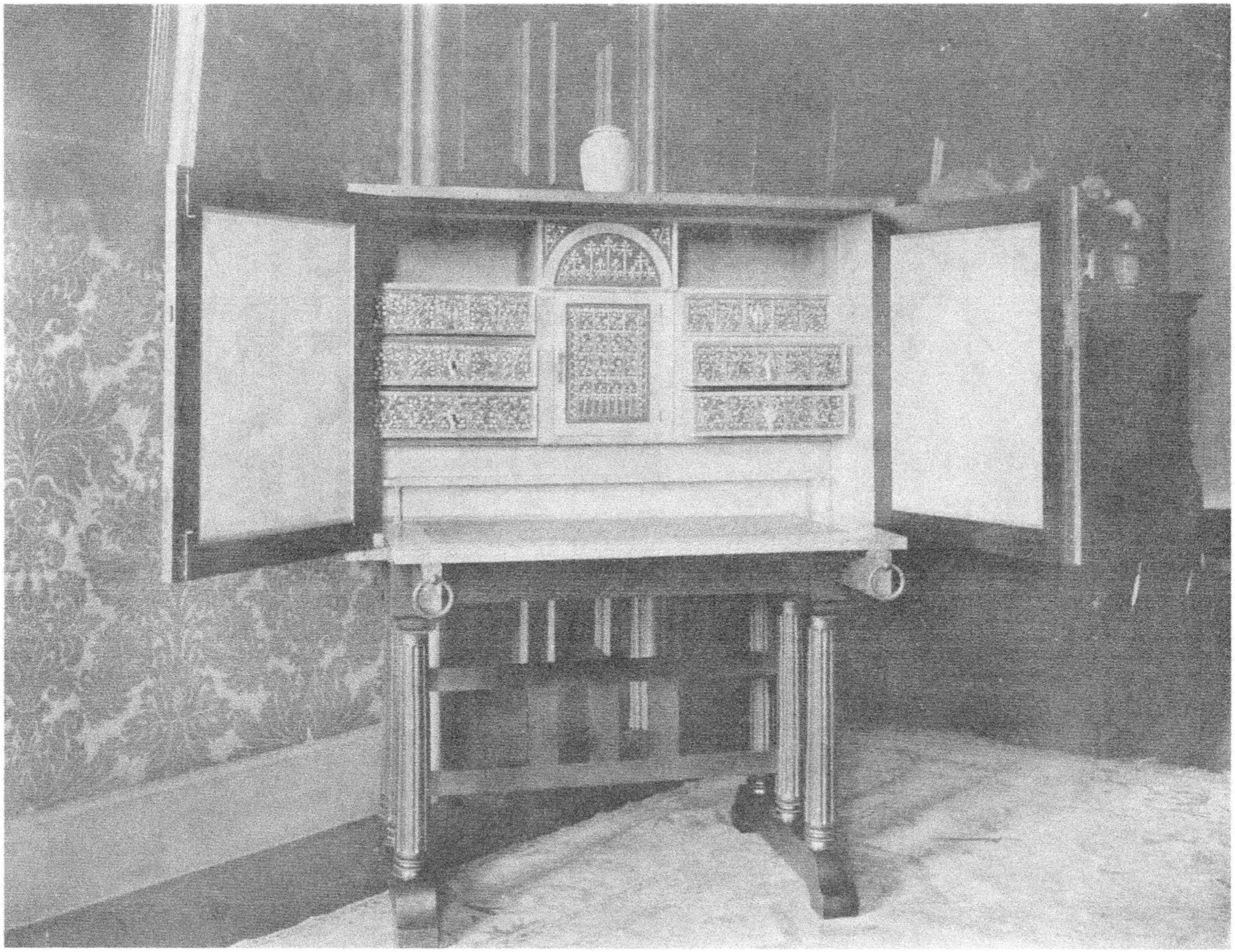

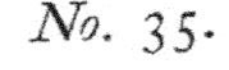

Cabinet in walnut, the interior of silver-grey wood and red morocco leather tooled with gold. Designed by C. R. Ashbee, executed by J. W. Pyment of the Guild of Handicraft; the leather work by Statia Power.

No. 35.

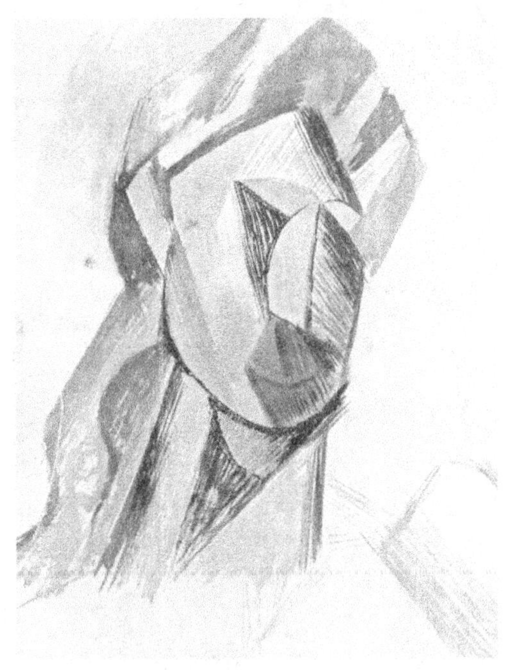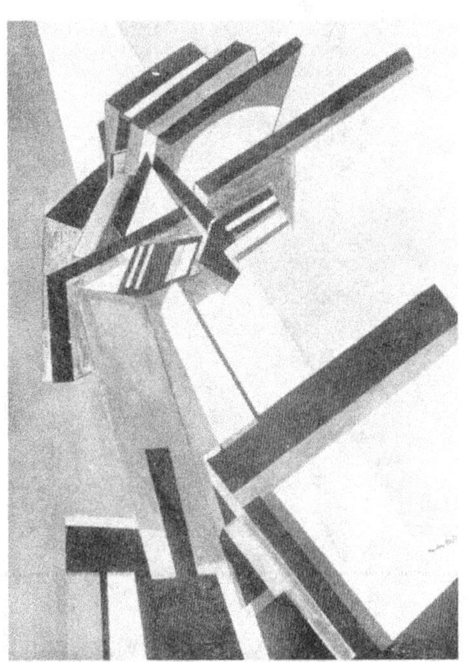

No. 36.   *No. 37.*

Head of a Man.
By Picasso.

Portrait of an Englishwoman.
By Wyndham Lewis.

No reason whatever. Therefore the only possible answer to this line of argument is that we whose appreciation the artist challenges inhabit our own solar system, and it is our own bodies we are interested in. I once asked a Post-Impressionist painter why he had painted six fingers on one hand. " Why not ? " was the reply. There was no more to be said ; the answer was conclusive, for it was the March Hare's reply to Alice, when they discussed drawing in " Wonderland."

It is no good pretending that our attitude is Oriental—that there is some symbol, some god behind, whom the artist is interpreting to the community—when it is still Occidental. *Symbolism and " signifi- cant form."*

" The Post-Impressionists," says Roger Fry, " do not seek to imitate form, but to create form ; not to imitate life, but to find an equivalent for life. By that I mean that they wish to make images which by the clearness of their logical structure, and by their closely knit unity of texture, shall appeal to our disinterested and contemplative imagination with something of the same vividness as the things of actual life appeal to our practical activities. In fact, they aim not at illusion, but at reality."

Granted that we accept that as a working philosophy for the Arts of our time, the difficulty is still its application to ourselves, to the work of the artists who challenge our attention. " Le véritable objet de l'Art c'est l'expression de la vie." The French psychologists had said it before. Post-Impressionism indeed was a French movement, the art of painting was being pursued by the irresistible logic of the Latin mind, and here was the mirror being held up. If you have something to say it is well ; if not, then no formula, whether of lines, or cubes, or masses, or squares, is of any use. Significant form must signify something worth while. It is life that teaches us.

" The logical extreme of such a method," Roger Fry goes on to say, " would undoubtedly be the attempt to give up all resemblance to normal form, and create a purely abstract language of form— a visual music ; and the later work of Picasso shows this clearly enough. The Post-Impressionist painters may or may not be successful in their attempt. It is too early to be dogmatic on the point, which can only be decided when our sensibilities to such abstract form have been more practised than they are at present. But I would suggest that there is nothing ridiculous in the attempt to do this. Such a picture as Picasso's ' Head of a Man ' (see No. 36) would undoubtedly be ridiculous if, having set out to make a direct imitation

POST-IMPRESSIONISM AND FUTURISM

of the actual model, he had been incapable of getting a better likeness. But Picasso did nothing of the sort. He had shown in the 'Portrait of Mlle. L. B.' that he could do so at least as well as anyone if he wished, but he is here attempting to do something quite different." *

We have here got to the point where it is essential for us to know what Picasso's symbol really means, much as we want to know the meaning of the symbols of some god in whom we believe and whom the artist is interpreting for us. The vital difference between the symbol "interpreted" by the artist and the symbol "invented" by the artist is that the latter has meaning to the artist alone, the former has meaning to the whole community.

The suicide of the Art of Painting. The Italian Futurists make the same effort to create "an abstract language of form." They tell us : "What must be rendered is *dynamic sensation;* that is to say, the particular rhythm of each object, its inclination, its movement, or, to put it more exactly, its interior force." They add, with an almost Eastern touch : "We thus arrive at what we call *painting of states of mind,*" and they tell us that the spectator "*must in future be placed in the centre of the picture!*" † Stripped of metaphor, this means that the spectator must understand what the painter is trying to say : the picture must have meaning to him. But there are thousands of paintings by Post - Impressionists and Futurists to which not even the most stimulating title or catalogue will ever give him the clue, e.g. the "Portrait of an Englishwoman" ‡ (see No. 37).

By withdrawing thus from life, and into an abstract symbolism of their own, the painters have cut off their own right hands; and so it is that, in our search for the Great City, they can only take us on a little way. It is the whole of life we want to change. Art is a greater thing than painting. It is difficult indeed to resist the conclusion that the Art of Painting is in process of disintegration. Perhaps, like the phœnix, it is destroying itself for some finer purpose.

"We wish to glorify War," says the leader of this youngest school ; "War, the only health-giver of the world—militarism, patriotism, the destructive arm of the anarchist, the beautiful ideas

* Roger Fry, "Second Post-Impressionist Exhibition Catalogue,". 1912.

† "Initial Manifesto of Futurism," 1912. F. T. Marinetti, Umberto Boccioni, and others.

‡ Blast, 1914.

34

that kill." The Italian seems to have studied Nietzsche. But the death he invokes may, for an Art with centuries of tradition, be suicide.

"Look at us. We are not breathless . . . Our heart does not feel the slightest weariness! For it is fed with fire, hatred, and speed! That surprises you? It is because you do not remember ever having lived! We stand upon the summit of the world, and once more we cast our challenge to the stars." *

* "Initial Manifesto of Futurism," 1912. F. T. Marinetti, Umberto Boccioni, and others.

CHAPTER XII.—THE HOUSING AND TOWN PLANNING MOVEMENT.

The Art of Painting, just as the Art of pseudo eighteenth-century Architecture, had lost its grip on life. This was brought home to us when we discovered that what we needed was not so much "fine houses for rich men" as decent houses for poor men, and clean and beautiful cities for all men. That meant a need for readjusting the planning of our towns to the life we lead in them. Town planning, as now understood, implies such readjustment. There is little consistency in town planning. Cities have sprung into life and continued, and history shows unmistakably how they have periods of efflorescence and disintegration.

Look, for instance, at the great story of London—Roman London, Norman London, the London of Richard II, the London of Sir Christopher Wren and of the Whig aristocracy, Mid-Victorian London, and the London we are now striving to reconstruct (see No. 38). They are six distinct cites, each often obliterating those that passed before. But what of the periods in between? They were often times of confusion and chaos. Out of this chaos the new life took shape. The Saxon upheaval when classic civilization broke down, the struggle of the Guilds to give shape to the mediæval city life, the plague and fire which ended the Middle Ages, the welter of the Industrial Revolution from which we are just beginning to emerge— they were often dreary and terrible, these periods in between. But when we think of the completed plan, whether of Norman Fitz-Stephen, or of Richard Eveleigh when he built Westminster Hall, or of Sir Christopher Wren with his vision of the new London (see No. 69), or of some dreamer in a progressive County Council, it is of a new life that we think. The plan has been readjusted to this new life; it is the heart of the community that has been changed.

So it is with every great city; and each city should be studied, and, so to speak, mastered diagrammatically. The diagram I show of the City of Dublin, upon the proposed reconstruction of which I was at work when the War broke out, is another illustration of the right historical method (see No. 39). Whether in London or in Dublin, we must know first what were those cities that have gone before. Here in Dublin was a problem set to us architects in which we were asked, besides saving the amenities of the old city, to make proposals for the

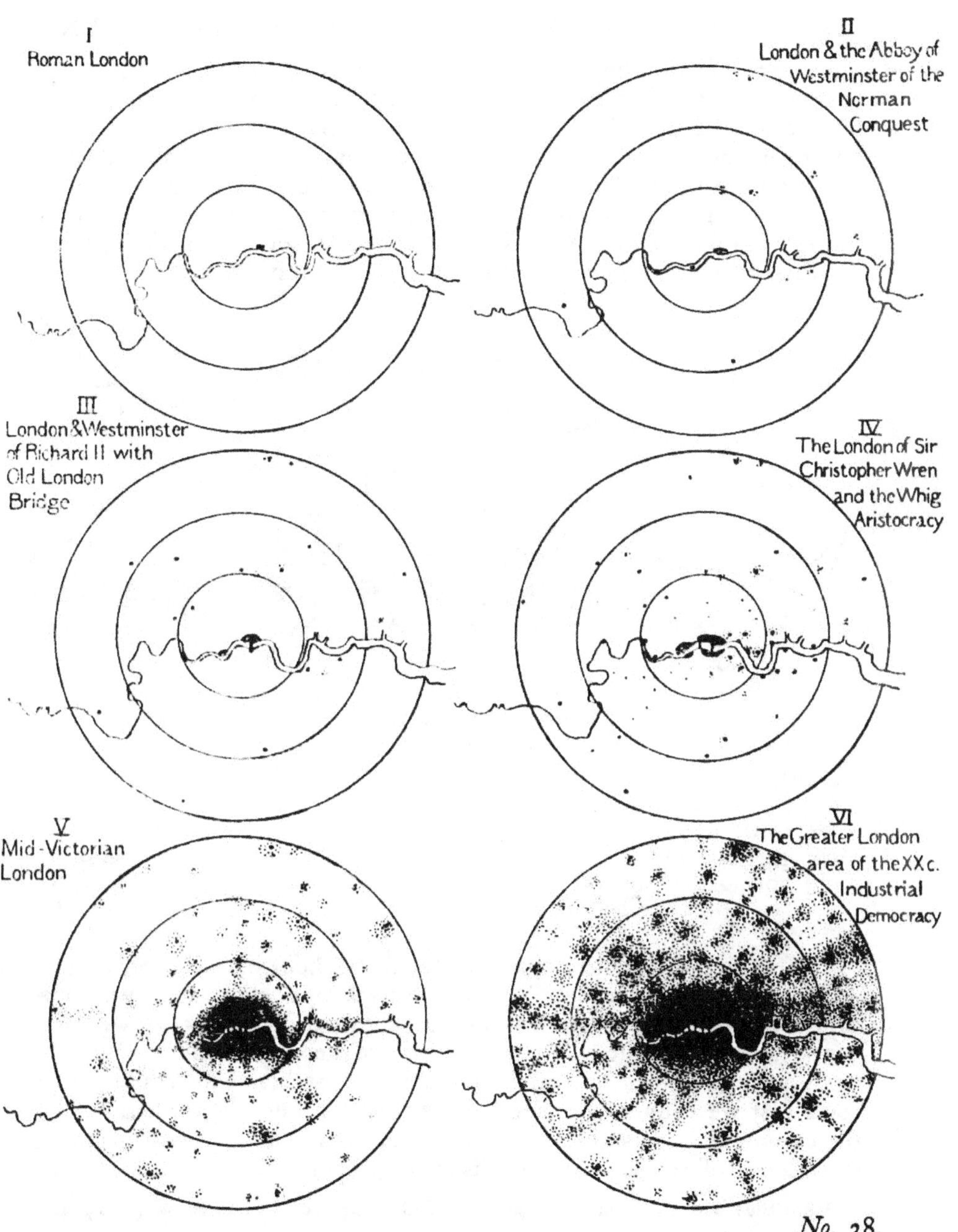

Diagrammatic plan of the expansion of London in six periods of its history.

housing of 150,000 human beings who were improperly housed.*   And then came the War, and not only ended all our plans, but set a red line across the period of industrial chaos that brought the old and beautiful Dublin of the eighteenth century to ruin and disgrace. The period of disintegration has now itself been circumscribed.   In the light of history the break is only momentary, and the twentieth-century Dublin, even as the twentieth-century London, is likely, when the War is over, to inaugurate a new period in civic history.

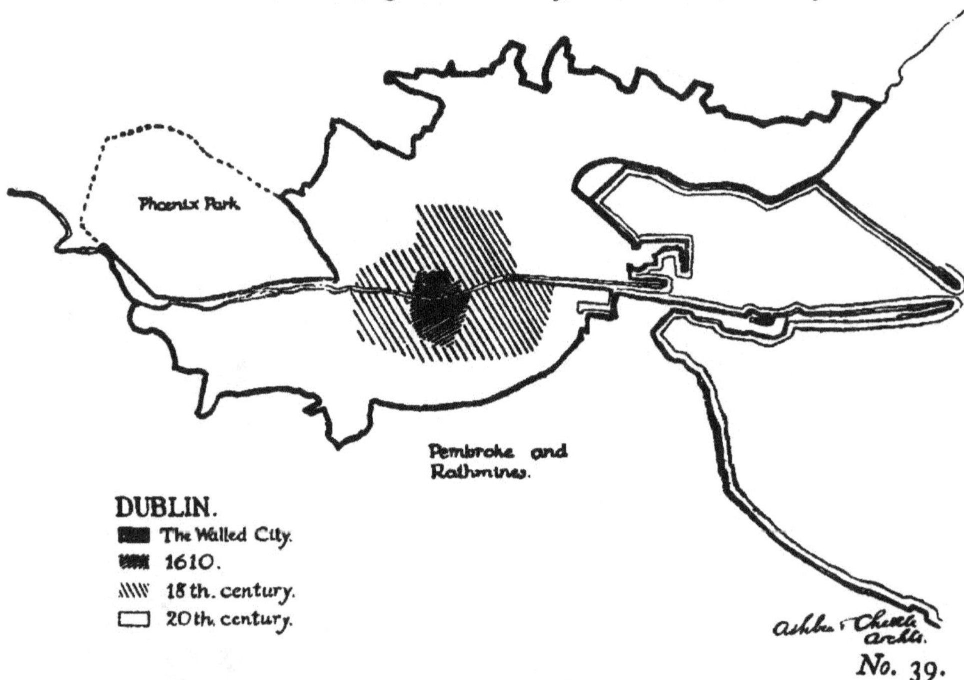

Volumes of architectural and technical books have been written on the planning of cities, but all resolves into this: that we must adjust our building to the life of our community, and that we must consider first the life.   To this point we keep returning.   For the town planner ethics and æsthetics are inseparable, and while ethics come first we cannot visualize them except through æsthetics.   That the community is awakening to the fact that it needs town planning is evidence of its having so far lived no proper communal life.   Some

* See Blue Book.   Report and Appendix of Dep. Com. on Dublin Housing.   1914.

38

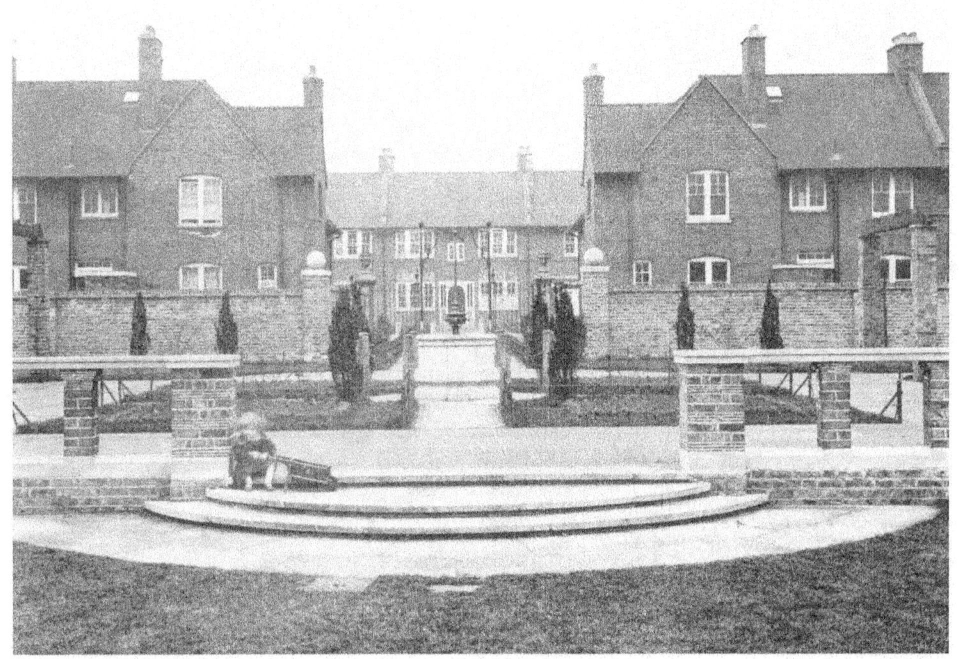

No. 40.

The Tower Garden, London.   View looking east.
W. E. Riley, Superintending Architect L.C.C.

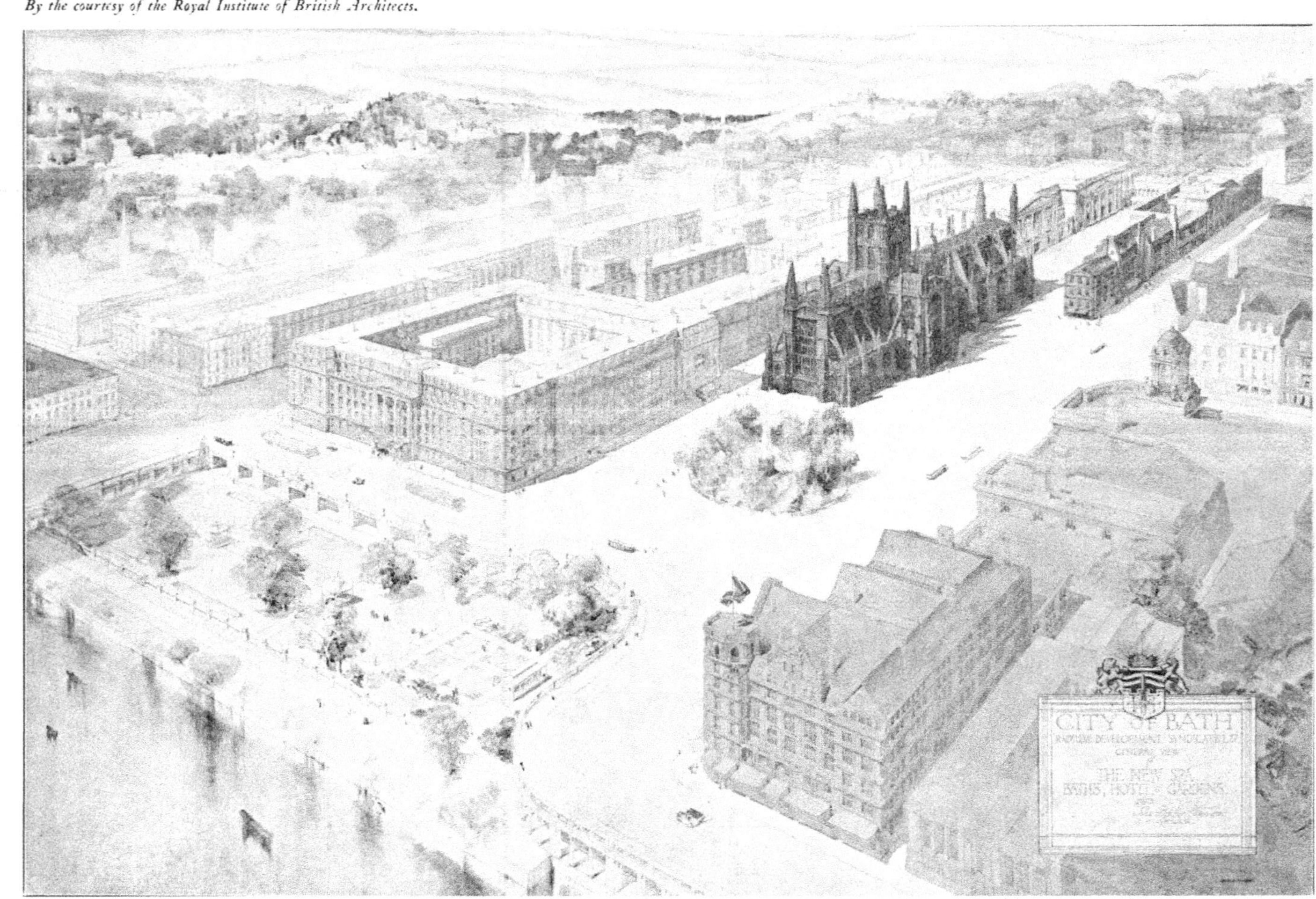

No. 41.

Proposed Scheme for the reconstruction of the City of Bath.
By John Belcher and J. J. Joass.

few of our cities, such as the beautiful City of Bath (see No. 41), *An illustra-*
where there are two distinct building periods, a mediæval and an *tion from*
eighteenth-century, have been spared the industrial humiliation of *Bath.*
the last century. They make the town planner's work easy; he has
but to follow tradition, note what remains of the finer life; but with
our industrial cities it is otherwise. They all tell the same story, that
of an absence of any finer life. And now suddenly, and rather mis-
trustingly, the community calls upon its architects and bids them
express in stone and iron something it has not got. The architect
tries, but he does not know enough. He knows about styles, but he
does not know about life. He tries styles, and they fail. Dimly
he realizes that each style is the crystallization of a life that was.

To take other examples that I show : Eighteenth-century Phila- *An illustra-*
delphia, with Penn's prim and dignified planning, was a city of quiet *tion from*
little squares and rectangles, two-story red-brick houses crowned with *Phila-*
its exquisite Independence Hall (see No. 58); it is now ruined by *delphia.*
tall buildings. The Dublin of Gandon's Custom-House, another of
the masterpieces of eighteenth-century building, was an even lovelier
city, with a salt and quality all its own, the city of a fine aristocratic
life. Now that those things are slipping away from us their lost
beauty grows clearer. The average man is no poet, and beauty for
him lies in the past. But the architect needs a finer understanding,
and his knowledge, if he is to interpret well, must be of his own
day, of a life generous and sympathetic. He must try to understand
Industrialism and Democracy.

And yet how grossly ignorant, not only of the technicalities of town *An illustra-*
planning, but of the needs of Democracy, are our Government depart- *tion from*
ments. Here is the criticism of the Garden Cities and Town Planning *Rosyth.*
Association upon the English Government's scheme for the building of
the new Industrial City of Rosyth, where with intelligence and foresight
—such, for instance, as the Germans showed at Essen—we could have
had the model dockyard community of the world. It was proposed that
the Admiralty should put upon seventy-four acres of land 2,225 houses !
"The figure works out at the rate of thirty houses per acre gross,
and no provision is made for open space; while, when the area required
for roads is deducted, the amount of garden space to each house will
be still less. In these times, when man-power is such an urgent
necessity, and when we have to think of the future of the race, with
all that this involves in the matter of the most complete physical development, surely it is unthinkable that, in connexion with

Government work, it is to be permissible to erect potential slums and to encourage the overcrowding of houses upon the acre. The principles which this association laid down eighteen years ago have been almost universally adopted, and it is everywhere agreed that the maximum number of houses to the acre should be twelve, and that one acre in every ten ought to be reserved for open space.

"The history of the housing problem at Rosyth is one of the most damaging indictments of Departmental muddling that could be written. As far back as 1903 this association offered its services to the Admiralty and made tentative arrangements for providing for the housing of the people who we could foresee would be housed there. From that time onward we never ceased to try to get something done. Successive Civil Lords were seen and consideration was promised many times, but always the permanent staff blocked the way. Ten years ago we could have started building cottages at Rosyth at at least half what they cost to-day, and we would have done so had the Government made up its mind to let us have land; but our efforts were ignored and our warnings were disregarded."*

Sailors are good on the sea, and clerks in Government offices may, within certain strict limitations, fulfil useful functions; but to us architects should be committed the work of planning and building the new cities, and we should ourselves be better trained than we are to build them.

As a set-off against the unintelligent muddle of Rosyth, we ought to put the excellent housing work in the Tower Garden area of London (see No. 40), where again *poverty* and *architecture* came into close contact. We do not want architecture till we have mastered poverty, but nothing justifies a Government department in continuing unintelligently the traditions of poverty.

From nineteenth-century chaos to twentieth-century co-ordination.

When John Ruskin, speaking of English decorative art in the 'eighties, said, "The best decoration for an empty house is a flitch of bacon," the architects did not understand him and thought the saying an irrelevant folly. We see it differently now, and the inspiration for which he and Morris stood has led to one of the vital æsthetic movements of our time. Achievement from the point of view of standard is not yet great: the greatness lies in the solid social force behind; only in the consciousness of this is it now possible for us to use that greater historical knowledge that enables a twentieth-

* Ewart G. Culpin, "The Times," 23 December 1916.

century writer on practical civics to say unchallenged: "The theory of the town, the pattern or model of what a town should be, is to-day being slowly pieced together out of the chaos left by the nineteenth century. In that ruthless time the towns emerged from their ancient

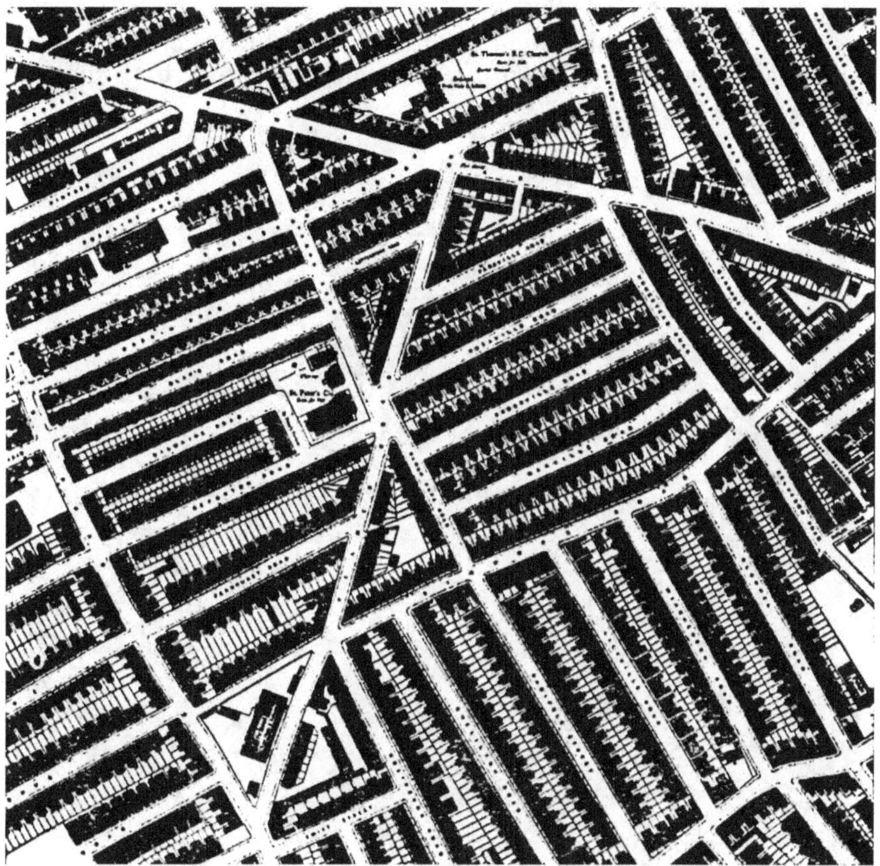

No. 42.

A Corner of Nineteenth-century London, showing the absence of any intelligent planning. Compare this with the plans shown in Nos. 46, 48, 54, 55, 56, 69, 74, 91.

place in the State, and became formless things of mighty power and dreadful horror. They lost all the fine orderly and homely qualities they had ever had, and took to themselves every evil weapon which could

THE HOUSING AND TOWN PLANNING MOVEMENT

menace human life.   To-day we are seeking to recover the town from
what the last century made it, and to bring it back to order and beauty." *

This formlessness and horror may be illustrated from the Ord-
nance Survey map of any English industrial city.   No. 42 shows a little
corner, taken at random, of nineteenth-century London.   I could give
a hundred such.   No. 43 is Greater London as a whole, in its formlessness, with its various, and often conflicting, district authorities.   In the
light of the new co-ordination of the twentieth century both illustrate
what is blind, wasteful, ignorant.

*C. B. Purdom, " The Garden City."

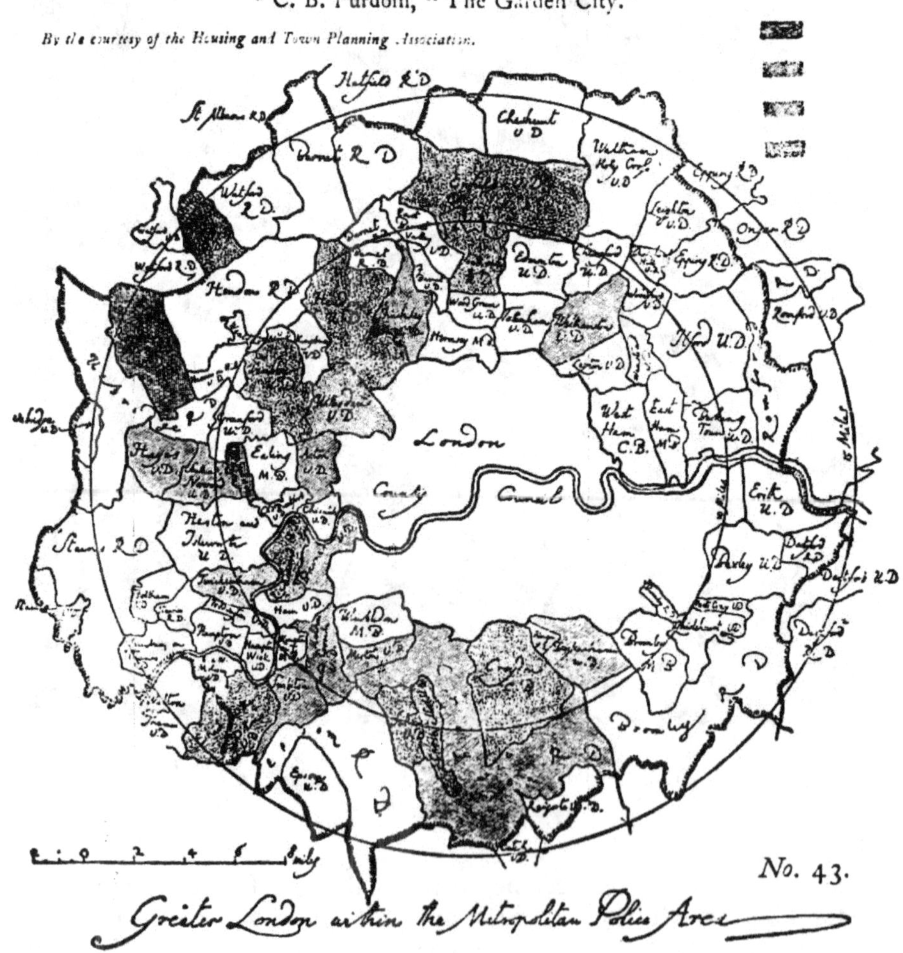

CHAPTER XIII.—The Garden City Idea.

The Garden City movement implies two conflicting ideas : the break up of the great city on the one hand, and on the other its more intelligent expansion. These two ideas are sometimes confused ; but they are quite distinct. Letchworth Garden City, Port Sunlight, the experiment of the Guild of Handicraft at Campden, belong to the first. The idea behind was the breaking up of the great town, the starting of a new community with a healthy life of its own in the country. Hampstead, Ruislip, Romford, Bournville, Forest Hills New York, and numberless others in Europe and America, are examples of the second. In them the idea behind is the intelligent expansion of the great city.

We see the essential " Garden City " idea best in Letchworth (see Nos. 44, 45, and 46). The Letchworth " first Garden City " was a development conscious and consistent. Its underlying principle was the limitation of the personal interests of land and capital in favour of the community. This principle has been variously stated, and by different idealists, at different times—Robert Owen, Thomas Spence, Silk Buckingham, Joseph Fels ; the profits resulting from the increase of population and people's improvements shall go back to the people.

Great ideas are often accepted in principle before it is expedient to put them into practice, and in England it was only the temporary depression of agricultural land values that made the purchase of the Letchworth estate possible by a company of not over-wealthy enthusiasts.

" The point of first importance in connexion with Garden City," says its historian,* " is that it is based upon a change in the ownership of land. It is essentially an attempt, not at land nationalization, or of ownership by the central authority, but of local ownership or municipalization."

There is, of course, nothing new in this. There are still mediæval cities, for instance in Germany, where the bulk of the land is under local ownership; the novelty is in the application of the idea to modern methods, especially of finance. The Articles of Association are of the greatest interest : " In the face of physical degeneration, the existence of which in our great towns is incontrovertible, imperialism abroad and progress at home seem alike an empty mockery. Sound physical condition is surely the foundation of all human development, and the

* C. B. Purdom, " The Garden City."

directors submit to the public a scheme for securing it in a particular instance which they believe to contain all the elements of success, and which, if carried to a successful issue, will lead to that redistribution

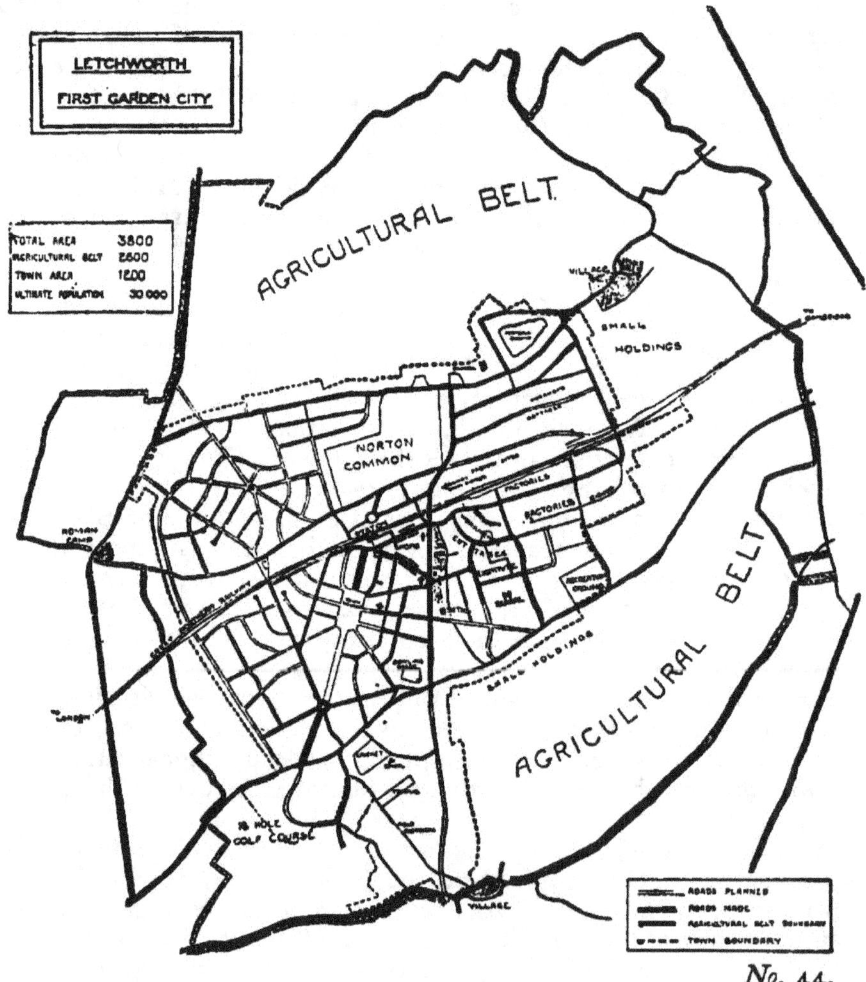

No. 44.

of the people upon the land in which, and in which alone, as they believe, is to be found a solution of the problem, how to maintain and increase industrial efficiency without impairing the national physique."

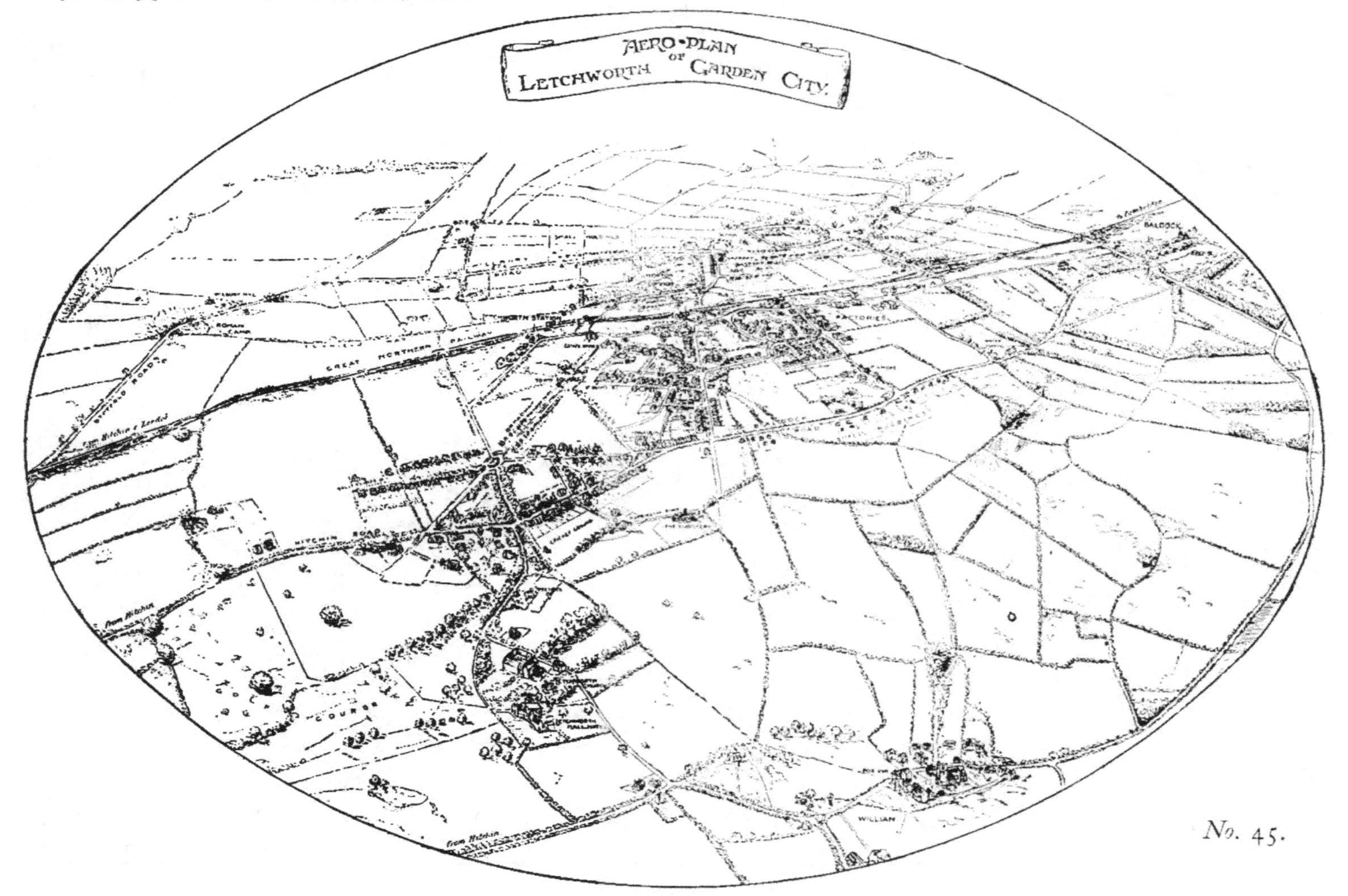

By the courtesy of the Garden Cities and Town Planning Association.

No. 45.

KEY TO COLOURS
Norton
GARDEN CITY TENANTS LTD
1905 COTTAGE EXHIBITION SITES
EAST HOLM
FACTORY AND SITES
G.N. RAILWAY GOODS YARD
FACTORY SITES
PLANS MODELS BUILDING TRADES EXHIBITS OF 1907 EXHIBITION
LETCHWORTH STATION
MAIN AVENUE
TOWN SQUARE
SOUTH VIEW
GOLF COURSE
Letchworth
FIRST GARDEN · CITY · LTD
PLAN · OF · PRESENT · DEVELOPMENT.
— SPRING 1907 —
This plan is subject to modification and must not be taken as the basis of any contract.
ESTATE OFFICE, LETCHWORTH
FROM PLAN MADE BY BARRY PARKER & RAYMOND UNWIN ARCHITECTS. BUXTON. & BALDOCK. HERTS.
1000 FEET   500   0   1000   2000   3000   4000   5000   FEET
1 FURLONG   0   1 MILE

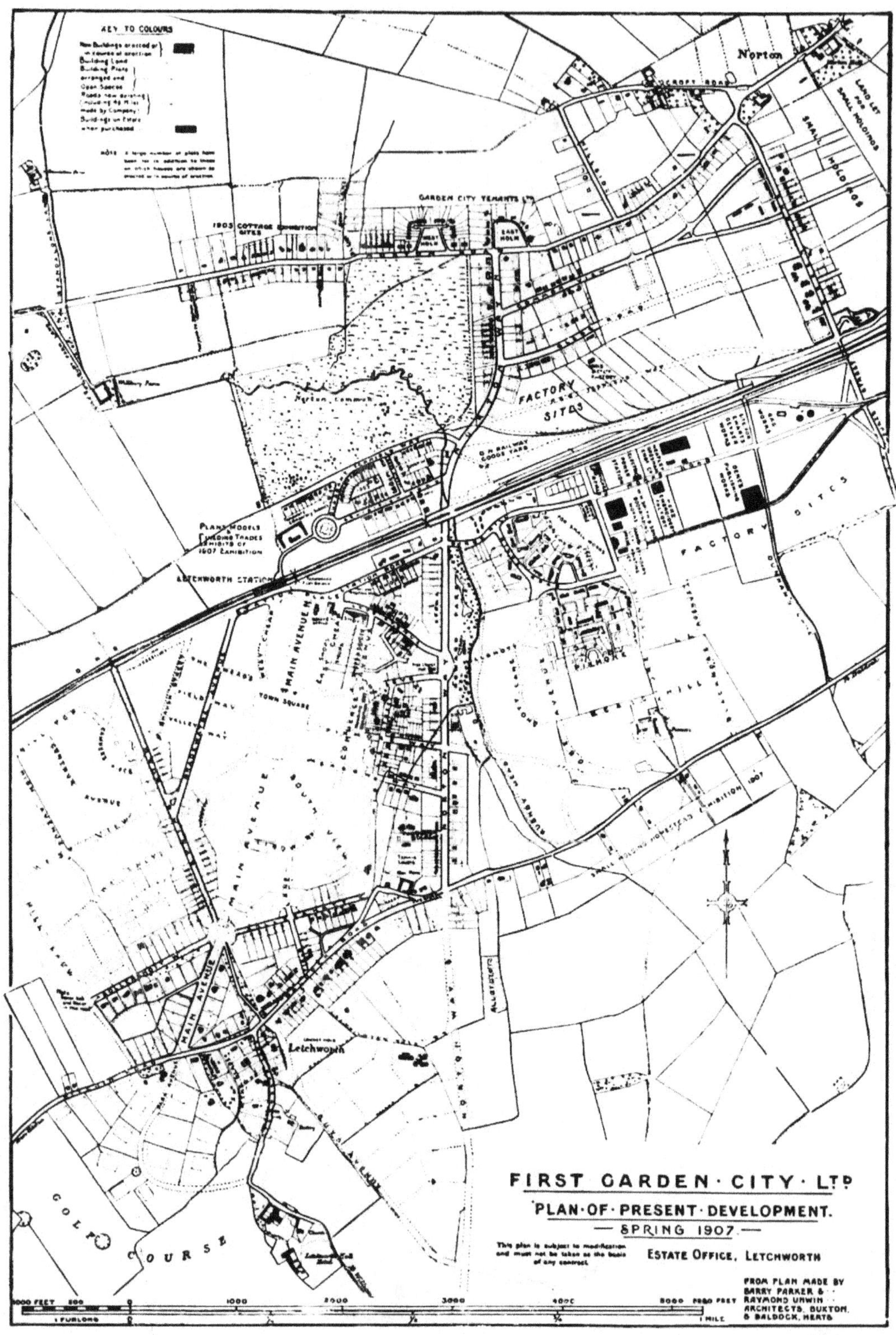

No. 46.

"The Articles of Association of the Company provide that all profits beyond a cumulative dividend of five per cent, which is regarded as a fair return to the shareholders, shall be used for the benefit of the town and its inhabitants. As the profits therefore cannot be retained by the Company, they will go to the tenants in one way or the other. . . . As the greater part of this increased value is due to the social activities of the people as a whole (i.e., in their collective capacity), it is in this capacity that they should receive the benefit, and not as private individuals."

The two conflicting ideas in the Garden City movement are very *The value in* clearly summed up thus : "It was to put an end to the extension of *civilization* towns and the building of suburbs that Garden City was founded. It *of " little "* was to stop the great towns growing that the new town was begun. *cities.* The essential idea of town planning as it is practised in England is the antithesis of the Garden City idea. The town planner says : 'We want to lay out in advance the land over which our towns are to spread; we want to schedule these green fields for the town more easily to swallow; we want to prepare for the endless growth of the huge monster.' The Garden City says: 'We need to put a limit to the size of the town; we need to preserve those fields so that they shall not be destroyed; we need to remake town life in small towns in the midst of the country.'"

The finest human civilization, it has been said, was evolved in cities not much bigger than Cork, and a population of 10,000 has been set as a convenient limit within which to enjoy the finer privileges of citizenship. Failing this, new and smaller groups must be built up within the great cities themselves—groups that stand not for wealth or class differences, but for civilization. The idealists are feeling their way in both directions, and we architects who are called in now to build new cities, now to reconstruct old ones, are but the antennæ of this idealism.

As for the great town, we are only at the beginning of its *The disinte-* disintegration; we still need it. Until there is some fresh distribution *gration of* of mechanical power, or until some social reconstruction enables *the great* smaller groups to hold and control mechanical power, the great town, *town.* as the nineteenth century knew it, will remain. That "clearing of homes" which Morris outlined in his "News from Nowhere," the Utopia of a hundred years ahead, assumed the social reconstruction, and on this we idealists are still at work. The break-up of the great town is not an isolated question, nor is the escape from Industrialism

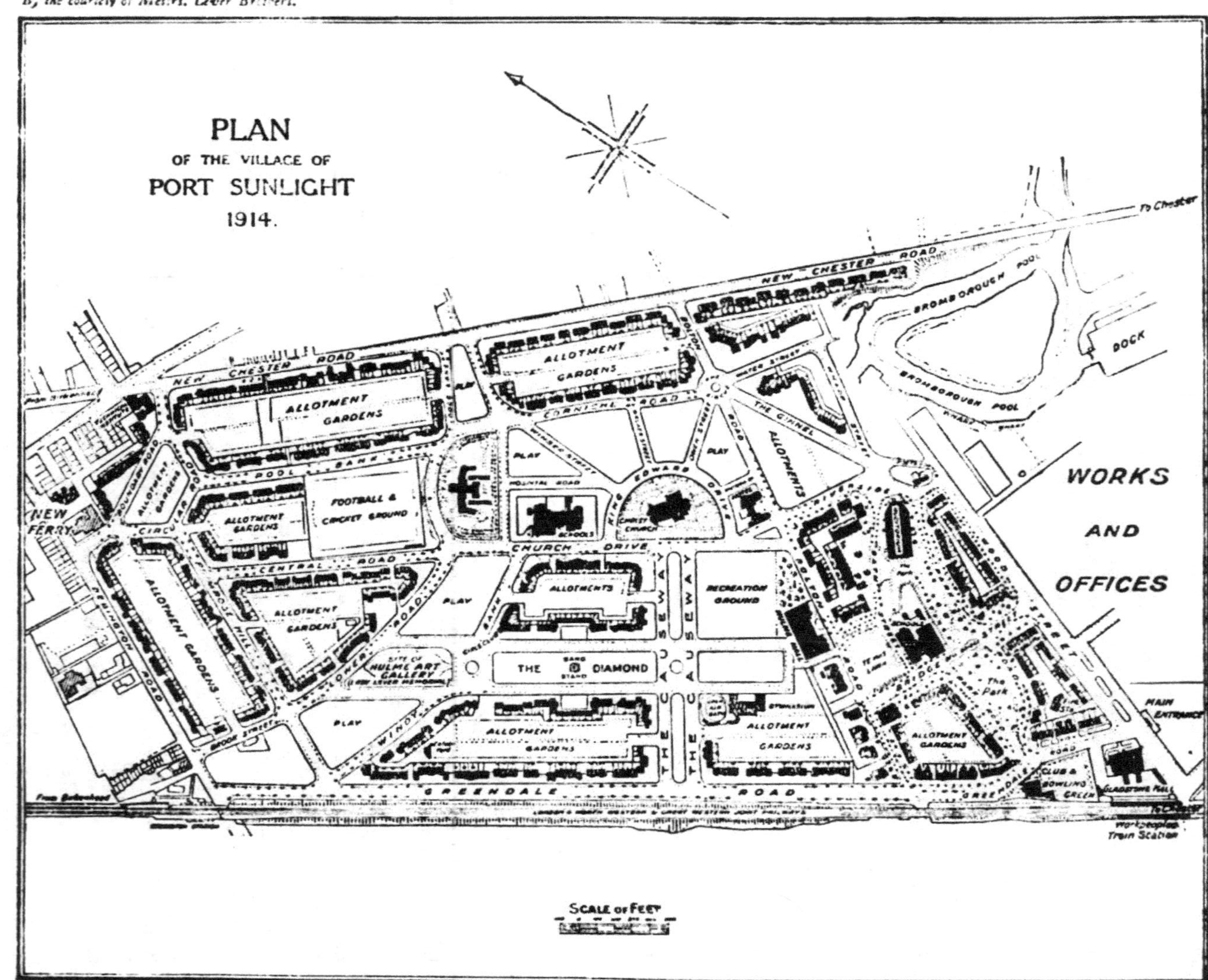
By the courtesy of Messrs. Lever Brothers.
PLAN
OF THE VILLAGE OF
PORT SUNLIGHT
1914.
To Chester
NEW CHESTER ROAD
BROMBOROUGH POOL
DOCK
ALLOTMENT GARDENS
ALLOTMENT GARDENS
CORNICHE ROAD
THE GINNEL
ALLOTMENTS
NEW CHESTER ROAD
PLAY
PLAY
WORKS
AND
OFFICES
NEW FERRY
ALLOTMENT GARDENS
FOOTBALL & CRICKET GROUND
SCHOOLS
CHRIST CHURCH
KING EDWARD
CHURCH DRIVE
CENTRAL ROAD
CIRCULAR ROAD
ALLOTMENTS
RECREATION GROUND
THE CAUSEWAY
SITE OF HULME ART GALLERY
THE DIAMOND
BAND STAND
PLAY
PLAY
ALLOTMENT GARDENS
ALLOTMENT GARDENS
ALLOTMENT GARDENS
The Park
ALLOTMENT GARDENS
WINDY BANK
GREENDALE ROAD
THE CAUSEWAY
MAIN ENTRANCE
CLUB & BOWLING GREEN
GLADSTONE HALL
Workpeoples Train Station
LONDON'S NORTH WESTERN & GREAT WESTERN JOINT RAILWAY
From Birkenhead
SCALE OF FEET
No. 47.

A View of
PORT SUNLIGHT
CHESHIRE
INCORPORATING THE PROPOSED
DESIGN FOR THE CENTRAL ROAD
WARD, PUBLIC LIBRARY AND
MUSEUM, BY MR E. PRESTWICH
AS SEEN FROM THE RAILWAY

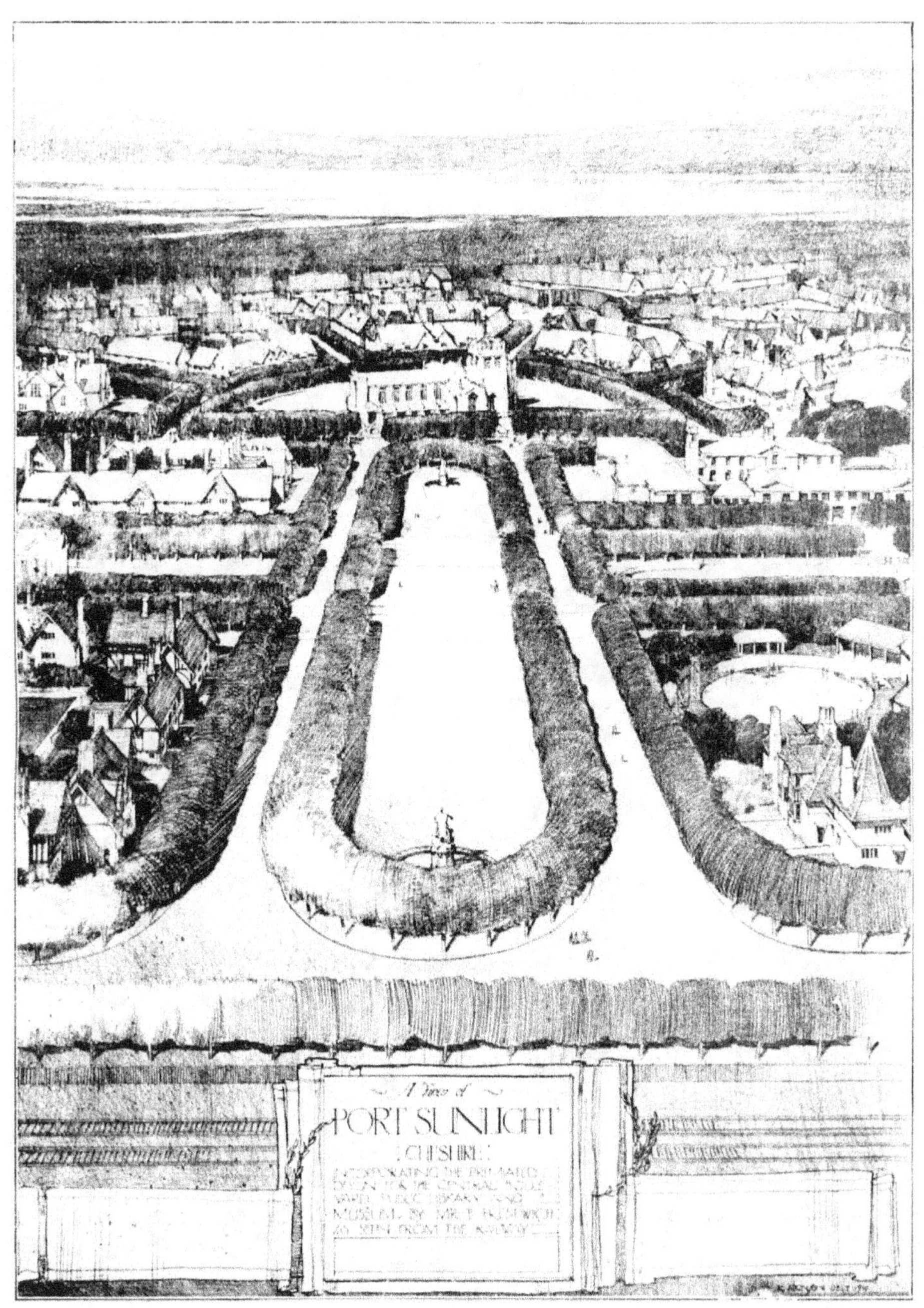

No. 48.

By the courtesy of Messrs. Doubleday Page & Co.

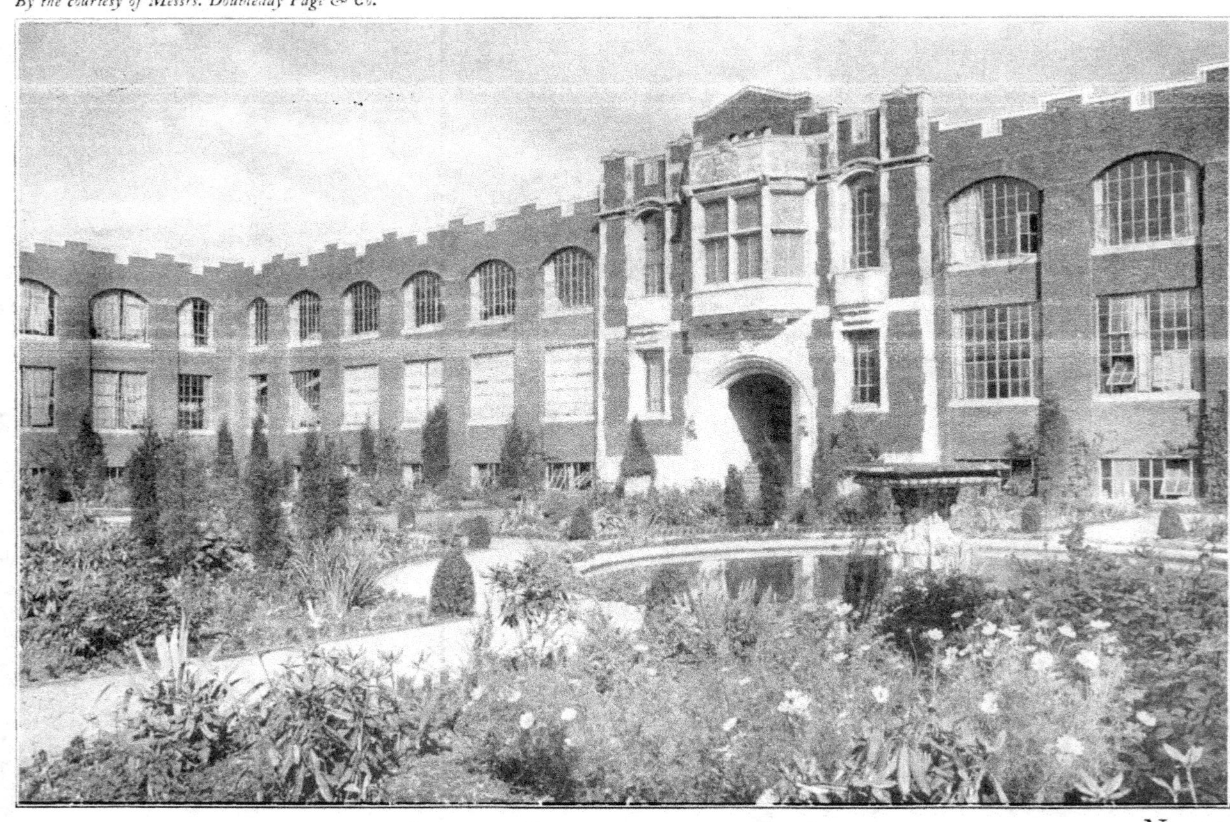

The Garden City Press, Long Island, New York.

No. 49.

into the cleaner life that is growing up merely a question of æsthetics; the Housing and Town Planning and the Garden City movements are two aspects of a greater tendency.

That good planning and clean housing pays the community is best shown by the statistical table I give (see No. 50), which shows the percentages of infant mortality in the unplanned as against the well-planned cities. That it pays great employers of labour of sufficient sympathy and foresight may be illustrated by Messrs. Lever Brothers' Port Sunlight in Cheshire (see Nos. 47, 48) or Doubleday Page's Garden City Press in Long Island, New York (see No. 49). Other examples could be given. We want more of those adventurers in "big business" who have the courage of their ideas and are prepared to relate them to life. And if such ventures can be carried out in cocoa, soap, printing, Pullman cars, and automobiles, why not in all the standardizable trades? And why not, subject to some newer, cleaner organization of life, also in the non-standardizable? To this I shall return again in Chapters XXIII, XXIV, XXV, XXVII.

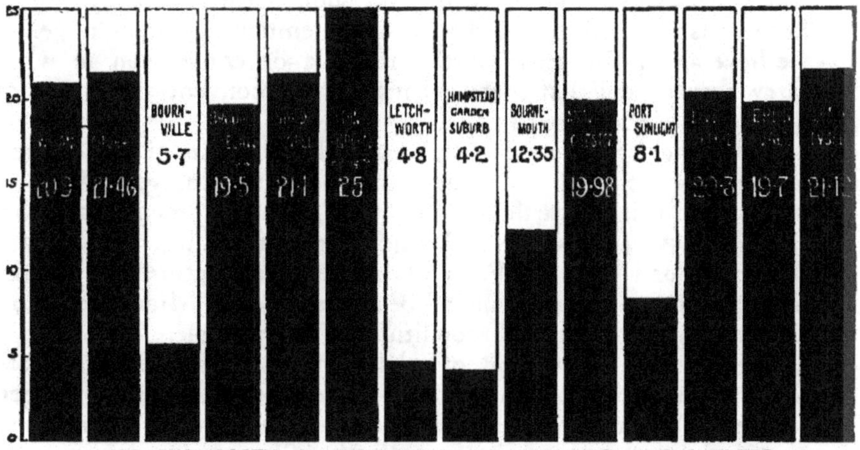

No. 50.

CHAPTER XIV.—Oriental Influences.

In Chapter III I said that the Art influences of our time had come to us in three ways: first, in the form of teaching and stimulus from the artists themselves; next as a part of the social enthusiasm, a force not primarily æsthetic; and last in the form of new ideas, or a quasi-religious nature, from the East. Of these I want now to speak.

The gift of convention. Japan, India, China, the Mohammedan with his Arab and Persian inspiration, the Buddhist, the Brahmin—from all sides they have been turned upon Western production and helped the change in us. The change is inward: here are some of the forms it has taken, more telling perhaps when we present them as episodes or pictures.

An artist—it was some twenty-five years ago—showed a business man, whose walls were hung with the ordinary, mushy, Mid-Victorian painting, a drawing by Kikumaro (see No. 51). Midas could see no beauty in it. "Get to understand that beneath the formula there is the form of a beautiful woman, and perhaps you will see it then," said the artist. And so it is. As soon as any new convention or formula is revealed to us, the thing it embodies comes alive. That we have again the sense of the formula or convention in which to carry beauty, and that there are many such conventions, is one of the great gifts of the East to us.

The gift of contempla-tion. Another gift is contemplation, the attitude of mind necessary for the appreciation of beauty and beautiful things. We in the West—and this is particularly so with our rich men—have the idea that in possession is the real enjoyment of beauty. But that is a false point of view. G. F. Watts in his great picture of "Mammon" showed what the possession of beauty meant to Midas (see No. 52). Contemplation under such conditions is not possible.

Here is an illustration of what I mean, and incidentally of how the East is educating the West. I was once in Seattle, where all the servants are Orientals, often with much greater refinement and sense of beauty than their masters. Staying one evening in an American house I noticed a Japanese boy bring in a lamp, and he set it on the table with such grace and distinction that I asked about him.

"Yes," said my host, "he is a charming boy, and we did him some kindness, and the other day there arrived this letter from his people in Tokio."

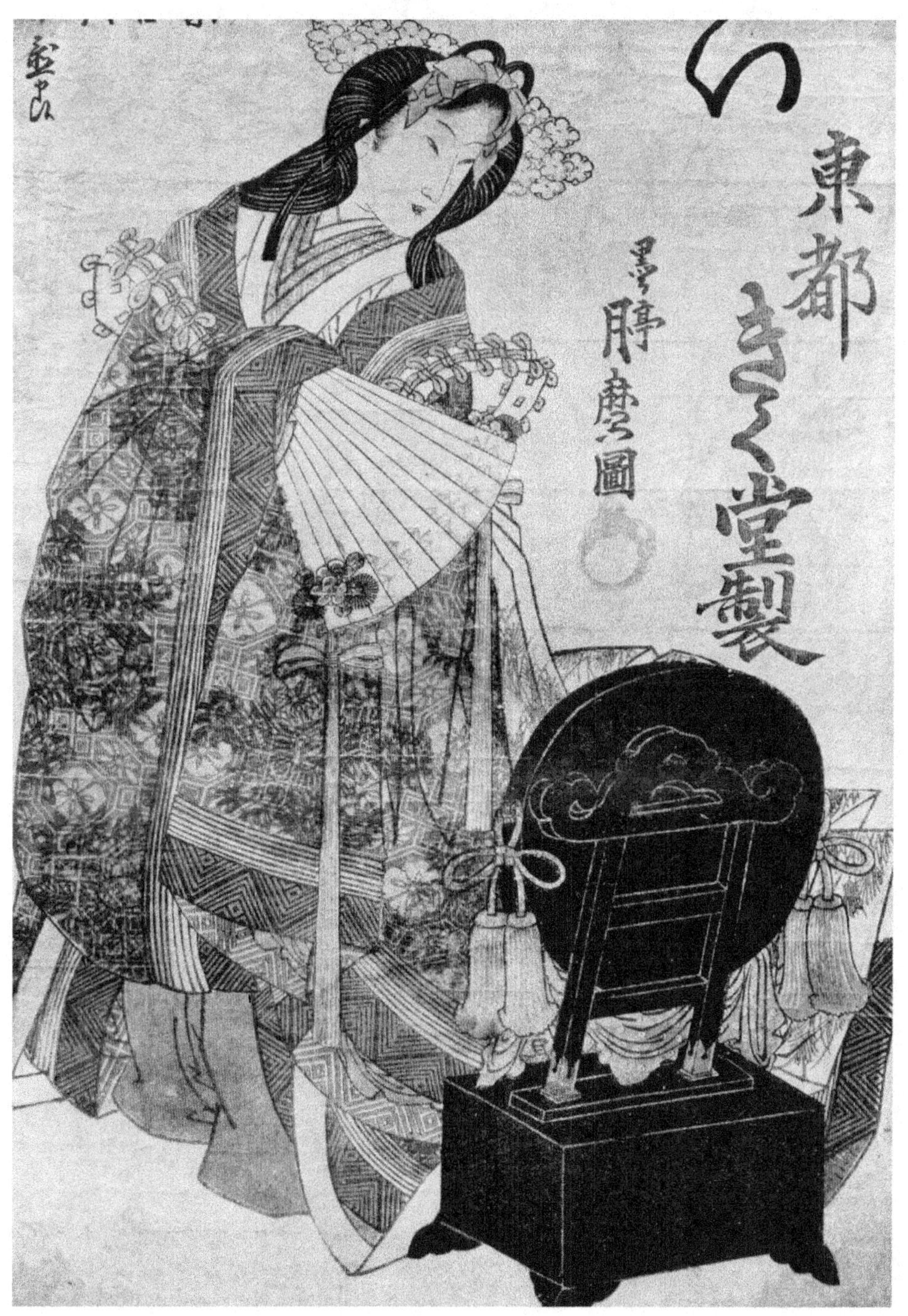

A Drawing by Kikumaro.

No. 51.

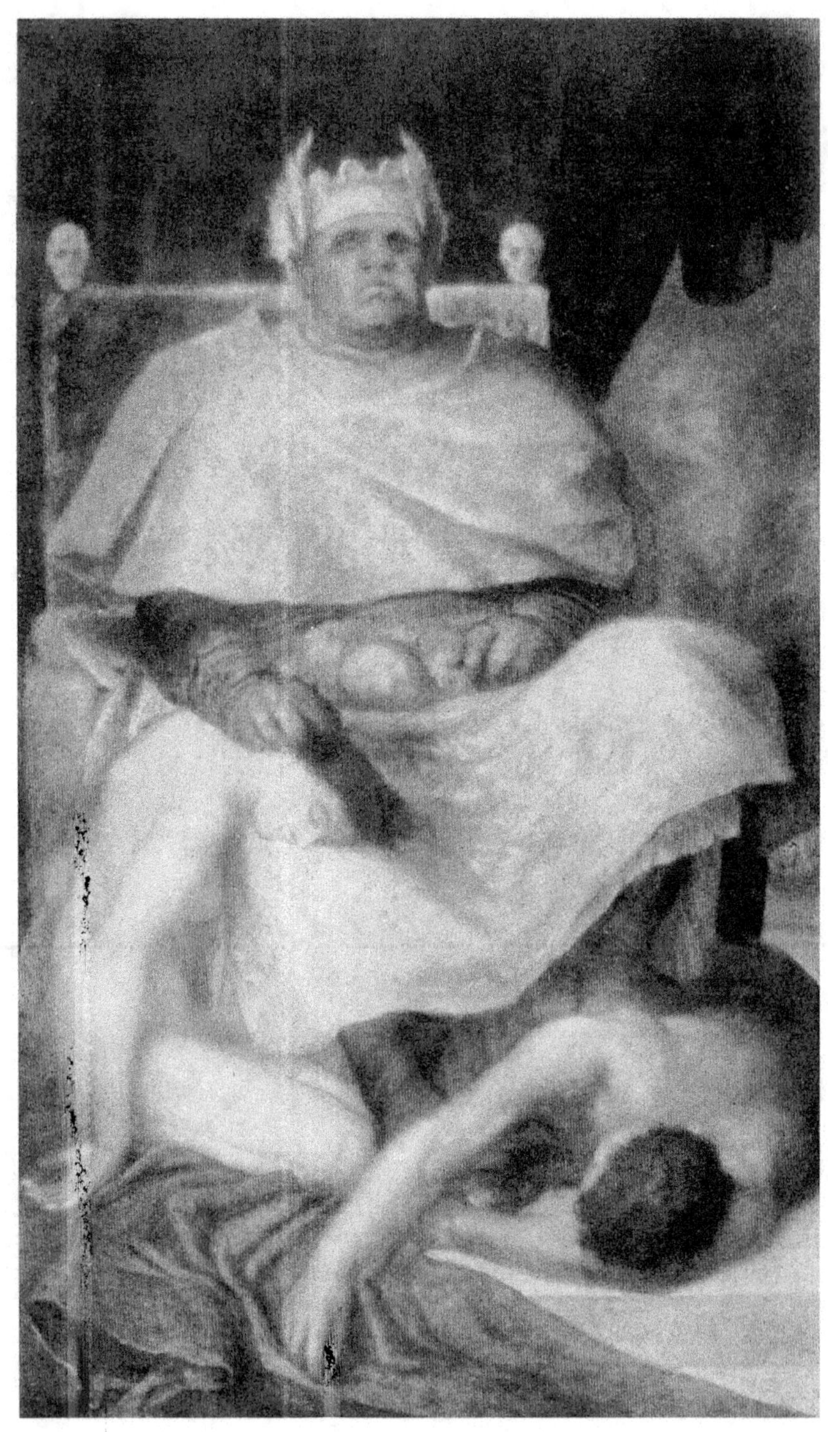

" Mammon."
By G. F. Watts, R.A.

No. 52.

ORIENTAL INFLUENCES

It ran somewhat thus :—

Honourable Sir :

    We are much touched at the kindness you have done to our son Shugio ; we want to make you some return for your honourable kindness, and so I am sending you herewith my two most precious possessions, a drawing by Hokusai and a drawing by Utamaro. Will you do me the favour of giving these your honourable contemplation, and when you have taken your fill of enjoyment return them to me.

There is yet another thing we are learning from the East—the truth that the Arts cannot be used for profiteering. It is an old truth; we understood it in the Middle Ages, in the great period of our Renaissance, the age of Shakespeare, and we held to it throughout the eighteenth century, when a cultured aristocracy planned our cities for us. In the nineteenth century we forgot it. But it is coming back to us again by way of the East, and in the words of the Emperor Akbar, who told us that no people could have the Arts whose first idea was to exploit them. *" Profiteering " in the Arts.*

In Egypt, for instance, there is still a live workshop tradition of Art and Craft; yet the provincial councils, under the mistaken notion that they are doing the "latest Western thing," are introducing machinery into the technical schools, and, by means of State-aided grants, are actually undercutting the local weavers and carpenters.* It is to be hoped that the Councils, or the Bureaucracy, not by any means unintelligent, which rule the country, will revert, while there is yet time, to the sounder Eastern tradition.

The words of the Emperor Akbar, as we shall see, contain a criticism not only on our point of view towards the Arts—the " Does it pay ? " point of view—but also a criticism of the social system in which they are set. Do we want the Arts? Then we must learn to love them for their own sake, and not merely that we may trade in them. Life, which the Arts connote, is more important even than Trade. (See Axiom III, Axiom VII, and Axiom IX.) Beauty, says the Oriental, is a state. We of the West, ever more concrete, say, Beauty is a condition of life.† *Axioms III, VII, IX.*

We want, indeed, some religious symbol that shall show the incarnation of the godhead in the arts of life. Perhaps it is the Japanese *A Japanese interpretation.*

---

  * The splendid little weaving school at Mehalla Kebir is a case in point. It began admirably, but is now (1917) on the high road to ruin, because economic and æsthetic principles are not understood.

  † See A. K. Coomaraswamy, " Burlington Magazine," April 1915. Also Ruskin, " Reade Lecture."

that will first bring the divine truth home to us, since it is they who have shown how it is not only the West that can use the foolish weapons the West has forged. We laugh wondering at their imitativeness: we should do better listening to their wisdom. Here is how one of them in quaint and gracious imagery would guide his countrymen from the all too slippery path of Western materialism. "The sad problems of Western Society turn us to seek a higher solution in Indian religion and Chinese ethics. The very trend of Europe itself, in German philosophy and Russian spirituality, in its latest developments towards the East, assists us in the recovery of those subtler and nobler visions of human life which drew the nations themselves nearer to the stars in the night of their material oblivion." *

Visvakarma the god of the Arts and Crafts. Or perhaps the symbol for which our Post-Impressionist and Futurist painters are so blindly groping will come to us again from India. There they have a god of the Arts and Crafts, and his name is Visvakarma (see No. 53). He is a deity of many hands and of five faces, the corded cobra is around his neck, and jewelled amulets and bracelets about his arms; he holds the book and the writing style, the adze and the citron; in his charge, too, are the garden flowers. He keeps the workmen's tools, the builder's compass and the mason's plumb-line, for he is the architect of the gods, the revealer of the science of mechanics, of the art of building. In the Mahabarata he is described as the Lord of the Arts, carpenter of the gods, fashioner of all ornaments, who formed the celestial chariots of the deities, on whose craft men subsist, and whom, great and immortal God, they continually worship. He has many names among his votaries—they know him as the "craftsman," "the wood-cutter," the "divine builder." It was he who first made bricks, it was he who first inspired the dome when his worshippers saw it floating as a crystal globe within the golden bowl. From him come beauty, rhythm, harmony, proportion; he understands and symbolizes what is in the artist's mind. He is not worshipped as other gods are, with ritual and ceremonies, with burnt offerings and outward services, but men sing of him at their work, or speak of him as their work nears completion; when the fire touches the jewel for the last time, when the finished vase is carried from the kiln, when the flag is hoisted

---

* Kakasu Okakura, "The Ideals of the East, with special reference to the Art of Japan," 1903.

50

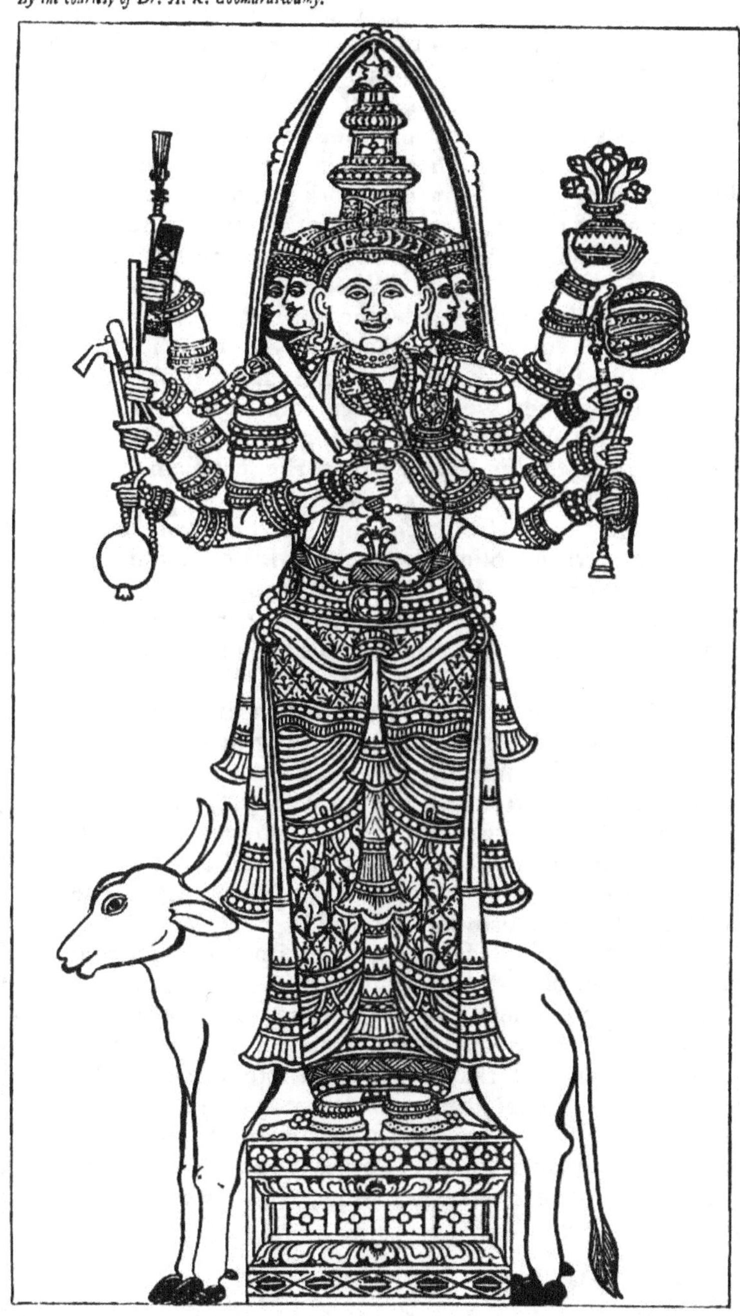

Visvakarma. The God of the Arts and Crafts. No. 53.

on the roof.   There is something about him abstract, aloof, impersonal, strange; something the artist alone understands, for it was the artist that fashioned the sacred thread about his neck, the splendid fire upon his head, and to the artist, his most intimate worshipper, reality exists only in the mind, not in the appearance.

It is from within that Visvakarma, the great Over-Craftsman of the Universe, goes about his work; and so comes he to be a personification of that Platonic Idea of Abstract Beauty which the East has known, and which for so many centuries has fitfully haunted the mind of the West.   Whether it be Plato or Plotinus, Pico della Mirandola or Rossetti, whether on the frieze of the Parthenon or among the mosaics of Monreale or by the Martyr's Crown at Canterbury, ever and again in the greater periods of our Western development, when we have done our noblest work, the Idea recurs. Perhaps when Visvakarma, looking westwards with his many eyes, shall touch with his many hands the problem of the Machine, he may help us in our search, straighten out our confusion with his gifted fingers, and from the lips of his beneficence blow a little upon our spiritual blindness, help a little in our reawakening.

The gift of repose.

One more gift the East has brought us, but as yet we barely understand it.   A few of our artists here and there may do so— Puvis de Chavannes perhaps, or Saint-Gaudens in the Adams tomb—it is the gift of repose, of being static.   Few things are so disturbing, or leave one so on edge, as an exhibition of twentieth-century painting and sculpture.   There is only one thing more distressingly restless, and that is the architecture of a modern garden city.   Everywhere is the desire for the assertion of the individual.   Cannot we get a little of the Oriental quietude?   Our artists do but interpret the aimlessness, the restlessness of a deeper want.   We had our warnings, yet knew not how to heed them.   "But now," says the East, "see whither your intellectual materialism has led you!"

"In the Orient from ancient times," wrote one of the modern exponents of Buddhistic philosophy over twenty-five years ago, "national government has been based upon benevolence, and directed to securing the welfare and happiness of the people.   No political creed has ever held that intellectual strength should be cultivated for the purpose of exploiting inferiority and ignorance.   The inhabitants of Japan live for the most part by manual labour.   Let them be never so industrious, they hardly earn enough to supply their daily wants. Surely it is monstrous that those who owe to labour the pleasures suggested by their civilization should forget what they owe to the labourer, and treat him as if he were not a fellow-being. But civilization, according to the interpretation of the Occident, serves only to satisfy men of large desires. It is of no benefit to the masses, but is simply a system under which ambitions compete to accomplish their aims."

This is the view of a man who knew the beautiful life of Old Japan :—

". . . That the Occidental system is gravely disturbing to the order and peace of a country is seen by men who have eyes and heard by men who have ears. The future of Japan under such a system fills us with anxiety. A system based on the principle that ethics and religion are made to serve human ambition naturally accords with the wishes of selfish individuals; and such theories as those embodied in the modern formula of liberty and equality annihilate the established relations of society. . . .

"Though at first sight Occidental civilization presents an attractive appearance, adapted as it is to the gratification of selfish desires, yet, since its basis is the hypothesis that men's wishes constitute natural laws, it must ultimately end in disappointment and demoralization. . . ."

And then comes this wonderful forecast :—

". . . Occidental nations have become what they are, after passing through conflicts and vicissitudes of the most serious kind; and it is their fate to continue the struggle. Just now their motive elements are in partial equilibrium, and their social condition is more or less ordered. But if this slight equilibrium happens to be disturbed they will be thrown once more into confusion and change, until, after a period of renewed struggle and suffering, temporary stability is once more attained. The poor and powerless of the present may become the wealthy and strong of the future, and vice versa. Perpetual disturbance is their doom. Peaceful equality can never be attained until built up among the ruins of annihilated Western States and the ashes of extinct Western peoples." *

After the struggle and the reaction of the War will there come to us a little of the Eastern quietude? It depends upon such new or old-time ethics as the sorrows of the War shall reveal. From the time of the break up of the Roman Empire, when Western idealism

* Viscount Torio, "Daily Mail," 19–20 November 1890. Quoted by Hearn, "Glimpses of Unfamiliar Japan."

became once more constructive—that is to say, all through the mediæval period to the time of the Industrial Revolution—economic conditions in the West were comparatively stable, changing gradually, shaping to a spiritual purpose. History is clear on this point. Kings and dynasties, wars and the intercourse of nations, do not materially affect them. The workshop, man and his labour, the guilds of craft, the apprenticeship system, what we called before *the workshop structure of society*, all this is much the same in the eleventh as in the sixteenth century; much the same in England as in Italy, in Germany as in Spain, and as it still is in the East. The great change, the devolution, the instability, begins with the coming of the machine. How shall our Democracy dominate the new power? That discovery is the aim of our Idealism. We do not know yet how far we shall be willing or able to take from the East the gift of repose.

CHAPTER XV.—THE NEW SYNTHESIS.

We have now in brief survey touched upon the leading æsthetic *What the* influences of our time. Let us recapitulate them. There were first *various* those that came to us through the teaching and stimulus of the *movements* artists themselves, the three groups of painters, the Pre-Raphaelites, *say.* the Impressionists, the Post-Impressionists and Futurists. In among these came the work of the Arts and Crafts under the inspiration of Morris the master craftsman, and of the Architects, influenced now by the Arts and Crafts, now by the Neo-Georgian revival. Revivalism, whether eighteenth-century or mediæval, meant the historic conscience, and men who were struggling with industrial conditions saw beauty not only in the future of the Socialist, but in the life and order of the past. We wanted that beauty again, in some modern form, as a corrective to the life of mechanism; and the housing and town-planning movement, the garden cities, the civic revival in England, Germany, and America, seemed to be taking us in the right direction; and last there came to us certain ideas from the East that went to the root of many of our problems, and brought us something in the nature of a new religious outlook.

Let us, then, try to make a synthesis of all this. What is the least common denominator of all these movements? It is not that they all say the same thing, for they do not. But they have qualities that all share. In their tangle of speech is a guiding thread of thought: I would put it thus.

Let us get back to the individual, let us find out what we feel, and let us be honest about our feelings. The genuine personal expression, that is where Art lies. On this all agree. It is in the method, the way of approach, that men differ.

"Nothing counts," says the Post-Impressionist, " but significant form."

"Quite true," say the Arts and Crafts men, "but you must make sure, not only what your significant form is, but of the right medium for its expression. Might not stone, glass, metal, mosaic, serve your purpose better? Try."

"We cannot; there is no livelihood in these things, because the machine blocks the way."

Here enter the social reformers. "That," say they, "is what we've always been telling you; only you Artists won't listen. The question is not merely one of æsthetics: it is social."

One school still demurs. "We settled that once tor all," say the Impressionists, quoting Whistler, "when we cut Art off from ethics. Art should be practised for Art's sake."

"Quite so," reply the Arts and Crafts men, the Post-Impressionists, the social reformers, together, "but we must distinguish. Art for Art's sake is a gospel for the Artist. What is true for him is not necessarily true for the man in the street. For the dilettante it is poison: it kills him."

"So much the better."

"We are all agreed, then, that Art means doing the thing—whatever it is—well."

Through the confusion ot argument come the voices ot the stylists, the men of classic scholarship and tradition, whether they paint, or build, or work with their hands. "Wait, not so fast. Where are you leading us to with your appeal to the emotions? These incentives to direct personal creation are like to cut us off from the past altogether. Art cannot live if cut off from the past. There must be continuity. At least let some of us preserve history, and what is best and most beautiful in the past."

But they are answered by the voices we have heard already. "Have no fear for Art. Unless it goes on producing it cannot live. And there always must be tradition, whether we like it or not. All our Post-Impressionists have come out of Cézanne. We could trace him further back. An early Whistler might be mistaken for a Pre-Raphaelite. Every bizarrerie of modern building has its antecedent. Of course, if you are not in earnest, and your idea is to run a bric-à-brac shop, or go in for dealing, we have no place for you. We leave that to the "drummer" and the Jew. It is, from our point of view, unproductive labour. We are here to create; we make our appeal to the individual."

There is still a protest trom the older generation. "But if we are to accept this appeal to personality—this Tolstoian appeal—haven't we got to go the whole hog, and, as Tolstoi insisted, submit the right and wrong in Art to the judgment of the Democracy, the common people; does it not become something the mere peasant must be able to understand? Surely an impossible thesis."

"Not necessarily. The Truth," say the psychologists, and those of us who try to synthesize, "is that Art is life. 'La loi interne de l'Art, c'est de produire une émotion esthétique d'un caractère social.' *

* Guyau, "L'Art."

Art is not merely painting nor making frills. Nor is it merely our life, the life of one nation or group of Western nations. The East also has its culture; remember Visvakarma the god of all the Arts of life. Thus understood, everything falls into place; the conflicting arguments and jarring schools coalesce."

Will not all then say together: "Let us build our cities nobly. *Where the* Let us have our drama, our dance, our music, our smaller personal *various* crafts, based on what is intimate and illusive, as well as our great *movements* architecture and engineering based on what is standardizable through *agree.* mechanism. We must master the mechanism that now enthralls us. We must free the individual from the machine."

The synthesis of our various movements, then, takes some such form as this: The freeing of the individual and the freeing of the Arts from the competition of mechanism are one. They are part of the same life process. The appeal to feeling is true, the appeal to personality is true, "Art for Art's sake" is true, if taken as an artist's gospel only; true also are the economic appeal and the ethical appeal; it depends on how they are presented. We cannot have the Arts unless we are worthy of them, until we actually have cleaner, fairer cities, until we are more sensitive to landscape, until we have stamped out poverty and squalor, until we have got back again to the purity and simplicity of nature as we see and enjoy it in the countryside, until we have men and women educated to the delight and understanding of beauty. And, lastly, the appeal to history and tradition is true; for, though the individual creates, it is the continuous and unfolding life of the community that finds the individual his place. The city brings us this continuity. To be a citizen (*civis*) in the full sense of the word is to be civil, civilized (*civilis*). In the last analysis, seeing that the Arts are life, what we make of it, the finer values we discover in it, the question *is* an ethical one. The architect, indeed, might answer it in the words of one of our leading political philosophers: "The *The city* science of city planning is rapidly developing into the Master-Science *survey.* of the material conditions of modern life." *

Let us then recall Axiom VII: "*The new relationship of man to Axiom VII. life which machine industry has brought with it, finds its fullest expression in the new life of our city. This implies that through the city and its proper adjustment to mechanical conditions will man realize again those finer values which the arts bring into life. Through the city we focus civilization.*"

* Graham Wallas, "The Great Society," p. 356.

THE NEW SYNTHESIS

To bring this about in practice we have to understand, and this understanding comes to us through what is known as "city survey." In
the city survey lies the method whereby the various functions of the
new life find intelligent expression. It is the scientific application to
life of such ethics as we artists preach. The city is one; the poor
have as much right to it as the rich, beauty and history are a common
heritage, the privilege no longer of "the king's counting-house" or
the "queen's parlour."

By the courtesy of the Consulting Architects of the Board of Public Works, San Francisco.

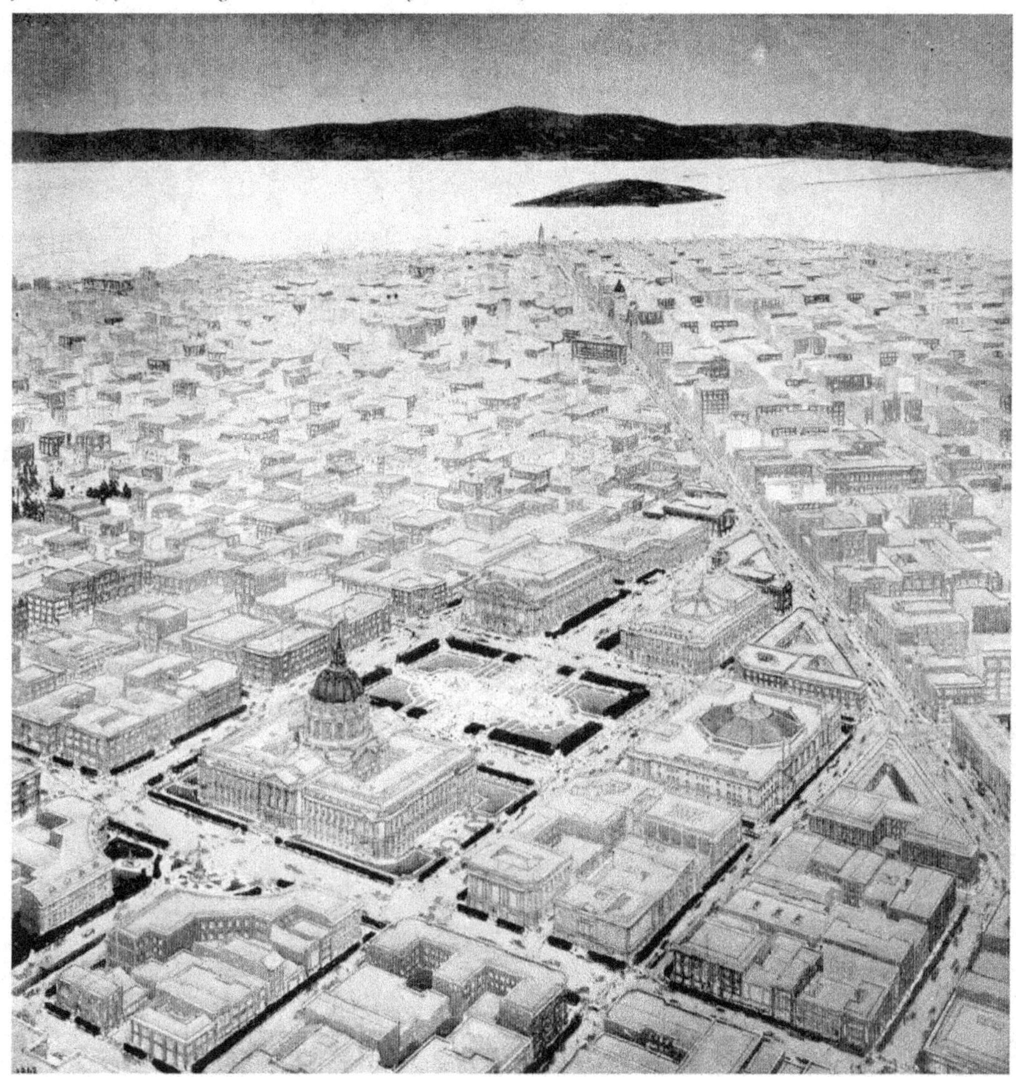

The new Town Plan and City Centre, San Francisco.　　　　　No. 54.

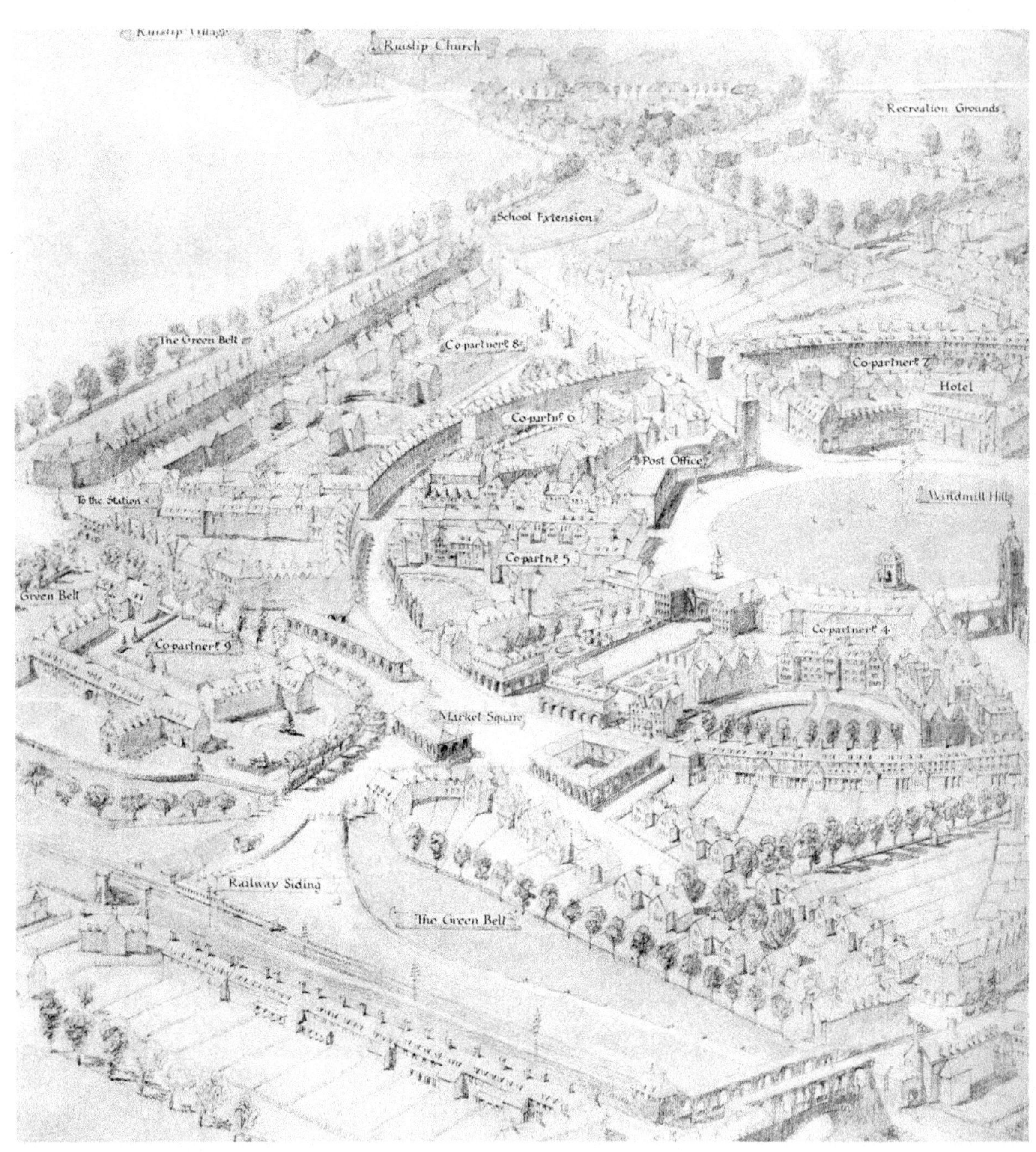

The Ruislip Garden City, for the estate of King's College, Cambridge, as designed by C. R. Ashbee.

The ride
The Pin Way
Park Way
Public Library
Co-partner 1
Co-partner 2
Co-partner 3
The Way to Eastcote
The Green Belt
Existing Poplars
Provost's
Square
The Green Belt
Co-partner 10
Kings' Way
RUISLIP GARDEN CITY

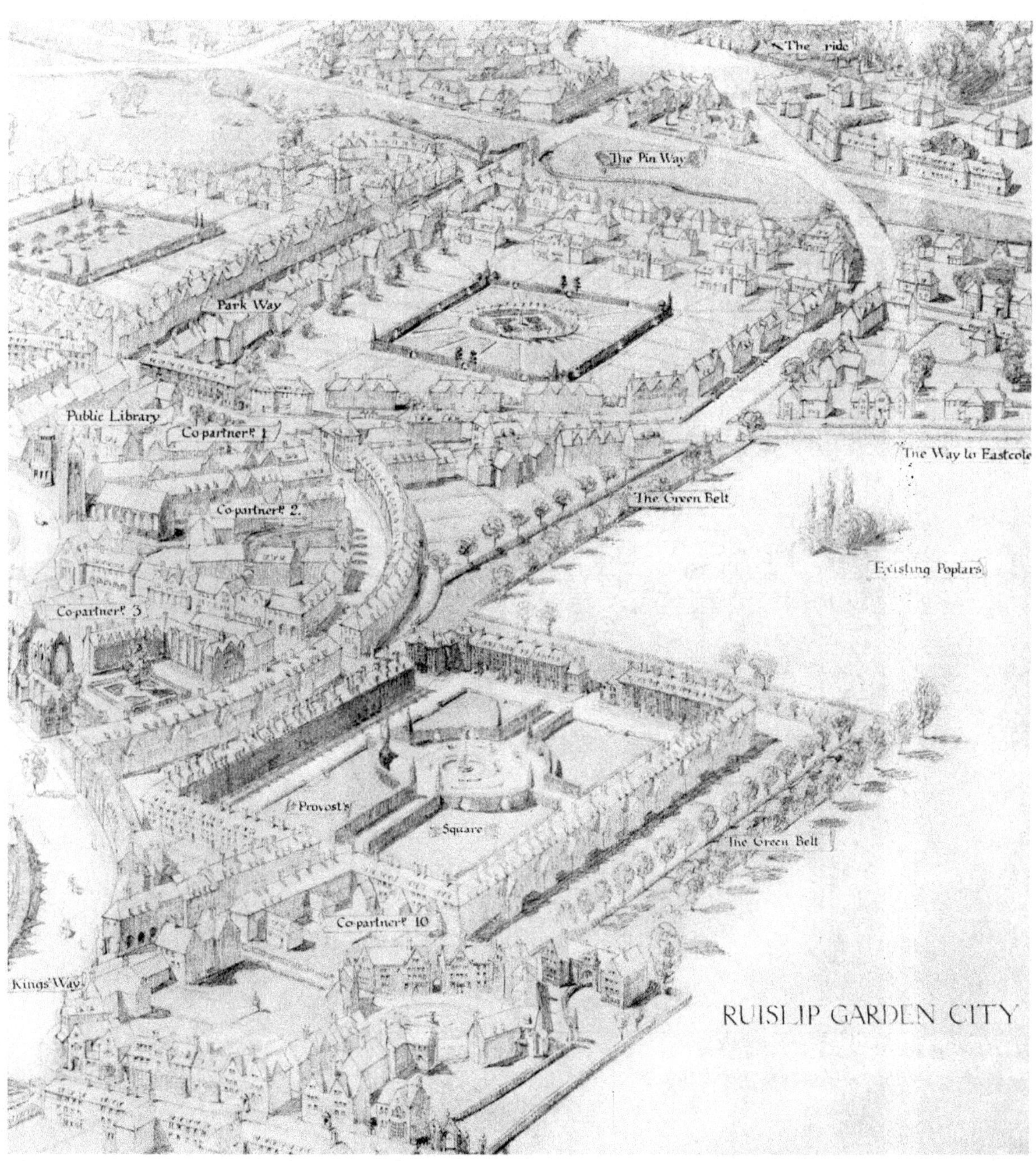

No. 55.

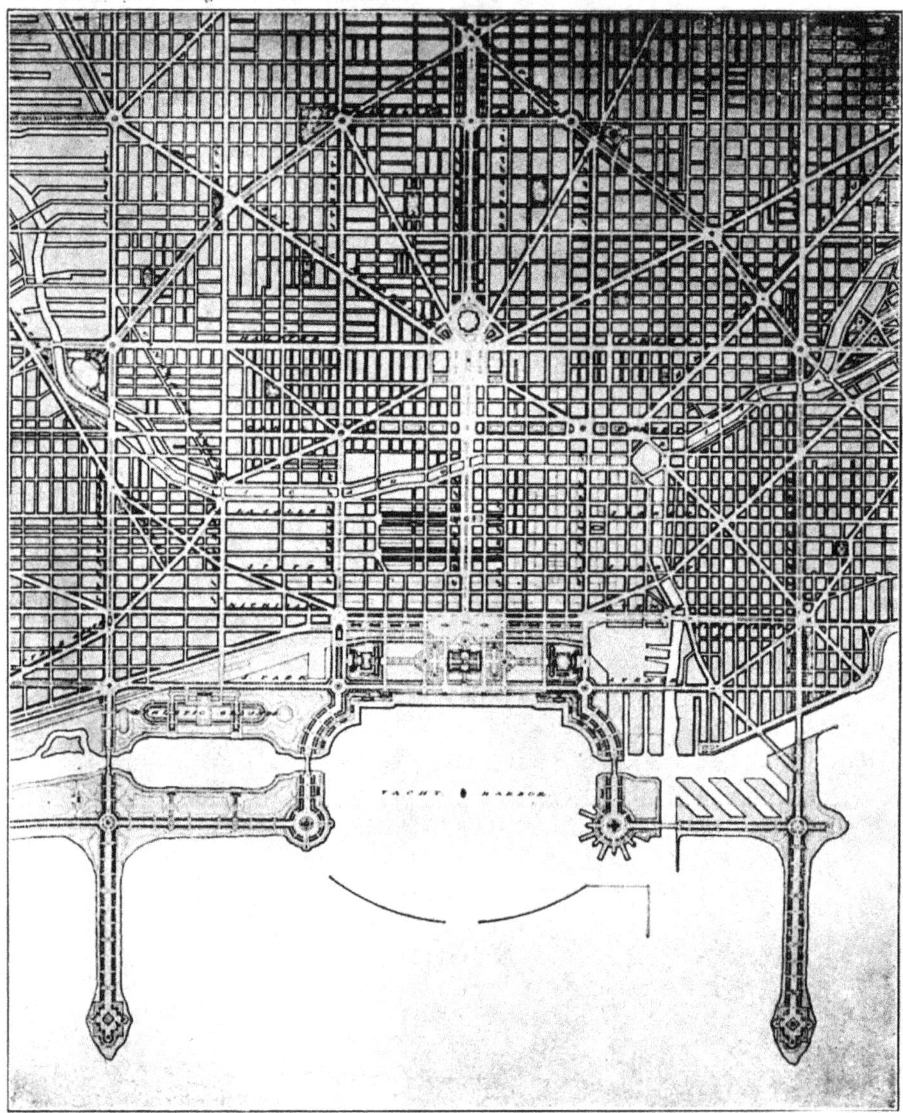

No. 56.

The Chicago Town Plan.

Plan of the complete system of street circulation, railroad stations, parks, boulevard circuits and radial arteries, public recreation piers and yacht harbours, treatment of Grant Park, the main axis and the civic centre, presenting the city as a complete organism in which all the functions are related.

CHAPTER XVI.—The City Centre, Zones, Lungs, and Open Spaces.

"And how," asks the practical man, "am I to give expression to all this? I want to see it take form in my city. How am I to do it?"

There are many answers, but one premise determines them all. In the crisis of the War, Rodin wrote a beautiful letter to a friend from which these words stand out as guiding stars to all human effort :—

"Cet orage rajeunera-t-il les fleurs? Ou bien seront-elles à jamais détruites sous la folle brutalité de son souffle?

"Dieu me garde de me rallier à cette dernière et désolante hypothèse. . . .

"Non, je ne veux pas désespérer bien que parfois, autour de moi, je sente monter la nuit.

"La France fut et sera, grâce à l'ardeur instinctive et à l'harmonieuse clarté de son génie, une source merveilleuse et toujours jaillissante, d'idées généreuses et d'élans infinis. . . .

"Que l'amour du travail, l'amour de la vérité nous redresse, plus grande que jamais, sur les ruines du monde !

"Sachons connaître, sachons aimer, sachons vouloir." *

Before we can achieve anything of any value we must premise that power of imagination without which no great civic achievement is possible.

Many answers have been suggested in recent years. In the *Practical* United States, for instance, every progressive city has suddenly made *expressions* the discovery that it must have a " Civic Centre." More than this, it *of the new* must have Zones—that is to say, be divided into districts where the *civic con-* different functions of the city life shall, or shall not, be exercised. *sciousness.* Further, it must not only have building ordinances : these must be devised intelligently, and in the true democratic spirit. Here, then, are ways of answering the practical man's question. In Nos. 54 and 56 I show some of these civic centres—San Francisco, Chicago. In No. 55 I show, in Mr. P. A. Mairet's sympathetic rendering of my designs, a civic centre that I myself projected for one of the new English Garden Cities. Whither is this study of "Civic Centres" and "Zones" leading us? What do they really mean? It is a

---

* Rodin to Armand Dayot in "L'Art et les Artistes," January 1916.

recognition of the fact that Democratic Government needs concentrating. It implies unity, order, co-ordination. We have too many authorities.*

Some rule of height for buildings is the first step in a co-ordination of modern industrialism. The principle involved must then be carried further into a system of Zones, or districting, by which we mean that the different functions of the city shall be so grouped as not to destroy each other, as is so often the case in English and American cities. It is to the Germans that we owe the most thoughtful development of the Zone or "districting." † It means method, cleanliness, economy of time and resources; it means that having learned the importance of these things in our own homes, we apply them also to the city in which we live.

"Scale," and what it means.

The rule of height and the Zone system have to be taken in conjunction, and without them any permanent architectural distinction is impossible. In architectural language the rule of height, and height in accordance with the Zones in which our buildings are placed, implies "scale," and scale in architecture marks the restraint and discipline we impose on ourselves. It connotes a human quality. Absence of scale, or being "out of scale," means that our building is badly designed, the detail out of relation to the whole, that one building is out of harmony with another, that in each street the general setting is marred by some impertinent or ill-mannered intrusion.

Here are ethical forces at work. A community that cannot impose scale upon itself has not realized its own corporate unity. A city whose buildings are out of scale is not yet civilized; it is, as the Greeks would say, "barbarian." In this restraint of the individual we have a fundamental question of manners, of good breeding, of culture applied to practical civics.

Let me give some examples of "scale" instinctively understood, of how our industrialism has destroyed it, and of how we are feeling our way into it again. Independence Hall, Philadelphia (see Nos. 57, 58), is one of the most beautiful buildings of the eighteenth century. As with most buildings of this type, the beauty depends on its symmetry and setting within a certain environment. All this—the essential scale—has been destroyed by the monstrous ten to fifteen story erections that now surround it. Illustration No. 58 shows the principle of

* Monro, "Principles and Methods of Municipal Administration," 1916.

† See Dr. J. Stübben's "Städtebau"; also, for an American study, George B. Ford's "Introduction to City Planning," 1909.

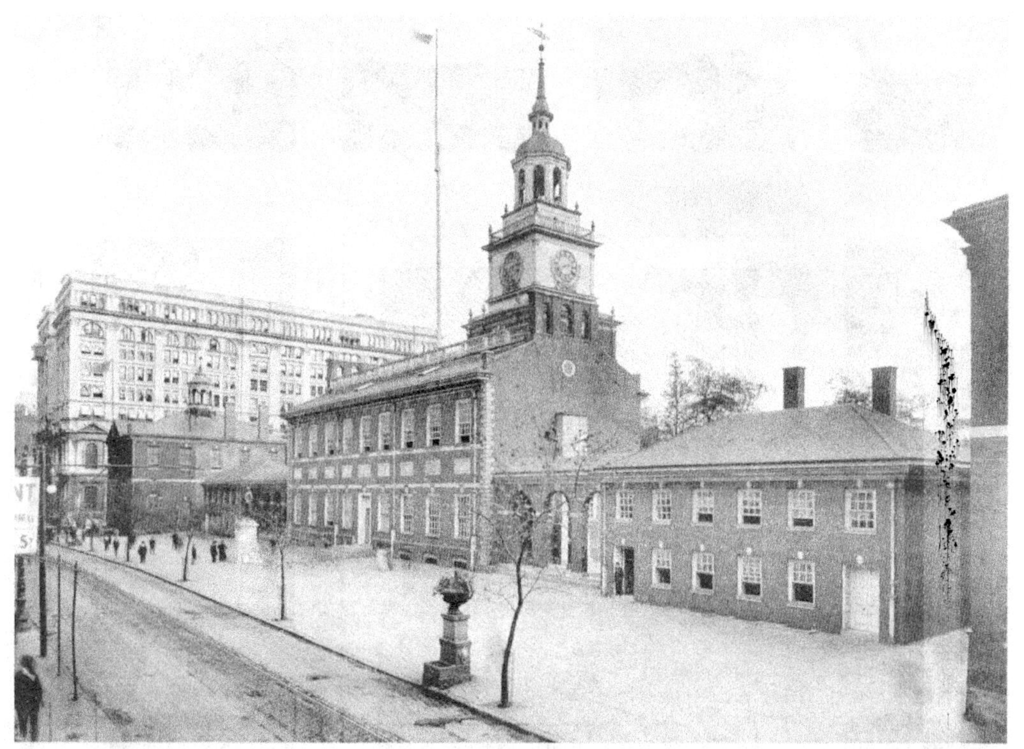

Independence Square, Philadelphia, Pennsylvania. No. 57.

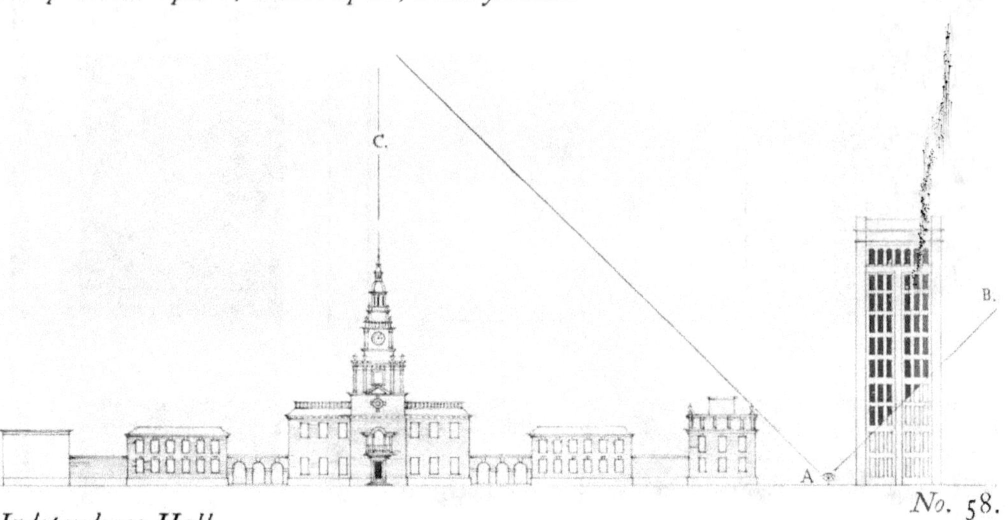

Independence Hall. No. 58.

To show the right principles of "scale" and the rule of height observed by the eighteenth-century builders.

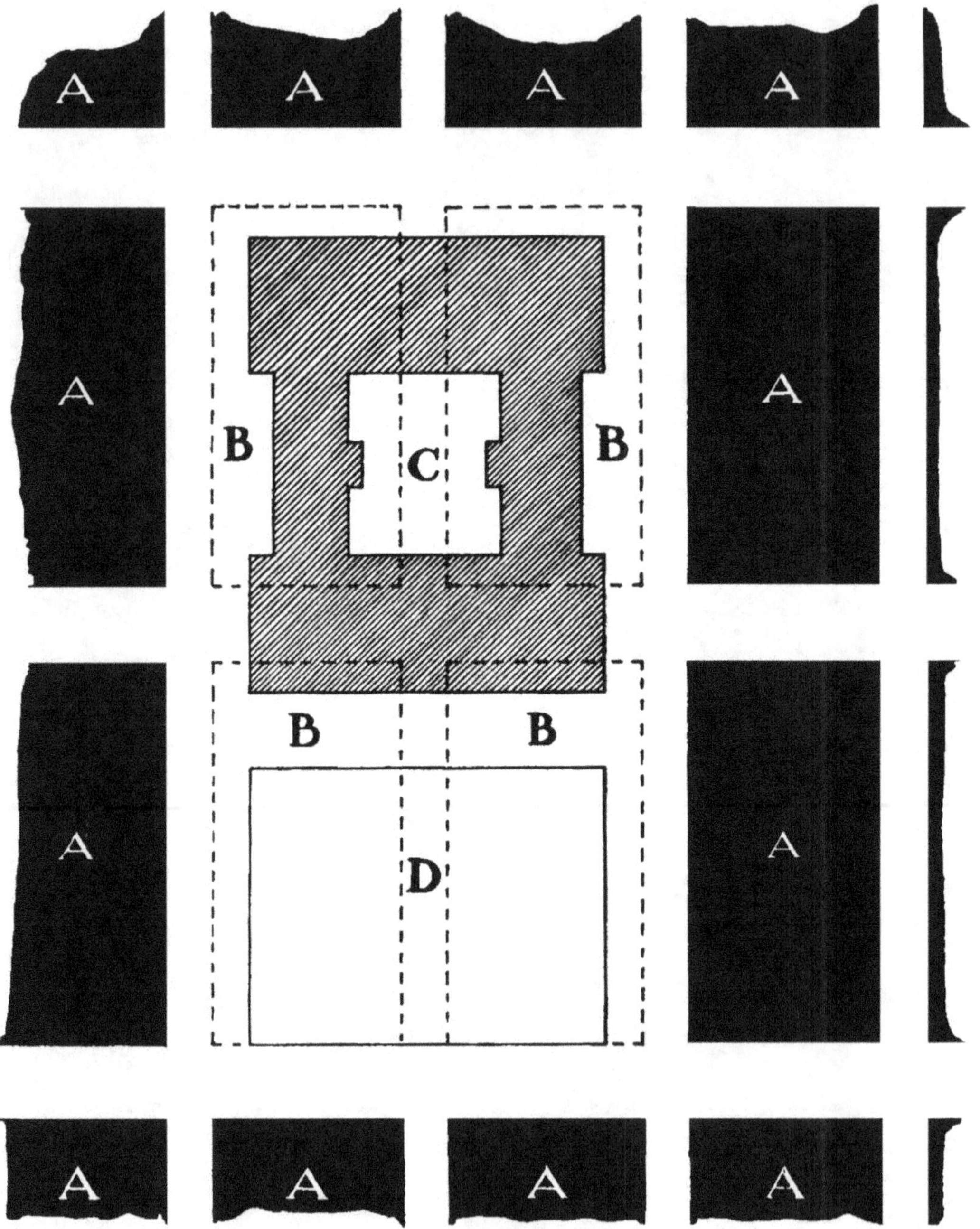

Diagram to show the gradual co-ordination of sky-scrapers into groups.   No. 59.

height adopted instinctively in some of the original buildings still standing in the square; that principle should have been observed in the new buildings which are now replacing them. There would have been no harm in the heights ranging, as did the old Philadelphia buildings, beneath the line A B, but the angle of forty-five taken from a point of vision within the points A, B, C should have been kept intact. The eighteenth-century community had the quality of reserve and good breeding, which the industrial community of the nineteenth century lost, and which the twentieth century is striving again to find.

Wren's rule of height. Sir Christopher Wren, the genius and scholar to whom we architects owe so much of the grammar of Civic Building, gave us a clear lead in his rule of heights for city streets. "In no street," said he, "should the houses touch if laid out on their faces." Illustration No. 60 shows the principle. If they are brought closer together, to the point A, or raised above the point B, our street loses its dignity and becomes an alley. Many of the finest streets in Philadelphia and New York have been turned into alleys.

No. 60.

But there is no reason, as Wren himself admitted, why, under certain conditions, we should not have alleys. This leads us to the question of placing tall buildings. The essential value of the skyscraper is its power of concentrating business. It enables the work of administration to be done so as to save time. If it takes the form of an apartment house, it enables people to live together more economically, and so helps to solve the difficulty of domestic service. But if we allow business houses, or apartment houses, to sprawl into other portions of the city, or to come too close together, it not only destroys the

61

amenities, as on Fifth Avenue, New York, and Independence Square, Philadelphia (see Nos. 57, 58), but it destroys property values and the effectiveness of the tall buildings themselves, as in Chicago. The development of the skyscraper therefore is æsthetically sound only if certain limitations are observed; where these limitations are ignored it is unsound.*

The grouping and gradual co-ordination of the tall buildings is best shown in the three illustrations Nos. 59, 61, 68. No. 61 shows the city in transformation out of the static or eighteenth-century type A, through the period of industrial individualism B, into the co-ordinated city of the twentieth century, still in process of realization. It represents the present skyline of New York seen from the middle

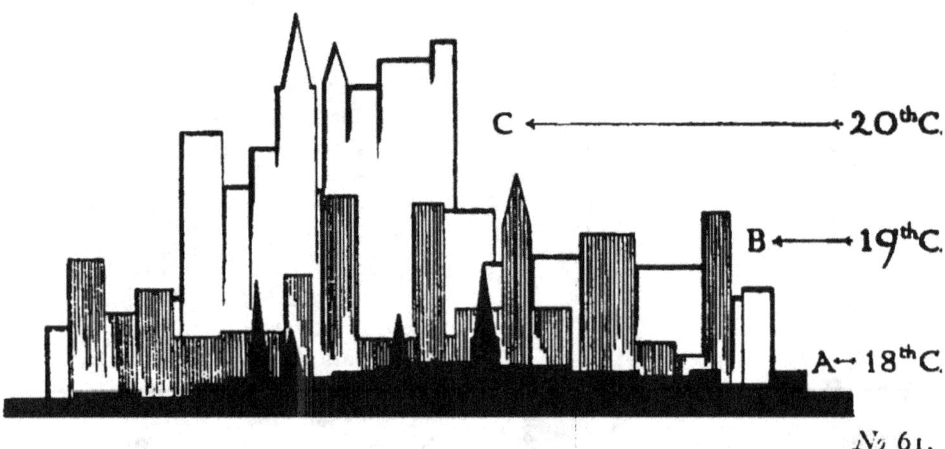

of Lower Harbour as we pass the statue of Liberty. The line A gives us the pre-industrial New York, the line B shows one of the many variations taken in the last twenty-five years. The great city is gradually achieving a conscious form.

The evolution of the New York skyline. Expressed in plan, this gradual co-ordination of heights—the intelligent arrangement into which we wish to grow—has immediate significance. Illustration 59 shows sixteen city blocks of the ordinary unintelligent and rudimentary type. On these sixteen blocks let us imagine the tall buildings struggling for mastery, buildings of four stories interspersed with buildings of fifteen or twenty, each

* As in the case of Madison, Wisconsin.

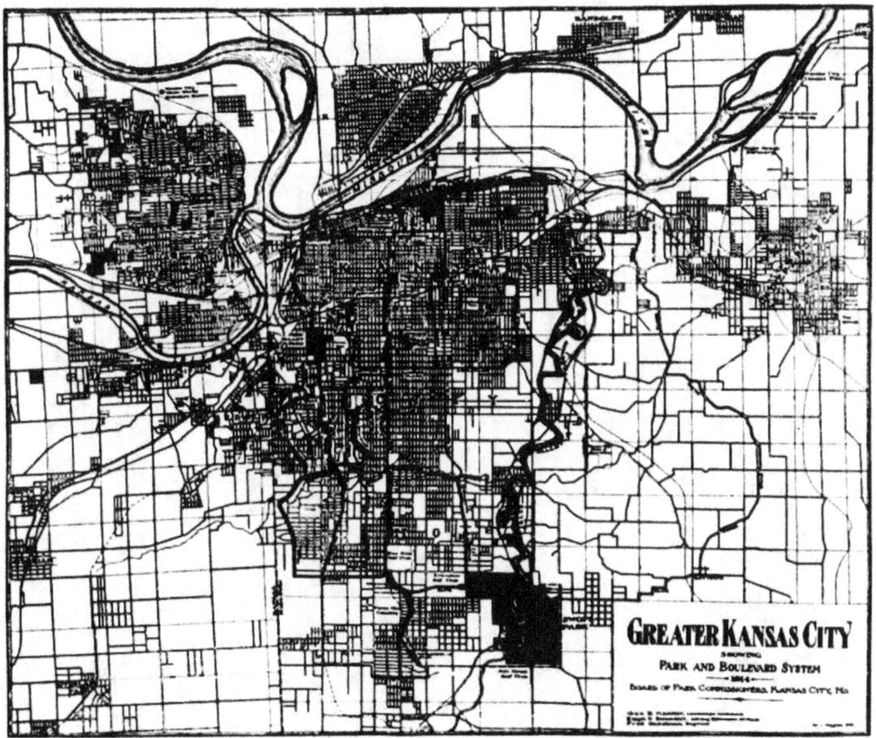

No. 62.

The park system is shown in black; the squares are square miles.

By the courtesy of the Royal Institute of British Architects.

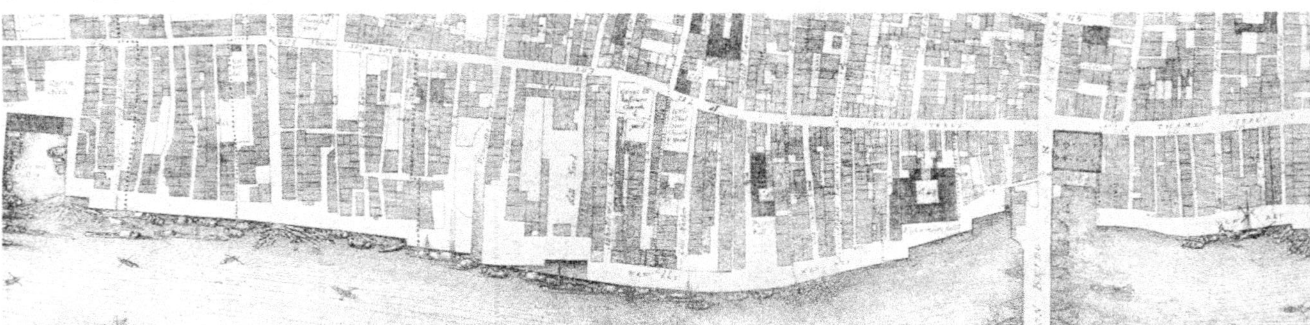

The Thames River Front in the Seventeenth Century.

No. 63.

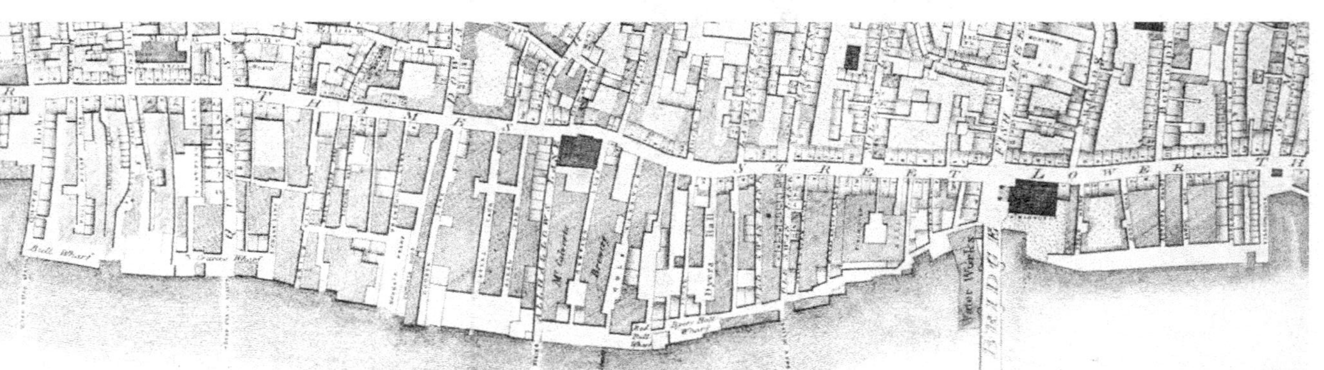

In the Eighteenth Century.

No. 64.

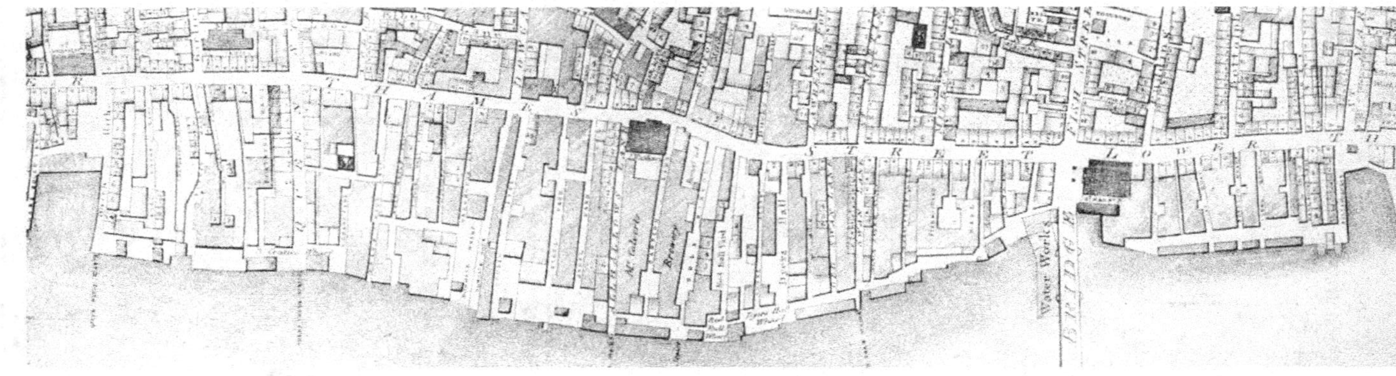

In the Nineteenth Century.

No. 65.

The above three plans show the gradual encroachments of the private over the public interests during the industrial period.

No. 63 is from Ogilby's Map of 1677, showing the "New Key" as completed.
No. 64 is from Horwood's Map of 1799, showing the commencement of encroachment on the river front.
No. 65 is from Horwood's Map of 1813, showing further encroachments.

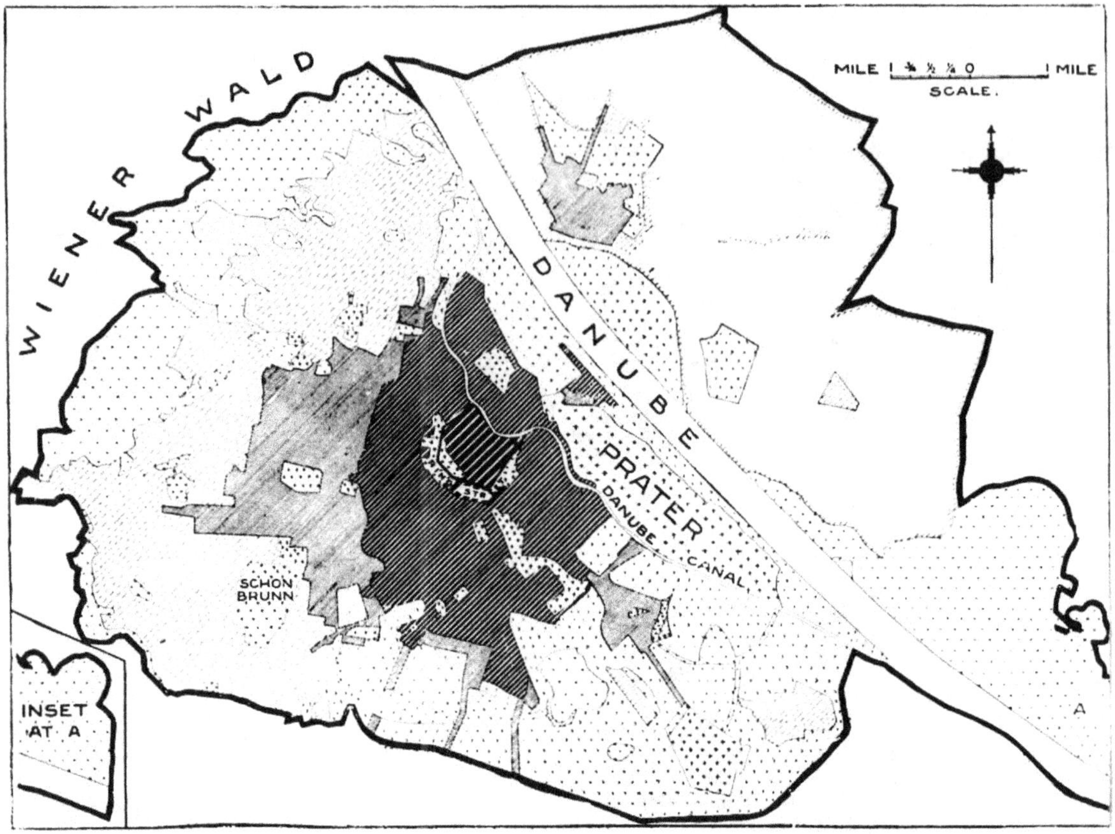

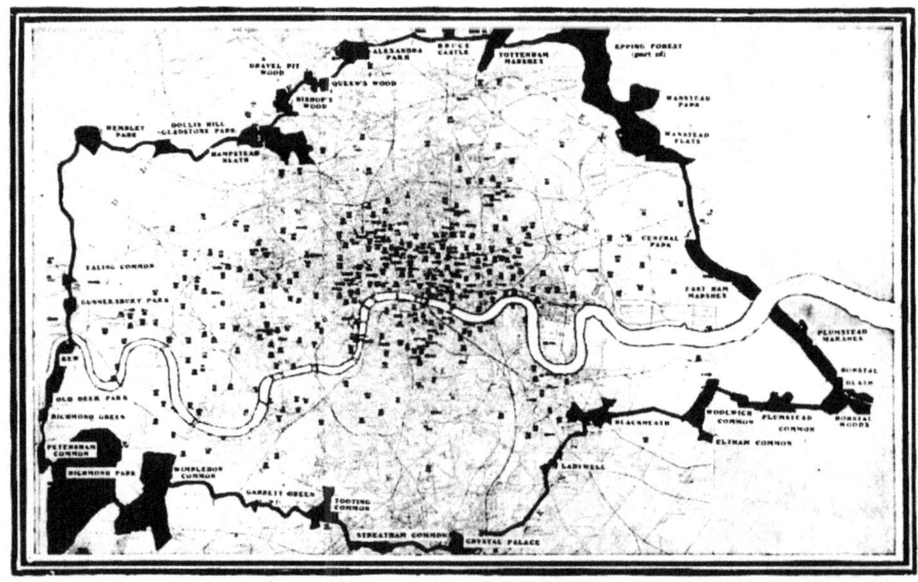

The Vienna Zone System.   No. 66.

Lord Meath's proposed green belt round London.   No. 67.

block having somewhat the look of a comb with broken teeth (see No. 61).

If, however, by means of wise building ordinances we limit the heights at A A in illustration No. 59, and pull down the four central blocks B, we can group in their place new and taller buildings C, perfect our business concentration, and throw D into garden, lung space, or amenities.

When propositions like this are first offered to the business mind, they are scouted as impractic-

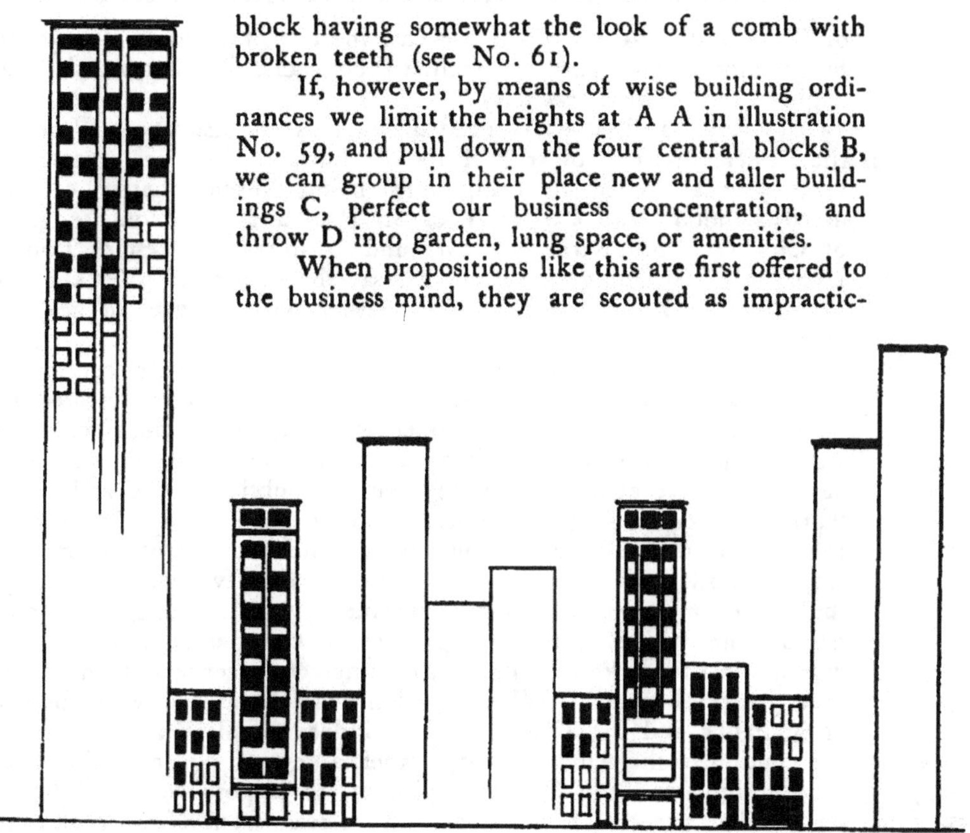

No. 68.

able; but many less practicable things have, in the last twenty-five years, been carried to triumphant achievement—such, for instance, as the Park System of Kansas City (see No. 62), or the American Library Association, as illustrated by Portland, Oregon (see No. 120).

To lay out a new city is an easier matter than to reconstruct an old one, such as London, Dublin, Edinburgh. Perhaps even here the reconstruction of decaying industrial areas, when once the creative idea has come to us, is not so wonderful an achievement as the Zeppelin airships or the Krupp Works at Essen, but it would certainly be more serviceable to mankind. Once again the problem is ethical, because it is a problem of the arts. We have to visualize it as one of Civic duty. Are the arts *our own* merely, or do they involve our fellow men? Not until we realize their social significance shall we begin to see " The Great City."

Wren's co-ordination of London.
Perhaps a disaster is needed, such as the European War; as the lesser disaster of the Fire of London in the seventeenth century was needed to bring into being Wren's better co-ordinated London: the Cathedral of St. Paul and the exquisite group of City churches with their surrounding spires—Protestant London (No. 69). " 'Oranges and lemons,' say the bells of St. Clement's "—London as a whole, all chiming together with a series of beautiful streets.

The City never fulfilled the dream of Wren, who complained then as we complain now, that the private interests defeated the noblest public schemes, e.g. the open embankment to the river which London only started two hundred years after the great master's dream, or the quays that he wanted to save for public service and which " private enterprise " gradually filched away (see Nos. 63, 64, 65) ; or the opening of the main thoroughfares which at the cost of millions we are now striving to carry through. But we gained through the vision of Wren something supremely worth having—the traditional sense which, despite the pressure of commercial and anti-social interests in the darkest hours of the nineteenth century, made us rise to a greater London. When London was threatened with the ruin of St. Paul's and the City churches, indeed of all Wren's work, by

London's lesson from New York.
the coming of the American skyscraper, a few of our councillors had the foresight, and the City the wisdom, to impose a rule of height on London streets. London learnt its lesson from New York ; but only just in time.

The Zone system implies intelligent unity.
What applies to London applies in greater or less degree to every city in the world. The rule of height, with the Zones, the distribution of building groups, the placing of parks and open spaces, the preservation of amenities, implies the beginning of a new period in city life. It will, as we shall see later, Chapter XXIV, postulate new civic and human groupings with control over mechanical power. In all this there is a logic that grows inevitably out of industrial life. We are brought nearer to that civilization of the past which the Græco-Roman city reveals to us. Writing of the ancient town and its planning, a classic scholar says: " As in modern England, so in fourth-century Greece B.C. the appearance of building regulations suggests the growth of a care for well-ordered town life and municipal

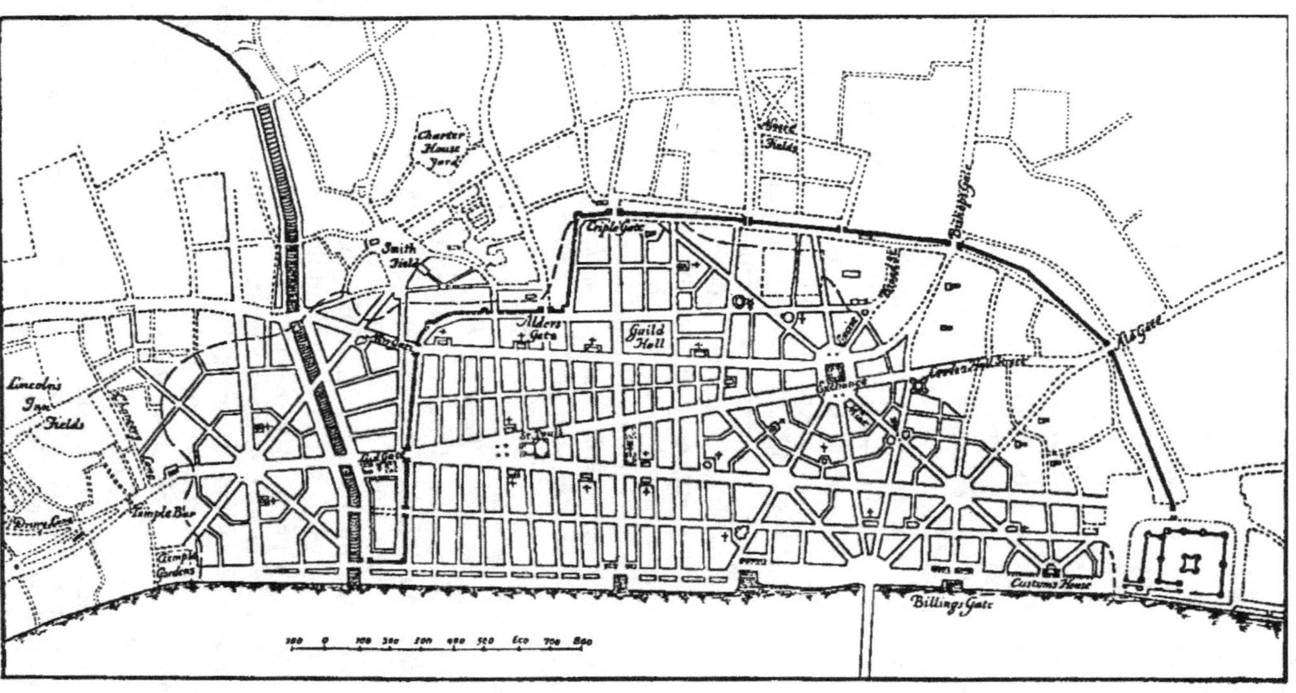

Wren's Plan for a co-ordinated London.

No. 69.

well-being, which leads directly to a more elaborate and methodical oversight of the town." *

Nor can the Zone, the Civic Centre, the Rule of Height, the Park, the Library system, or the Garden Suburb be taken as a thing by itself. Each has to be regarded in relation to the whole—and that whole is the city. We have to consider the idea behind. Here again we learn from the Germans, and perhaps one of the finest *An example* examples of Zoning is the City of Vienna (see No. 66). The Zone *from* system, so far as it embraces all these things, and the machinery *Vienna.* for making them effective, brings intelligent self-consciousness and distinction into the city of industrialism.

The city of Seely once made a famous generalization : he told us of the City *interna-* state—the Nation state—the Empire state. We might rewrite it thus, *tionalism.* with a sense less political, more human ; and say, our study of the new civics shows us the Autonomous city, the National city, the city *VII.* of Internationalism.† In this newer type of city the vital force on *Axiom* which civilization depends (see Axiom VII) is kept within view. We no longer risk losing the reality, the actual life of men, for the shadow of great empire, or the conquest of other cities and states. It is impossible to imagine the world reconstructed after the War without visualizing it through the city of Internationalism. Our axiom holds. "*The new relationship of man to life which machine industry has brought with it finds its fullest expression in the new life of our city. This implies that through the city and its proper adjustment to mechanical conditions will man realize again those finer values which the arts bring into life. Through the city we focus civilization.*"

The old cities had distinction because they had a life—a civilization that had found expression. We have but to look at such as are, or were until a year or two ago, left to us. Furnes or Nieuport, for instance, or Louvain, or Arras or Nancy, or Ypres, that classic city of the Flemish guilds. With the cities of the Post-Industrial period it is otherwise. How many can we not recall! They are merely vast villages industrialized, and the life led in them is a monotonous and commonplace life, uncultured, uncivilized. It we trace the men and women who live it, back through the last two generations, we shall find not the Puritan father, nor the idealist of revolutionary Paris, nor the citizen of the dignified little German

* Haverfield, "Ancient Town Planning," 1913.
† This question of the City of Internationalism is curiously illustrated by Hébrert, "Town Planning Review," Vol. IV.

66

eighteenth-century State, but the European peasant. Throwing off what culture his ancient peasant order gave him, his peasant garb, his folk music, his handicraft, he is now mesmerized by mechanical power and the apparent freedom of a new world. His essential peasant quality alone he retains, the power meanly to grow rich. But he has no city—he remains uncivilized.

And so the practical man's question remains only in part answered, because he is himself only in part civilized. These things are accomplished little by little and from within. They have to be understood first, and as a whole. Let us have a wise body of ordinances, a park or lung here, the gradual development of a Zone system first in this, then in that city ; let us have green belts round all our cities, even that splendid green belt around London which Lord Meath designed for us, and which we long for before it is too late (see No. 67). One city helps another, and the growth and decay of cities, as history teaches, helps us all ; but let us first understand the problem as one of civilized life. *Sachons connaître.*

CHAPTER XVII.—Dirt, Noise, and the Menace of Mechanism.

Naaman was told to wash in Jordan, and objected that the rivers at home were finer and larger. We never care to consider the problem of dirt. Dirt is most terrible in large cities such as London, Liverpool, Pittsburg, where they burn soft coal. The constant, hopeless effort, especially among the poor, to keep clean in these cities, is pitiful. Smoke consumption and dirt in the city is one of our industrial problems. We have to master it much as the problem of chamber hygiene was mastered at the end of the sixteenth century, when the great humanist, Sir John Harrington, was lampooned by the dramatists as the "Knight of the Stool" because he carried a necessary reform through the Court of Queen Elizabeth.

Illustration No. 70 shows the significance of the soot problem. Any city might be taken. There are many aspects of the same difficulty of dirt. An American city I know has one of the cleanest, most quickening atmospheres of any in the world, but when I last walked the main street they seemed to be battling with an insuperable difficulty. The Danaides, in the form of hundreds of Dagos, of many races and languages, were working in gangs, undoing each other's work. At one point the gangs were picking up and opening out the roadway, a little farther along other gangs were ramming it down again. I counted ten, twenty, thirty rows of service pipes: gas, water, light, telephone. Scarce had the pipes been opened out by one gang when another gang was burying them again in masses of rubbish and waste. It was cheap foreign labour that was doing all this, and meantime there was a blinding drift of dust blowing up town on the cool sweet harbour wind. Obviously the right method where, as here, the streets were straight and serviceable, was to construct a permanent subway to hold all these services, so that the mechanic can have access to them without this endless picking up of the roadway. We shall come to this, and the Danaides will be put to more useful service.

Noise is first cousin to dirt. The abominable din of our streets merely means that mechanical contrivance is out of control. It implies bad manners. It is as ill-mannered for a motor-car as it is for a human being to go belching and snorting down the street. When we apply the æsthetic test to life it takes us farther than we think. The world has learned of late that it is ill-mannered to rattle the sword—

68

mechanism expressed in terms of militarism.   So it is with all mechanism ; we have to subdue it.   One of the objectives of a society

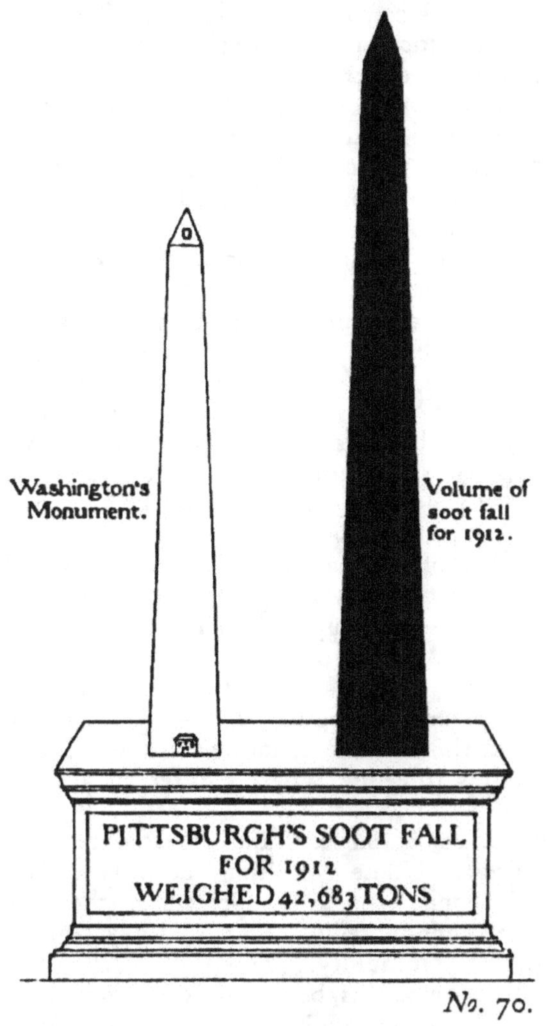

No. 70.

that desires the arts is to keep street noises under control, in order to retain the beauty of the human voice.   Barrel-organs, hooters, whistles, bells, overhead cars, automatic machines, the incessant tearing

DIRT, NOISE, AND THE MENACE OF MECHANISM

and rattling of trolleys and trams—all this we must subdue if we are
to have beautiful cities again. All this is ugliness and waste—waste
of what is most precious—nerve force ; and without the beautiful
voice the beautiful city is inconceivable. The high-pitched, tin-plate
quality of the American woman's voice is largely the result of the
noises of American streets.

A sensitive woman asked a New York snipe why he sold papers.
" Because I likes to 'oller," was the reply. A community thus inspired
wastes lung, nerve, and ear. We begin to doubt if it is really "getting
anywhere," and the sensitive Englishman or Frenchman creeps out
of the noisy child's way.

In the city of Pittsburg I once attended a masque given by the
students of the Carnegie Institute. It was a beautiful piece of work,
well constructed, charmingly staged, delightfully rendered in colour
and movement ; but it had two blemishes. The English language
was badly spoken, and when the voices came clear enough to be
heard they were drowned by the far-off din of steam hammers,
hoists, trolleys and trains. One of the scenes was a glorification of
James Watt. He had created a new world and brought it to Pittsburg, but also he had brought soft coal, soot, dirt, noise, and a
number of nervous diseases. It is for the engineers to master the
noise and filth of mechanism. They, by their inventiveness, have
made life the dirty, noisy thing it is. Let them now make it quiet
again and clean. It is "up to" them.

The
Chicago
discovery.The city of Chicago has recently made the discovery that to
master dirt and noise is a part of the great town plan. One
of the finest pieces of popular civics, a manual used in the Chicago
schools, states this view.* Another expresses it finely thus : † (I put
my own italics to show where I differ in the interpretation of the
spirit.)

"The noise of surface and elevated road cars is often excru-
ciating. (*True.*) These conditions actually cause misery to a large
majority of people, who are subjected to the constant strain, and in
addition they undoubtedly cause a heavy aggregate loss of money
to the business community. (*True.*) For the sake of the State, the
citizen should be at his best, and it is the business of the State to
maintain conditions conducive to his bodily welfare. (*True.*) Noises,

---

* Whacker's " Manual of the Plan of Chicago."
† C. Moore, " The Plan of Chicago," page 74.

70

ugly sights, ill smells, as well as dirty streets or workshops or offices, tend to lower average efficiency. (*True.*) It does not pay the State to allow them to continue. (*True.*) Moreover, citizens have pride in and loyalty to a city that is quiet, clean, and generally beautiful. It is not believed that " business " demands that our present annoying conditions be continued. (*Unfortunately it is still very widely believed.*) In a state of good order all business must be done better and more profitably. (*This is but half true.*) With things as they should be, every business man in Chicago would make more money than he does now." (*False.*)

All these statements, then, are true except the last three, which are false teaching. Unfortunately it *is* believed that business demands that our present individualistic conditions be continued. Fortunately, however, *in a state of good order*, a great deal of business—the bulk of the cutting, wrecking, competitive business—will not be carried on more profitably, will indeed not be carried on at all. *With things as they should be* every business man in Chicago would *not* be making more money. But why base the appeal on an increase of material goods? Men will be making something better, realizing the finer values in life. When we appeal for the great city, why should we not do it at once on the highest ground? The petty material motives are in the end not the strongest. When men once have a clear vision it is only necessary to state the facts. Writing of the intersection of Chicago Avenue and Halstead Street, this heroic champion of the Chicago Town Plan says: "There the smoke from railroad shops and yards and from standing locomotives combines with the soot sent up by nearly four hundred trains that come and go each day. Steamships, tugs, and other river craft add their contribution ; the nearby tanneries and the garbage wagons contribute their odors ; the great coal docks, with their noisy buckets and intermittent engines, increase the din ; and the streets are covered with sawdust, coal, and dirt spilled from the thousands of wagons that constantly use this crossing. Close to this intersection is a cosmopolitan district inhabited by a mixture of races living amid surroundings which are a menace to the moral and physical health of the community." *

And Chicago is merely one of the great cities of Industrialism, where Naaman has got to perform certain preliminary duties before

* C. Moore, ibid., page 108.

he can find salvation. I do not know that its strident offensiveness is any worse than the dull horror of London, say at some point by King's Cross, Houndsditch, or Queen Victoria Street ; and there are few things so humiliating to an Englishman as the smug self-sufficiency of an English industrial town—Coventry, for instance (of which I give an illustration, No. 94 : observe its sordid streets), or Birmingham, which, for some reason known only to itself, used to call itself "the model city."

The need for Temples of Silence. We need once again in modern life Temples of Silence ; not as the Parsees, places of the dead for the pleasure of the vulture, but live places for the spirit and its contemplation, places where we can be refreshed. We might even use our existing churches more for such purpose. And perhaps we should if they were less the property of priests and vergers, if they were less part of an ecclesiastical system that had to be kept up for class purposes, if they were there more for the service of the community. We need these churches, their splendour and their beauty, for "silent prayer," where the spirit can find us again, and where we do not have perpetually thrust at us the priest's challenge on behalf of a body of doctrine that no longer squares with Truth as we understand it. "Now that the streets are nearly as noisy and as full of moving machinery as a factory, some one must arrange the provision of quiet places . . . . where lads can talk and play together ; or tram committees or railway companies must grant new facilities for carrying them to the spots from which country walks can begin."* It is not only lads that need these things, and perhaps the best temple is the green field; but of this I shall speak below (Chapter XXX). The cities of the past, for all their shortcomings and their want of comfort, were gems set within green fields.

* Graham Wallas, "The Great Society," page 352.

CHAPTER XVIII.—Poverty, Disease, Drink, Privilege, and the Glut of Wealth.

The immediate problem before the English, as before all democracies, is the conquest of poverty. The Fabian Socialists tell us they have discovered the formula. Perhaps they have. But they have not yet convinced their fellow men, nor shown us that the conquest may not be too dearly purchased. What is the trouble with Socialism? Simply this: it ignores the individual creative appeal in man—the desire for personal expression. Hence it is concerned only with men in large industrial groups. It has never fairly considered Agriculture. It has never faced the problem of the Arts, and that means all those trades and human occupations to which the Arts apply. Socialism, moreover, is now up against a greater problem still, the woman question—the life of the home disintegrated as the result of Industrialism. Half the human and personal interests of life have been in the care of women; the continued exploitation of women by factory industry is merely accelerating a process that must inevitably break down. Socialism, as taught by Fabian economists, by politicians, by stump orators, is itself the outcome of an industrial system we have to reconstruct. Socialism therefore helps us only in certain directions. In order to make it effective we need the complementary things: the ordering of Agriculture, the ordering of the Home, and, above all, the ordering of the Arts. A system for the reconstruction of the State that leaves out these needs is necessarily imperfect: they are too deeply rooted in life to be ignored.

But this, thanks to the Fabian Socialists, we now know: that poverty, and more particularly that form of it sociologists call pauperism, is kin to parasitism in biological science, a disease of character. Its origin is less economic than moral.* It results from our sick mental condition. We have outgrown our morality, and a charitable system originating in Christian morals that may have been sound in Judæa in the year one, or in the monastic age of Europe, is unsuitable to Industrial Democracy, if it brutalizes a large part of the community. In Socialism as a faith, this Christian morality is re-incarnated; in Socialism as a political theory, the stamping out of pauperism and the conquest of poverty is a cardinal point.

* See Hunter, "Poverty," p. 69, also citing C. S. Loch.

POVERTY, DISEASE, AND THE GLUT OF WEALTH

This fact of poverty, indeed, is the warp of the industrial system. Most masters of Industry, and all who preach the comfortable doctrine of success and reward through personal endeavour, with its obverse—failure and the workhouse—are blind to the fact that Industry as at present organized depends upon cheap surplus labour. It is this fact that inspires the workman's "limitation of output." "If there is not enough work to go round," says he, "we will make less of it in order to make it go round." He is wrong, of course, in not taking a broader view; but so is the master of Industry in not realizing the fundamental Christian postulate at the root of the workman's attitude. The answer to both is mechanical power, with its unlimited possibilities, provided it is organized with a view to the whole life of the State —that is to say, the æsthetic and ethical as well as the economic life.

Disease.

We cannot get rid of disease, and death comes to every man; but we can circumscribe the former. We can destroy occupational diseases, we can clean up our cities, we can stamp out sweated labour. In England, for instance, medical officers of health are still appointed by the owners of property whose drains they have to condemn; thus we premiate fever and diphtheria in our villages and slums. It was the vision of a brilliant Irishman that first helped the public to see what a professional class having a vested interest in disease really meant. The ethical basis of the new civics will be a physical basis also, and the health of the children will come first. We are feeling our way into this through our garden cities and our military discipline. During the War the English statesmen taunted the Germans with their enslavement to militarism and their surrender of purse control. The retort of the Germans was that the English were enslaved to certain political formulæ of which the control of the purse was one; and they added, "Look at the English cities! What is your control of the purse worth?" Doubtless each side was right and can learn from the other; and each was blind to the fact that it was confusing a principle with privilege. The social organization of Prussia—based on militarism, sweated Polish labour, or a school system in which child suicide is common—may be neither better nor worse than one based, as ours, on sweated labour in slums and farms, or on a condition where property is held more sacred than life. In neither case has a free citizenship been evolved.*

* In my district of England agricultural wages ran, until the War, at from 10s. to 15s. a week; the labourers' cottages are tied to the farms, and the children often can get no milk.

74

POVERTY, DISEASE, AND THE GLUT OF WEALTH

Drink and disease are first cousins.   There is no subject, unless *Drink.*
it be religion, about which men and women grow so fanatical as
drink.   Drink, as we artists see it, is the result of " baulked disposi-
tion "; let there be more colour and interest in life, and then there
will be less drink.   There is reason as well as joy and service in "wine
that maketh glad the heart of man."   But when I was in California
in 1915 I found vine-growers rooting up their vineyards for the reason
that they feared the inevitable abolition as the result of the women's
vote.   Unreason was meeting unreason.   The women pointed to the
facts, and these I also knew ; for, when the year before I had been
working on the Survey of Dublin, I tried to make a " drink " diagram,
as I had made a " slum " diagram and a " parks " diagram.   The
public-house properties were marked with black dots on the portions
of the city to be reconstructed.   The difficulties were all but insuperable—the plan illegible for black—and I was warned by Dublin
bankers that no plan stood a chance that touched the one profitable
industry.   This lay like a nightmare at the city's heart.   The Dublin
brewers were not only in possession, they were the philanthropists.
And so it is in our English cities.   We cannot have the great city
till we have mastered the drink problem, but it cannot be mastered
by fanatical abolitionists who do as much harm as good to the cause they
advocate.   A community that had created this gilded " beerage " was
faced, during the War, with its Frankenstein.   To be a "beer peer " was
found to be no longer creditable, and we grew uneasy in our conscience
as to the rightness of a monopoly of brewing or spirits that went hand
in glove with a magistracy that was a social organization, controlled
licences, and was interested in the selling of drink.   The first thing is to
be honest with ourselves, and if we want to root out the evil of drink
and the poverty and disease that comes of it, we must first root out the
social class—the monopolists and profiteers who are interested in the
maintenance of the evil.   After that we have to consider the advisa-
bility of State revenue based on the encouragement of drinking.*

* A wise and well-known brewer friend of mine writes to me (1916) on this
thorny question thus : " Most people forget that the Pub is the great working-class
tax-gatherer.   Whisky is worth about 1s. 6d. a gallon ; the Government tax is well over
10s. a gallon (I forget the exact figure).   So that most of the money paid over the
counter for whisky passes from the working man to the Exchequer.   Government *won't*
allow spirits to be sold below a certain strength, because that would at once reduce the
income from spirits.   Which is an indirect way of making people drunk by Act of
Parliament !   It is a very expensive way of collecting taxes from the working classes, and
causes a good deal of drunkenness.   If that high limit on strength were removed, the

75

The artist's attitude in this as in all kindred questions is the reasonable attitude. My personal experience, and I have known hundreds of workmen, is that drink and the arts should be more implicit. The arts correct and ennoble. They should be used to help us out of this dirty alley of life. A workman, inclined by heredity to drink, will be kept for years, perhaps permanently, from drinking. If he is interested in his work, he is too interested to drink. He has found the necessary colour and heightening of life.

Privilege. As for privilege—that citadel built anew by mechanical power, which the American Democracy is now attacking—it is akin to pauperism in this, that unless it justifies itself in some social duty it is parasitic.

We have been brought up in the belief that this justification may be left to the individual conscience. If a man "gives" or fulfils a social duty, as for instance did Sir Roger de Coverley or John Halifax, Gentleman, we need not concern ourselves with the underlying privilege on which his income is based. Thus our fathers taught.

It is improbable that the great city of the future will continue to see it so, for it will have other ethics. Sir Roger may keep his tenants' cottages in perfect order and John Halifax be a model employer, but what about the great cities as they are and the land on which they stand? I gave above my own practical experience in the housing of Dublin, where 150,000 need new houses; I have not lived for thirteen years in East London without knowing how the same is true there. Some of the latest estimates of this need

ordinary forces of competition would soon reduce the strength of spirits. . . . But it is inaccurate to speak of what is spent on whisky as *waste*. Whisky is a very cheap form of stimulant—it may be a wasteful and bad system of tax-gathering, but that is another question. Brewers make very little profit out of the spirit trade, and with the development in recent years of the jug and bottle and outdoor trade in beer, they are not nearly so dependent as they once were on the Pub; so that they can afford to look at the question without self-interest quite blinding them to any other consideration. . . . I see nothing to be gained by the State taking over the drink trade. The fact that so large a revenue comes from it, and that arbitrary interference with people's habits is sure to be reflected at the polls, are fatal objections. Local magistrates have for thirty years had, and *actively used*, the power to control all alterations to public-houses. . . . The existing Pub is the direct outcome of the united wisdom of magistrates and police; brewers have never had any trace of a free hand. I am certain that Pubs would have been more sensibly planned if brewers had been given a free hand and there had been no magisterial or police interference. Brewers would have supplied such premises as were *required* by the people, and the people have far more sense than magistrates, police, parsons, and temperance faddists." In short, what my friend suggests is Guild syndicalism applied to the craft of brewing.

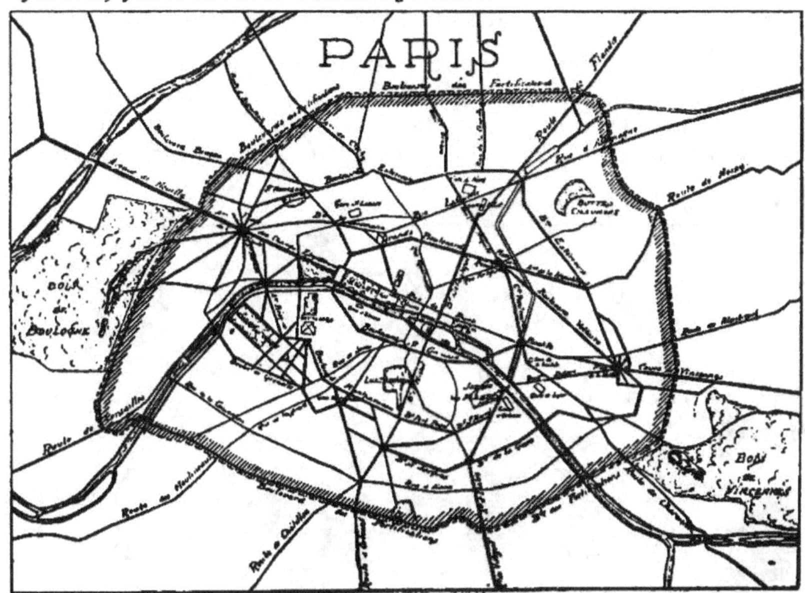

Haussmann's reconstruction of Paris.   No. 71.

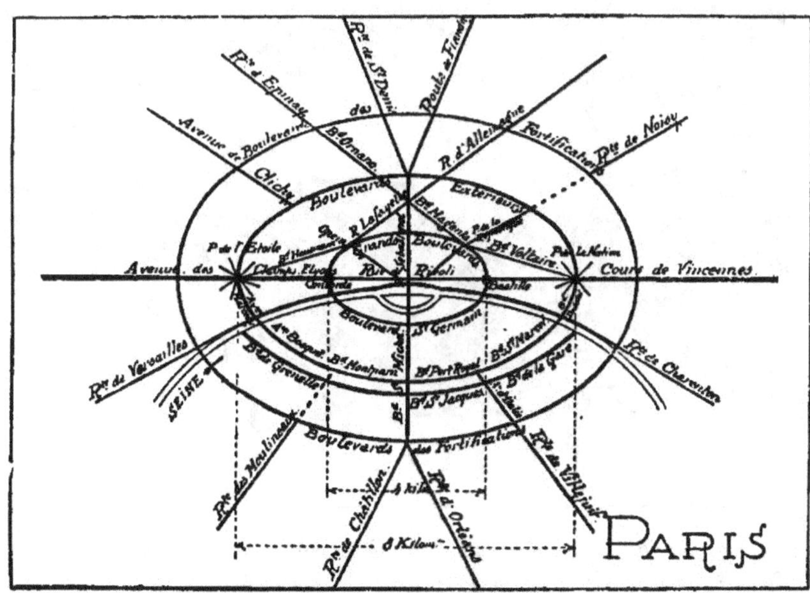

The " schematic " plan of Paris.   No. 72.

are as follows: "From 'reliable statistics' it appears that no fewer than 2,500,000 of London's population require better housing. In Scotland 22 per cent. of the families live in single-room homes . . . . while in Glasgow the proportion runs up to 33 per cent. In Chicago,

By the courtesy of the Editor of "The Town Planning Review," and Mr. F. Howkins.

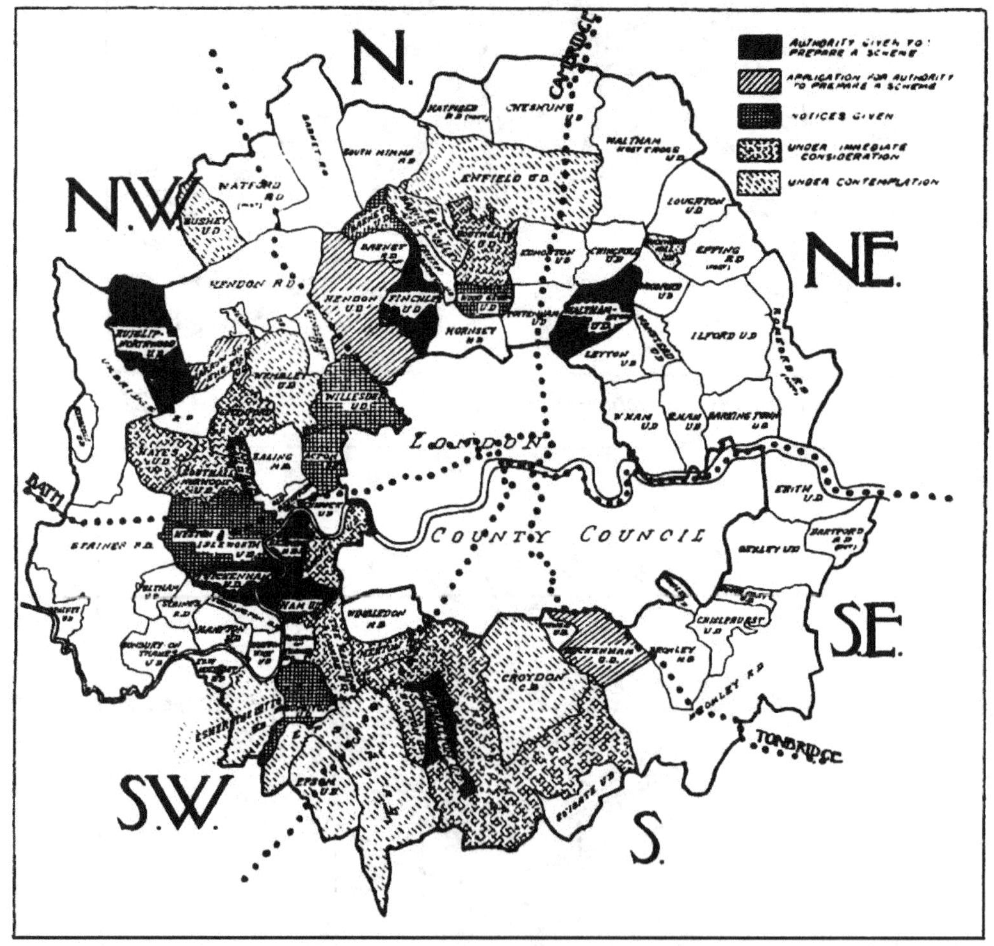

Greater London, showing the authorities in various stages of procedure under the Housing and Town Planning Act on 31 December 1913.　　　　No. 73.

in certain sections, the overcrowding exceeds that of the densest portions of London. In New York the conditions are three times as bad as they are in London." *

It is sometimes argued that this is not always the result of privilege. If it is not, the two are dangerously akin, and we run the risk of losing the beauty and culture of life that a privileged class has given us and can give, unless we cut out the canker that lies at the root. I do not want to see the English gentry destroyed, the cultured life, the history and tradition for which it stands, the public-school system on which it is based. I do want to see it transformed, grow more intelligent, have more sympathy with, more understanding of, Democracy. Here again the solution to our difficulty—in this case how to keep what is good—is mechanical power. We must learn how to use it for menial service, instead of using and wasting so much human labour. We want a closer knowledge of what the machine can and should do. We need a larger vision in history and æsthetics, and to learn that these things must be no longer the enjoyments of a class. I have known the time when English country gentlemen—friends of mine—used the flag as a party election badge, and then wondered why workmen—also friends of mine—who were of the other political party, misprized the flag. The War, let us hope, has changed this, and shown us that the history, the tradition of the flag in our own or any country, can no longer be the privilege merely of a class. As soon as it becomes that, either it is doomed, or there is an end to Democracy. In England we still need our gentry, but what our gentry need is more sympathy, more wisdom. "I like educated people," said an old labourer to me in my village, "but what a pity they're so ignorant!"

The glut of wealth affects all our great cities, and it affects them *The glut of* in inverse ratio to the scholarship and science of their planning. *wealth.* We notice it least in Paris (see Nos. 71, 72). For what, after all, is a glut but a want of clean passage through the system of life? It means that where nourishment should pass easily and pleasantly we have instead a congestion. The intestines are clogged. We notice it most in London (see No. 38, also No. 73), where the chaos of the nineteenth century has made out of two mediæval cities, London and Westminster, and some hundred surrounding hamlets and villages, a swarming area of human life with its self-governing authorities. What a little gem was once the City of Westminster, and how tragic has

* F. C. Howe, "The City of Democracy," pages 188-190.

been its obliteration! (see No. 74 *).   In the New World, again, the glut is at its worst in Chicago.   Here, until the coming of the new town plan (see No. 56), there was practically no planning at all; and

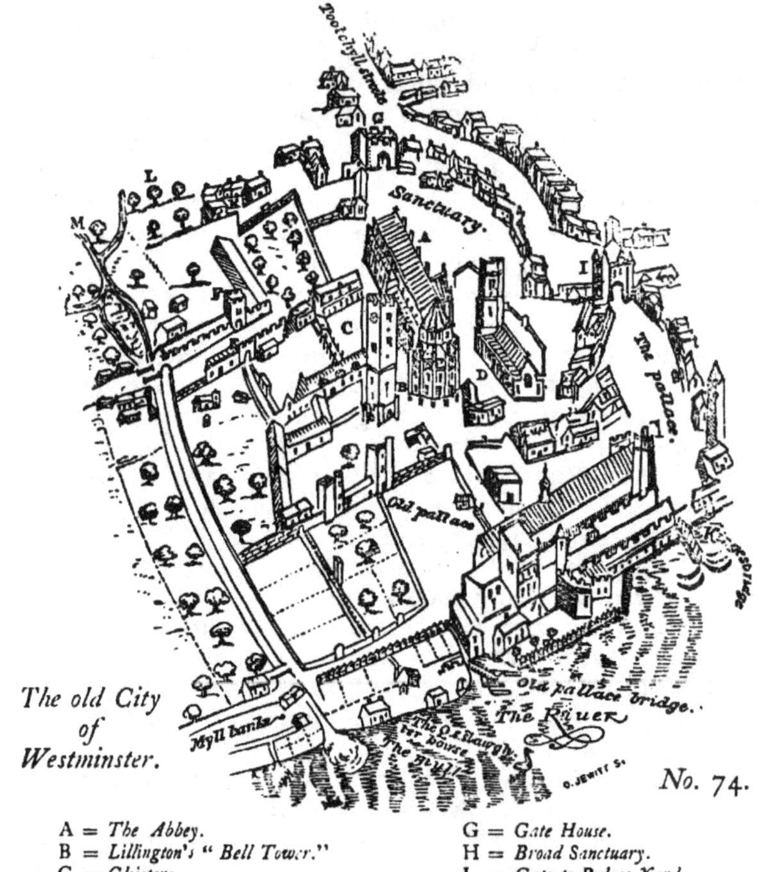

The old City
of
Westminster.

No. 74.

A = *The Abbey.*
B = *Lillington's " Bell Tower."*
C = *Cloisters.*
D = *St. Margaret's Church.*
E = *Tower over entrance to Little Dean's Yard.*
F = *Granary and Brew houses.*

G = *Gate House.*
H = *Broad Sanctuary.*
I = *Gate to Palace Yard.*
K = *Almonry.*
L = *Orchard.*
M = *Stream of Water.*

it is not possible to drive, and barely possible to walk, through the heart of the city and its square mile of congested streets.

*An illustra-
tion from
Berlin.*

Every great city has its own problem, and brings its lesson to the art of life.   Of modern Berlin it is written: "The carrying out

* From "Scott's Gleanings."   See Trans. R.I.B.A.

of the projects which were elaborated in the 1862 scheme was probably prevented by the sudden rush of prosperity that followed on the successful issue of the Franco-Prussian War. Whereas other German towns experienced an influx of wealth sufficient to enable them to undertake colossal schemes of enlargement, Berlin was over-glutted; its efforts at bestirring itself and looking after its true interests were paralysed by excess of nourishment . . . At the two extremes Berlin is found deficient; in the broadest sense her plan was never controlled and brought into order, as was that of Paris by Haussmann (see No. 71); and at the other end the actual habitations, the units from which the town is built up, were left to take care of themselves as best they could. The explanation of this curious condition is comparatively simple. . . . The treatment that should have been urging Berlin into a mighty unified organism was absent . . . Added to this was the fact that so much of the work necessary to be done was outside the actual city boundary . . . there was the important and also rival city of Charlottenburg provided with its own royal palace, and other populous townships inclined to resent interference from the central city. . . . Finally, in her housing conditions Berlin has developed a very remarkable method, one which to a large extent might have been expected throughout Germany as a natural result of the traditional planning and the universal provision of wide streets; but here intensified . . . A rush like that of adventurers to a mining camp is deterred by nothing, so that we find a close packing and a congestion in the population of Berlin which would otherwise be inexplicable. Since the refilling of the old original fortifications, she has been an "open city" . . . her powerful army giving her protection instead of fortifications . . . The most important cause of the congestion was the land speculation, and the formation of a ring of landowners forcing up the price of land to the amazing figure of £15,000 an acre. The poor suffered to the full from the injurious effect of tenement dwellings. The figures quoted by Professor Eberstadt of fitness for military service in the year 1910 illustrate this. Whereas the percentage for the whole German Empire is 53 per cent., and for the medium-size towns about 50 per cent., for Berlin it is 27·6."*

Here we have a curious and profoundly interesting picture drawn by an English architect and town-planner writing before the War without any national or political bias. It is that of a glutted and

* Patrick Abercrombie, "Town Planning Review," 1914.

imperialistic city, on the one hand amazingly successful in her military Industrialism, the gathering of material goods, but failing in the essential quality, the physique of her people for that military fitness which was the supreme boast of Prussia.

All the great indus-trial cities glutted.

Hundreds of examples of the glut of wealth could be given from the great cities of America, but in this respect all great cities are alike. One of the leading landscape architects of the United States who has studied the problem yet again from another angle, that of the laying out of Parks, Streets, and Gardens, puts the same thing thus: "We are concerned with a single complex subject, namely, the intelligent control and guidance of the entire physical growth and alteration of cities, embracing all the problems of *relieving* and *avoiding* congestion—congestion of people in buildings, and of buildings upon land, congestion of transportation facilities, or of recreation facilities, congestion in respect to the means of supplying light, air, water, or anything else essential to the health and happiness of people."*

The artist's study indeed, when we look at it from that point of view, becomes the master study, "L'objet de l'art c'est l'expression de la vie."

Axiom VIII

We get back therefore to our eighth axiom. Whether we deal with the drink question, or with disease, or with poverty and its obverse privilege that brings about the glut of wealth, the central question always faces us—How shall mechanical power be socialized? Our axiom is insistent: "*Man's control of mechanical power has yet to be made effective. The making it effective is not merely a matter of inventing or exploiting new processes, it is the discovery of means whereby it shall be best used in the public service; in other words, how it shall be 'socialized,' and not merely used to enable men to exploit each other.*" The end of the axiom brings us to the gentleman in democracy. He will not drink, nor be stricken with poverty, he will be free of disease that comes from squalor or ill-breeding, and he is not to be the product of privilege. If he is to be made with the aid of the machine, it must be because through democracy he has mastered the machine. "*As Hellenic civilization made the gentleman with the aid of the slave, so we may make the gentleman with the aid of the machine.*" To throw away, as we have been doing during the War, so much of the best of what we have, unless it yield for all the heroism and sacrifice some fairer world for man, is mere waste. Let us consider now what waste means to the city in Times of Peace.

* F. Law Olmstead, at Philadelphia, 1911. C. A. Beard, "American City Government," 1912.

82

CHAPTER XIX.—Waste in Education.

Waste is largely want of imagination. Christ made that clear *Waste is* once and for all when He rebuked Judas about the box of precious *want of* ointment. Daily, when we have the chance of bringing right into *imagination.* the City, into life, we go on with our schemes and doles for the poor, our privileges for the rich. Men, especially Americans, cried out at he horrors of the War, but there are as many lives lost yearly in the United States from preventable accidents and disease as were lost at Verdun and Ypres ; * and more babies under one year of age died in England during the first two years of the War than there were Englishmen killed during that time in the War.† The old gods, the old beliefs, the old conventions, make it so hard for us to focus, and in these high matters of life and death we fail in any right sense of proportion.

In England the supreme waste is in our education system—or *The* want of system : the antiquated class divisions ; the armies of officials *English* and inspectors ; the ridiculous water-tight compartments—" elemen- *muddle.* tary," " secondary," " art," " higher," " technical," " agricultural " ; the mobs of unintelligent committees ; the obscurantist parsons and churchwardens clinging to ancient trusts ; the want of organization and of purpose. We need some Thomas Cromwell to root the old system out ; but we also need an Erasmus and a John Knox to make the new system sympathetic and democratic. In the United States they are better situated ; for there, though the individual standard, when set beside that of the English gentleman, may not be so high, the average standard is infinitely higher. The people value Education more ; and, apart from that, the spaciousness of the country, its wide human range, is in itself an education ; but in both countries there is the same lack of æsthetic synthesis.

This English weakness has thrown us back for two decades, and will continue for some time to do so. Many of our failures in the War are directly traceable to our want of science—there lies the insincerity ; to our want of practical æsthetics—there lies the demo- cratic want. Æsthetics, as I have shown, imply the life of the community as a whole. The better organization of the Germans for war was largely due to their civic æsthetics. They had learned

* For confirmation of these figures see R. Hunter, "Poverty," 1905.
† Blue Book, Cd. 8206.

how to order their cities with more cleanliness, more discipline, less muddle and confusion. As the result of a war that has been fought for the democratic idea, we may find ways ot learning what the Germans can teach without paying the tragic price that they had to pay.

Class barriers.

In England the crying need is to create an educational system that shall meet the want of Democracy. The old system no longer serves. We must reform it, break down the class barriers, think less of property and more of men and women, give the children more chance ; until we do this we can have no City in the greater sense of the word.

Illustrations of waste.

I give here three illustrations of English enterprise and waste— efforts with which I have been closely associated during the last ten years. They represent achievement or failure, according as we look at results in their ultimate or immediate influence on life. Each has its meaning for the æsthetic education of Democracy, and shows the architect's share in it. I shall not go into details, as each has been dealt with elsewhere. The first was part of the greater enterprise for the University of London ; the next had to do with London's so-called "secondary" and "higher education"; and the third with county education in Gloucestershire. It is with the underlying idea in each case that I am here concerned, and how that idea called forth the architectural or æsthetic form.

London University education.

The idea underlying the "Fraternity House" on Chelsea Embankment (see No. 76), where I had done a good deal of building at different times, was to establish a community life as part of the University, and to link this up with the historic life of Chelsea, on the actual site of Sir Thomas More's garden, incorporating what was left of Shrewsbury House, the ancient Palace of Bess of Hardwicke, one of the greatest of the Elizabethan builders.* It was part of the larger scheme for the collegiate development on Cheyne Walk, the re-erection of Crosby Hall, and the existing buildings of " More's Garden." Only a fragment of the great enterprise is in being. What we wanted to do was to establish a college with halls of residence for men and women. But it was not to have only the Oxford and Cambridge tradition : it was to have some of the Scotch and some of the American quality, it was to be a creation essentially

---

* See Geddes's Reports ; also " Catalogue of the Universities Exhibition," University of London, 1912.

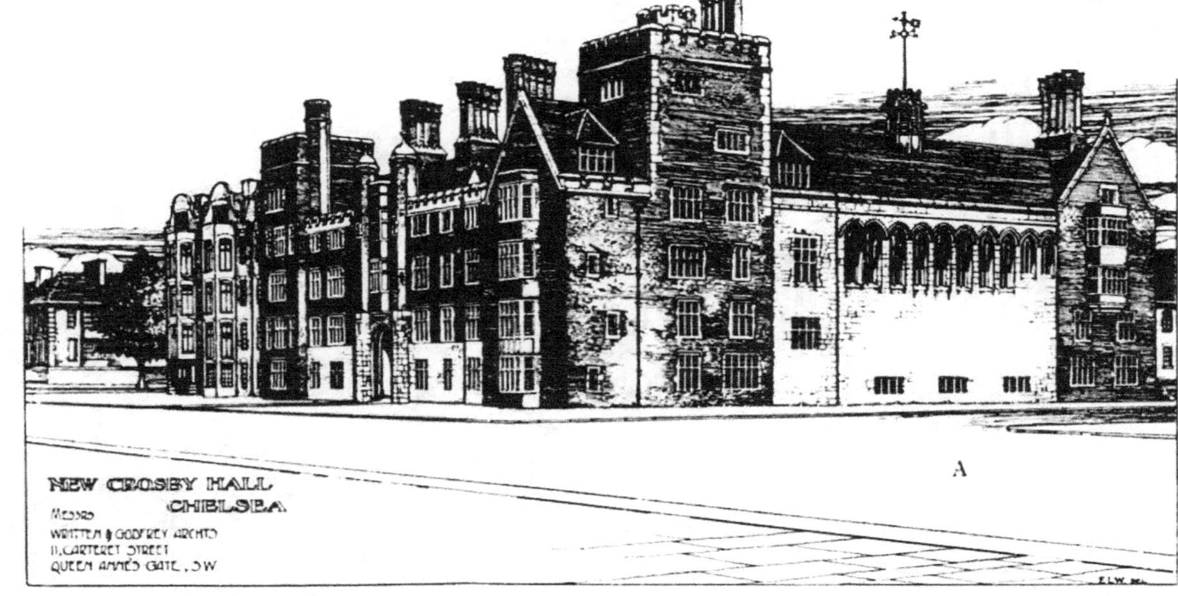

No. 75.

Crosby Hall at A is the only portion of this scheme that is built, with the exception of the corner portion at the south-western end of the block.

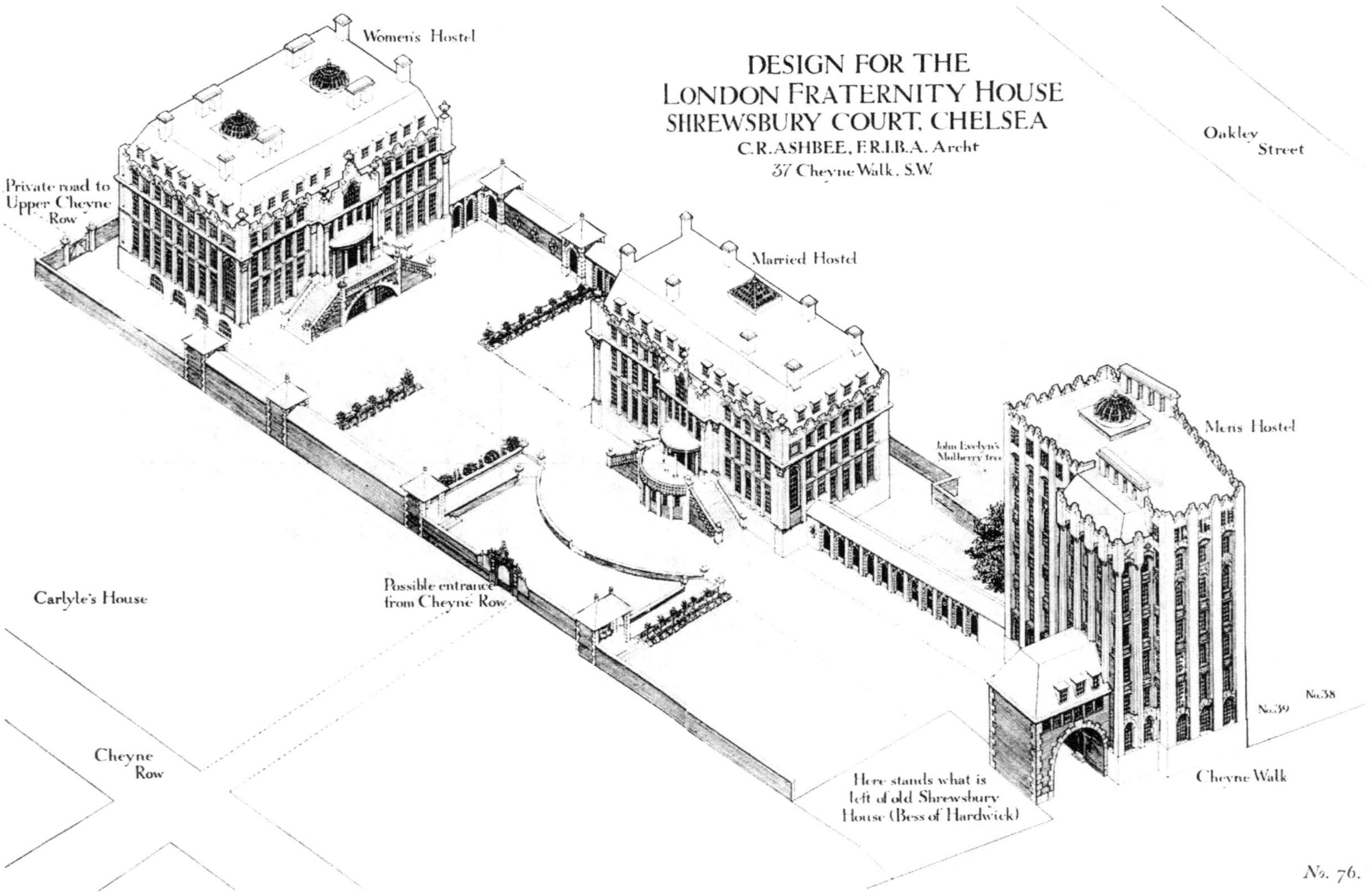

DESIGN FOR THE
LONDON FRATERNITY HOUSE
SHREWSBURY COURT, CHELSEA
C.R.ASHBEE, F.R.I.B.A. Archt
37 Cheyne Walk. S.W.
Women's Hostel
Private road to Upper Cheyne Row
Oakley Street
Married Hostel
Men's Hostel
John Evelyn's Mulberry tree
Carlyle's House
Possible entrance from Cheyne Row
Cheyne Row
Here stands what is left of old Shrewsbury House (Bess of Hardwick)
No.39
No.38
Cheyne Walk
No. 76.

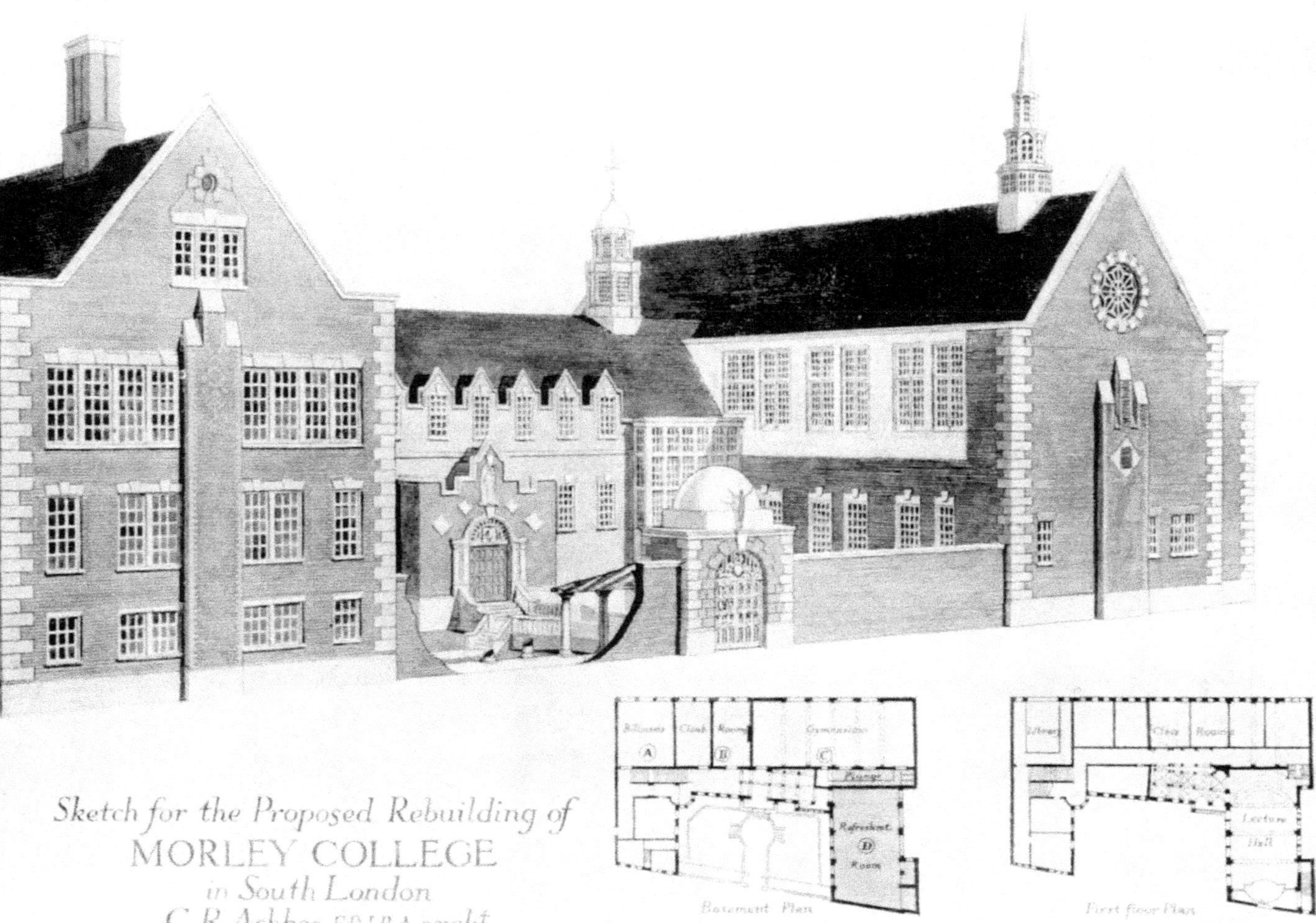

Sketch for the Proposed Rebuilding of
MORLEY COLLEGE
in South London
C. R. Ashbee, F.R.I.B.A. arch.

No. 77.

suitable to London. My colleague, Walter Godfrey, had, with fine scholarship, re-erected the old Merchants' Hall* at the corner of Danvers Street, when Professor Geddes saved it from being broken up for road metalling in Bishopsgate, and I give his sympathetic treatment for the new front to the embankment (see No. 75). My scheme for the development of this includes a " Fraternity House " somewhat on the American model—the southern group for men, the northern for women, the central block for married couples. The remains of the old palace, with additional rooms over the archway, was for various communal uses. Here was to have been the first great residential college within the London area ; its appeal was to have been to Colonial and American students. The elements of the life, indeed, were already there ; the students, men and women, housed in different parts of London in horrid lodging-houses, were there; the vacant land was there. The idea, admittedly, was live ; but, as so often with us in England, the organization for giving shape to the idea was ineffectual. It was impossible to get the various rival bodies to agree to work together. There was no means of launching the needful appeal, and the men of standing and finance who might have backed the enterprise were too timid. Perhaps they were thinking of armaments, of taxation, of vested college interests. Perhaps in another ten or twenty years the University of London, roused from its coma, may get its halls of residence, make its mark on the Great City, as a university should. Then the larger communal life of London will begin. The scheme waits for Democracy, but meantime the brains and enthusiasm of many able men, some of them now dead, have been wasted.†

In the Morley College enterprise (see No. 77) the problem was *London* simpler, and the scheme smaller ; but the difficulty of conflicting *secondary* Education Authorities, the want of vision, the internecine quarrels, *education.* were even greater. Here also the land, and in part the money, was at hand. The objective in this case was not the formation of a new life, it was to give architectural form to a life that had already grown up among the clerks, mechanics, and evening students in one of the most vigorous educational centres on the south side of the Thames. The type by which a far-sighted Education Authority might have been guided was what is known in American cities as the " Municipal

* See " London Survey Publications," 1908, " Crosby Hall."
† One of these was R. D. Roberts, to whom London, and indeed Oxford and Cambridge, largely owe the University Extension Movement.

WASTE IN EDUCATION

University."* The idea is that the education shall vary with the employment and the standing of the students. Of one of the great American cities we learn : " Its Municipal University is the keystone of the city's educational system, where other Universities are millstones to the secondary and elementary systems." The millstone is a metaphor with which English educational reformers also are familiar. It was hesitation and uncertainty that wrecked the Morley College enterprise— want of any clear purpose as to what the higher education in a great city ought to be. Here, again, we wait for Democracy, and perhaps it is as well. The sweeping out of dead-heads in high places is a preliminary to any educational reform. The present College stands, squalid and slovenly, in a region of London—Waterloo Bridge Road—the whole of which ought to be rebuilt, and treated as part of a comprehensive Town Plan for the linking up of the City north and south of the Thames. Education and civic reconstruction are part of one problem, and it is impossible, when we are considering the reaction of æsthetics and education upon one another, to consider these educational centres of life apart from their surroundings. In no other district of London have I noted Wagner and Purcell competing on even terms with the neighbouring public-houses; and workmen and their wives standing in queues outside the ticket office, because good music could be purchased at the price of a pot of beer.† Yet so it was here, and the Education Authority was not alive to the æsthetic influence—it let it go to waste.

English country education.
Of the third enterprise much has been written, and many Reports published from time to time.‡ The idea in this case was to give unity and purpose to English country education, centring it in a small town of 1,300 inhabitants, surrounded by some thirty villages, in one of the districts within the educational area of the Gloucester County Council. The plans here given (see Nos. 78, 79) show a Central School with its outlying gardens. The types of workshops and schoolrooms, gardens, etc. (Nos. 80–85), will indicate the kind of teaching given to country boys and girls. Here the

* C. Zueblin, "American Municipal Progress," 1916. See especially p. 225. "At the crown of the Municipal Education system is the Municipal University, represented to-day by the institutions in New York, Cincinnati, and Akron, Ohio."

† At the "Old Vic," the nearest approach to London's Municipal Opera House, such as they have in almost all German cities, this might often be seen. But it was all the work of one determined and fearless woman—Miss Cons.

‡ See the Reports of the Campden School of Arts and Crafts from 1903 to 1914 ; also Ashbee, "The Hamptonshire Experiment in Education," 1914.

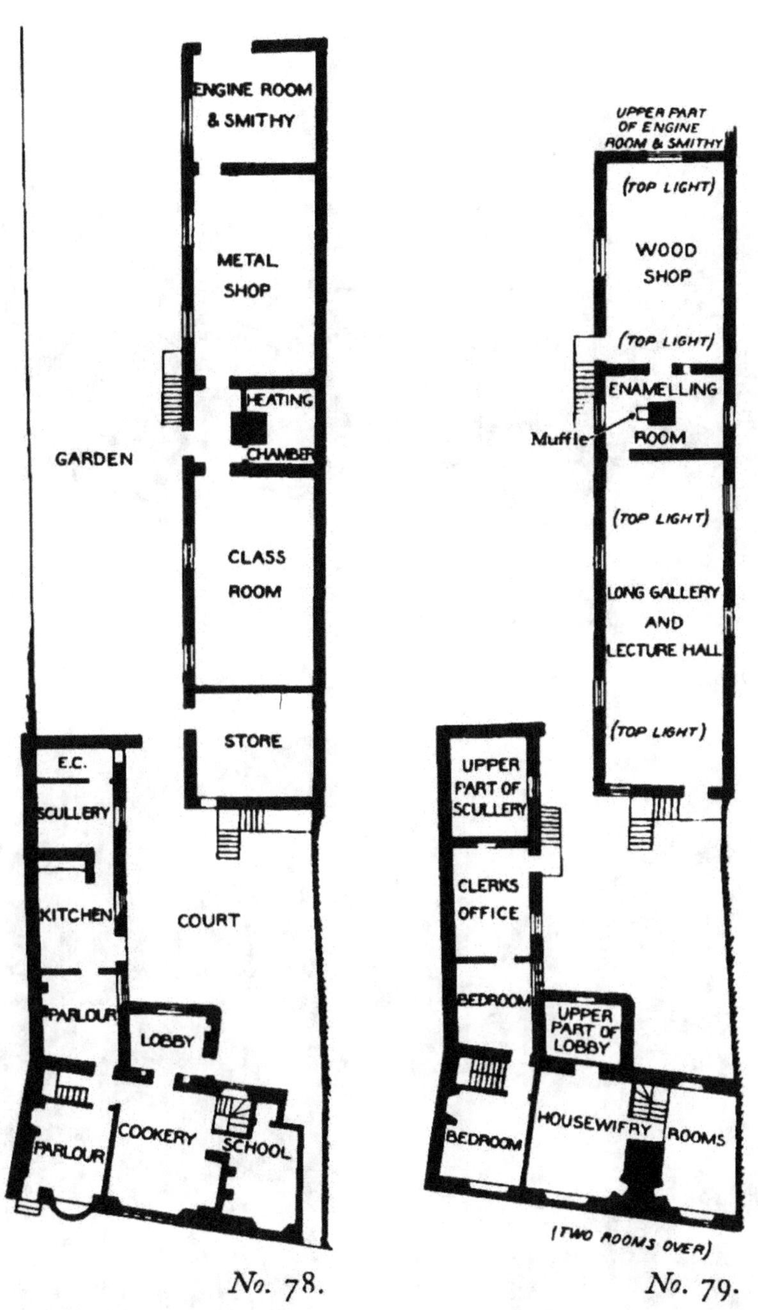

Plans of the Campden School of Arts and Crafts before the dismemberment by the Gloucestershire County Council in 1917.

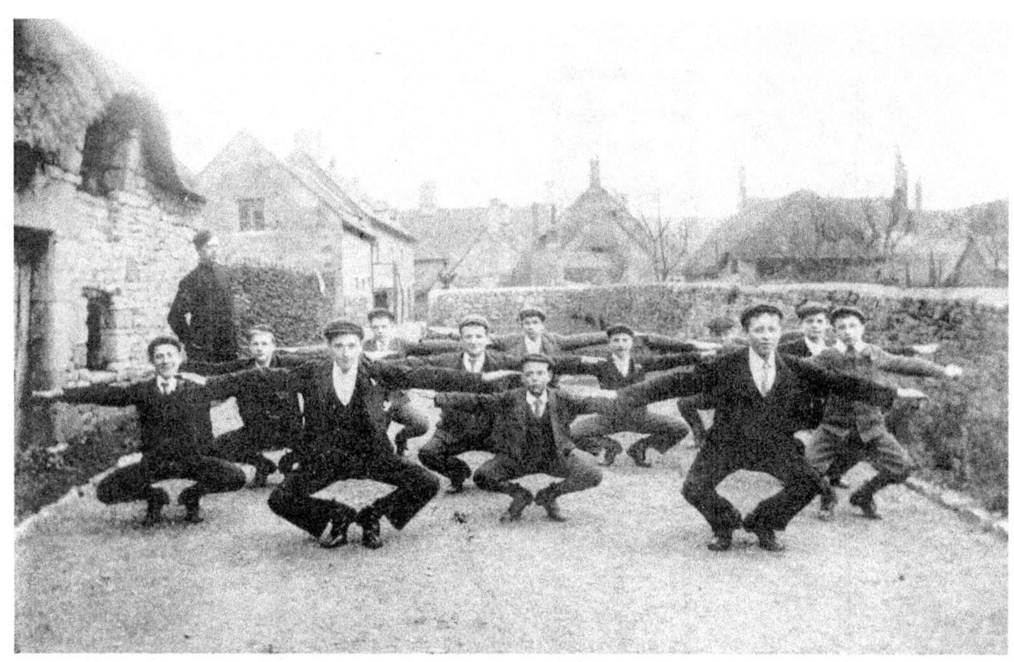

Physical Drill. No. 80.

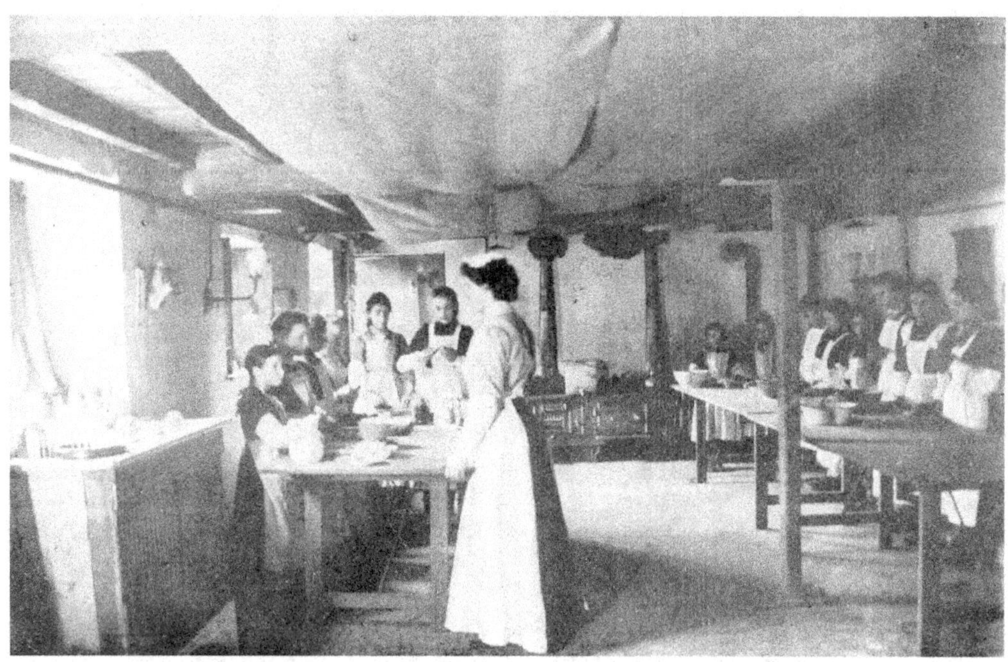

Cookery. No. 81.

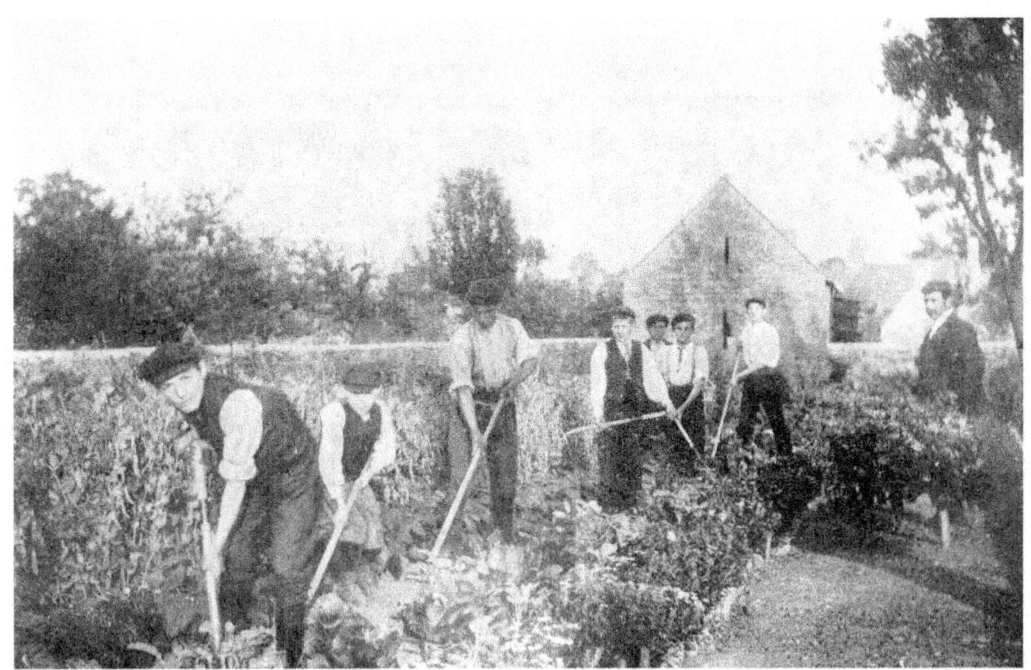

Gardening. No. 82.

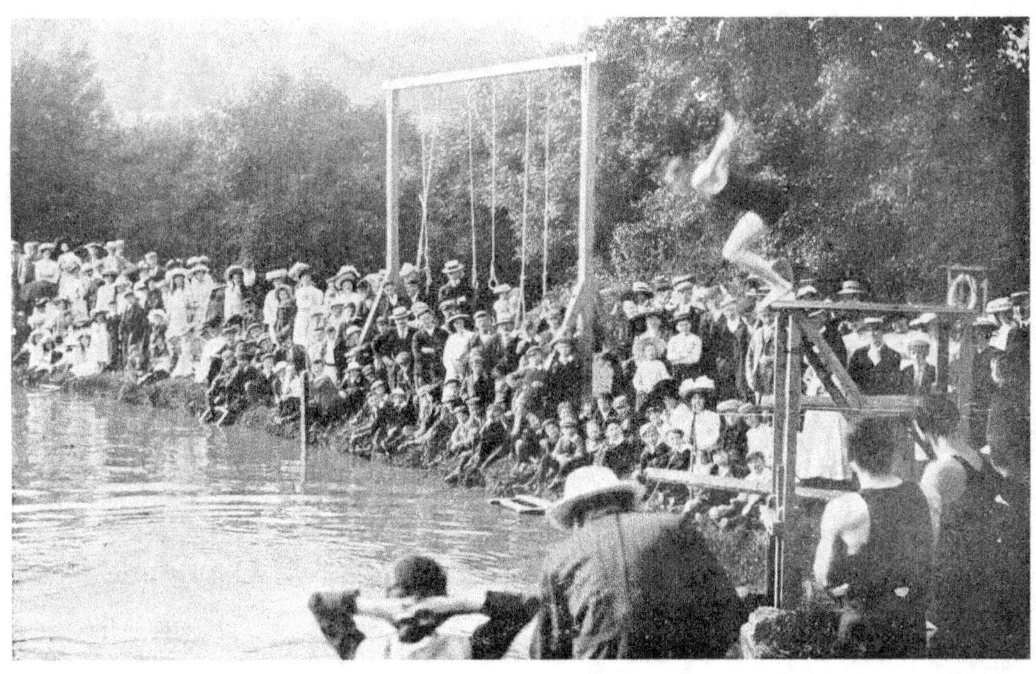

Swimming. No. 83.

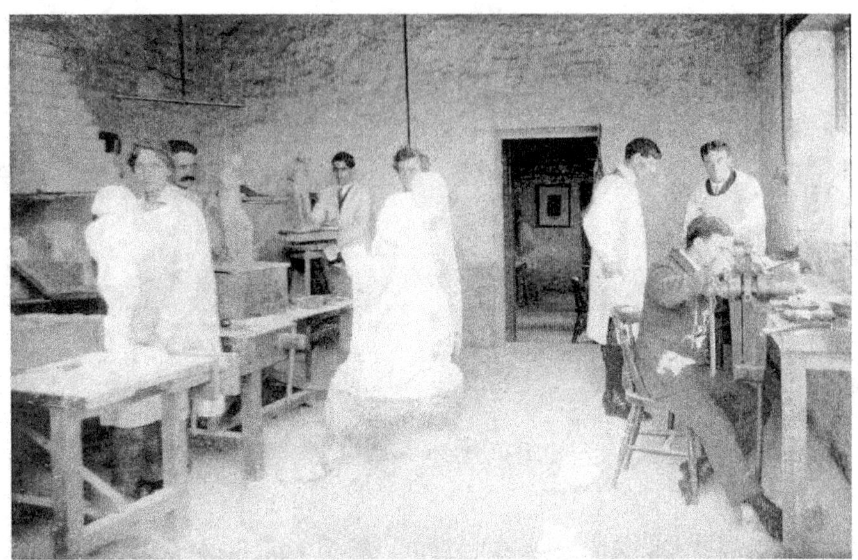

Modelling and Carving. No. 84.

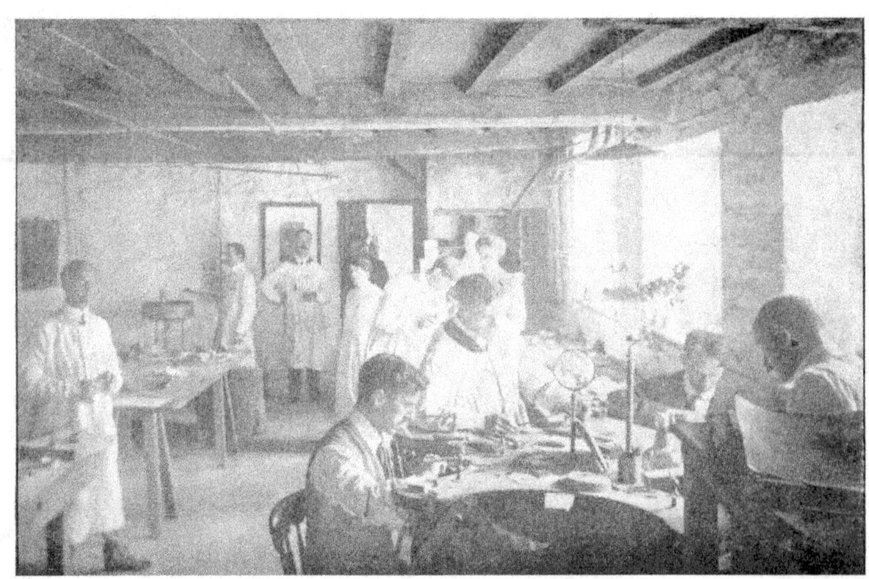

Jewellery and Metalwork. No. 85.

form was ready to hand; the exquisite building tradition of an unindustrialized English village dominated the whole conception. Intelligent conservatism was all that was needed. The life flowed instinctively into the mould. The School came to be, and the lives of hundreds of boys and girls, men and women, have been influenced by it. After fourteen years' successful enterprise, the bulk of this work was wrecked by the Education Committee and the officials of the Gloucester County Council, and in spite of the protests of the Board of Education, in a moment of panic during the crisis of the War. They anticipated the reduction of their grants—based mainly upon "whisky," or excise revenue—and they thought the wisest form of retrenchment was the destruction of Education. The traditions were scattered, the staff and teachers dismissed, the buildings abandoned, and the Government grant thrown away by the Local Education Authority. Here again we need the larger national reform before we can re-establish our work—that more logical "Education Act" to make possible intelligent enterprise and democratic teaching. Here again we have to unload the "dead-heads," to scrap the antiquated machinery of administration that hampers enterprise or gives power for destruction to men who do not understand, and who have no sympathy for, the labourer. The waste here *was actually of the labourer* and the *labourer's children.* The mills of Democracy grind slowly, and good results are perhaps never wasted. When a piece of sound constructive work is over-turned, it is not unlike an ant-hill—time is of little account; nor is the individual: the pile rebuilds itself. The destroyers sometimes get stung. "It might be discouraging," said Samuel Chapman Armstrong, one of the greatest American Educationists, of his Hampton enterprise, "if we were not working for two hundred years hence."

These three illustrations of waste in Education and the finer democratic life of England are given less for what they contain of personal experience than for what each stood for—democratic humanism and the æsthetic synthesis. There lie our needs; when we find them they will be a check to waste. If the democratic humanism is ever and again grudgingly accepted, the æsthetic synthesis is sometimes not yet understood by the community: certainly not by the three Education Authorities concerned in the illustrations given, in this case the University of London, the London County Council, and the Gloucester County Council. In each instance the plea, of course, was want of money; but those of us who know

Democratic humanism and the æsthetic synthesis.

are conscious of a much greater want. Rather was it a want of thought, a want of purpose, a want of imagination.

The Scotch Dominie tells in his delightful log-book that the only thing he aims at, despite the Code, is to get his bairns to think—and think through the imagination. "When one has stripped off all the conventions, and superstitions, and hypocrisies, then one is educated." But, pulling himself up in a moment of doubt, he asks : "Is it possible that I am overdoing the imagination business ? Shall I produce men and women with more imagination than intellect ? No ; I do not think there is danger. The nation suffers from lack of imagination. Few of us can imagine a better state of society, a fuller life." *

It is said of the English Tommy in war, that he quickly thinks for himself. I have certainly found among my skilled craftsmen that they have the democratic humanism, if they often lack the power of æsthetic synthesis. One of them, who had struggled on on the totally inadequate wage allowed in times of peace to men of his type of ability and imagination, but who within a few months of his entry into the war became second in command of his regiment, wrote to me during the Battle of the Somme, of that technical education our Mandarins at home were engaged in destroying :

"I wish we had the ' big bugs ' in Education out here ; I cannot conceive a better ground for their study of character. . . . The army in France has become one huge Technical School ; the past scholars of Eton and Harrow even have to become students in its various handicrafts. In short, the Nation out here is being trained to think and observe, which is all-important. . . . You see, in modern warfare we are up against very hard facts, and we have found out to our cost that we are not a thinking nation ; we have also found out that we can no longer win battles solely on the playing-fields of Eton."

In an inspired passage in his " Principles of Social Reconstruction," Bertrand Russell restates the words of the Scotch elementary teacher and of my Guild craftsman in terms of the philosopher : "The joy of mental adventure," he says, "is far commoner in the young than in grown men and women. Among children it is very common, and grows naturally out of the period of make-believe and fancy. It is rare in later life, because everything is done to kill it during education. Men fear thought as they fear nothing else on earth—more than ruin, more even than death. Thought is subversive

* A. S. Neill, "A Dominie's Log."

and revolutionary, destructive and terrible ; thought is merciless to privilege, established institutions, and comfortable habits ; thought is anarchic and lawless, indifferent to authority, careless of the well-tried wisdom of the ages. Thought looks into the pit of hell and is not afraid. It sees man, a feeble speck, surrounded by unfathomable depths of silence ; yet it bears itself proudly, as unmoved as if it were lord of the universe. Thought is great and swift and free, the light of the world, and the chief glory of man.

"But if thought is to become the possession of many, not the privilege of the few, we must have done with fear. It is fear that holds men back, fear lest their cherished beliefs should prove delusions, fear lest the institutions by which they live should prove harmful, fear lest they themselves should prove less worthy of respect than they supposed themselves to be."

Thought, indeed, is the great talisman, inevitable to democratic humanism. With it we resolve the evil of the world ; and if some of the good goes too, we need not fear, for the other talisman—the power of æsthetic synthesis, remains. So shall this world for ever be re-imagined and re-made ; so shall all things be given us—" beautiful things made new for the surprise of the sky children."

Thus our poets and philosophers have taught. Thus shall we build the great city. It was with fine insight that Granville Barker made his noble play, " Waste," deal with the failure of an English Education Bill.

CHAPTER   —WASTE IN INDUSTRY.

Waste in Education is merely the reflection of Waste in Industry. I have used the phrase "the æsthetic synthesis"; I mean by it the method whereby we artists would put together and test the various activities of life: as the architect or the painter says of his work, "Does it come together?"

"The ugly," says Croce, "is unsuccessful expression," and he adds, "The paradox is true, that in works of art that are failures, the beautiful is present as *unity* and the ugly as *multiplicity*."* He might perhaps equally well have called it waste. I was once sitting in the library of an American steel magnate, fingering with him the incunabula and vellum manuscripts, when he suddenly looked up at me and said:

"Why can't we produce these things any more? Why has our society been such a failure, and everything we produce so ugly? With our architecture, our painting, our books, it's all the same; our schools, Art Institutes, and cities cannot give us the result—in standard—of these old men. Why is it?"

The Italian philosopher supplies the answer. We do not go the right way to work. The system wastes the men, it does not allow them to work in the only way in which such things can be produced. Methods suitable to the production of steel cars are unsuitable to the production of incunabula.

Our Education system, as we have seen, does not stand the test of the æsthetic synthesis. It has no unity, it does not come together, still less so the Industrial system it reflects. If we want an object lesson in the failure of the latter, we have but to look at one of the ordinary architectural exhibitions. In England, for instance, they are microcosms of the actual face of the country for the last twenty-five years. What do we see? Houses for the rich, innumerable houses for the well-to-do and the middle class, a few stylistic churches rigidly clinging to a Gothic tradition, a few public buildings obviously produced officially, not spontaneously because the people really love or want them, while for the vast mass of the people—75 per cent. of the population—nothing. The people until quite recently in housing and town-planning schemes, which the War brought to a sudden ending, have been no concern of the Architect. For them

---

* "Æsthetik," Ainslie's translation.

he has had no message. The Architect has had nothing to do with the poor. Industrial England has meant nothing to him. There was no money in it. "Unfortunate, yet so it is," say the reformers and the politicians, and they add, "It is due to the wrong distribution of wealth." Some of us artists hold this to be a false view. We say that the happiness, the beauty, the divinity of life find expression without reference to either wealth or poverty, unless the latter be below the margin of subsistence.

It is not so much a redistribution or a better distribution of wealth *A less* that we need as a riddance of waste. The poor, the rich, the middle *wasteful* class, are all alike wasteful—wasteful of the amenities, of the health- *distribution* giving, the life-giving things—wasteful of beauty. If the Socialists *of wealth* would preach the elimination of waste, as Morris did, rather than the *needed.* redistribution of wealth, their appeal would be more effective, and have more spiritual force. We do not need all these dead mechanical things that are ever being thrust upon us by Ill-organized Industry. Our misuse of mechanical power has brought us, rich and poor alike, a wrong way of looking at life. We hold it desirable, happy, for its accumulation of "things," not for the possession of the real goods. We would in fact, like Judas, sell the precious ointment for purposes of slumming.

But the waste is not where we think it. The greatest waste is spiritual and human. All stuff that is made for sale rather than service, all stuff that in the making numbs or destroys a human being, is *ipso facto* waste. It may "fill a want," but it also is a waste, and the waste is often greater than the want. The mediæval craftsman may have had a narrow intellectual outlook, but his were the divine chances of the creative artist, because of the "standard" of his guild. The modern machine hand can seldom achieve this out of the quantitative standard of mechanism. In this numbing of the finer faculties is an economic waste beyond measure. Let us keep our eighth Axiom well in mind, for it is this waste and cheapening of men *Axiom VIII* that is implied in their exploitation of one another. "*Man's control of mechanical power has yet to be made effective. The making it effective is not only a matter of inventing or exploiting new processes, it is the discovering of means whereby mechanical power shall be best used in the public service—in other words, how it shall be "socialized," and not merely used to enable men to exploit each other. As Hellenic civilization made the gentleman with the aid of the slave, so we may make the gentleman with the aid of the machine.*"

WASTE IN INDUSTRY

Thus we approach the Arts from different standpoints, but the pull is ever in one direction: more sensitiveness, more appreciation, more response to what is vital and quickening, less waste of the finer things so that we shall better understand. "Pour comprendre un rayon de soleil," says the French psychologist, "il faut vibrer avec lui; il faut aussi, avec le rayon de lune, trembler dans l'ombre du soir; il faut scintiller avec les étoiles bleues ou dorées; il faut, pour comprendre la nuit, sentir passer sur nous le frisson des éspaces obscurs, de l'immensité vague et inconnue. Pour sentir le printemps, il faut avoir au cœur un peu de la légèreté de l'aile des papillons, dont nous respirons la fine poussière répandue en quantité appréciable dans l'air printanier."* It is the humanist speaking, and he appears in the latest vesture of the man of science: Erasmus might have spoken so; and the new humanism for us, with our greater knowledge of the physical sciences, is to save and dignify men and women—and their labour.

A workman once got up at a meeting of Fabian Socialists when the learned were talking economics. "All your talk, gentlemen," said he, "is neither here nor there. When we workmen actually *do* get control of Industry, we shall say not only what our wages are to be, but what we shall or shall not work at." This was no empty brag of Labour, it was instinctive prophecy. Labour was feeling its way out of mechanical Industry into something else. Was it Art? Religion?†

Whichever it is, we need it, in Industry as in Education, Democracy dumbly cries for it, for the means by which the individual human being, the man himself, shall come again into direct and intimate touch with life—no machinery in between. "Art," says the Oriental, "is the moment's repose of Religion, or the instant when love stops, half unconscious, on her pilgrimage in search of the Infinite, lingering to gaze on the accomplished past and dimly seen future—a dream or suggestion, nothing more fixed—but a suggestion of the spirit, nothing less noble."‡ It is hard for the Western mind to follow the speculation; but every now and then, when we realize it in the city, when we are conscious of the present effort, the past greatness, the dream of the future, we come a little nearer

* Guyau, "L'Art," p. xxxviii.
† See also the fine chapter on the "Organization of Happiness," in Graham Wallas's "Great Society," especially pp. 323–327.
‡ Okakura, "Ideals of the East."

92

understanding. The poets, philosophers, and scientists of the Post-Revolutionary age—Shelley, Browning, Arnold, Huxley—pruned in us the Puritan. In doing so they cleaned away the old beliefs, and prepared us without knowing it for the new humanism which is to be the basis of Industrial Democracy.

These intangible things—physical fitness, cleanliness, refinement, beauty, poetry, music, drama—these Arts of life, the contents of the box of alabaster, all of which we need in our schools and our cities, shall no longer be *given* to the poor, they are a human right. That is what industrial as distinct from political Democracy implies, and our control of mechanical power in the interest no longer of the few, but of the community, is the clue to their attainment. Thither inevitably does the æsthetic synthesis lead us. There is no need for 12,000 alley houses in Chicago, for 95,000 British mothers to lose their babies annually within a year of birth, for 150,000 people in Dublin to be ill-housed, for one out of seven of the boys who offer themselves for the British Navy to be discarded as unsound, for 73 per cent. of the young men of Berlin to be unfit for military service.* To live as we are living now is to waste them, and to waste the Arts is to waste the men and women who could be producing them. Waste of the product and waste of the producer are one and the same ; once again our ninth Axiom : " *The arts, postulating as they do the motive of joy in their creation, and the freedom of the individual to go on creating, do not flourish under conditions where men think it right to exploit them for profit.*"

Writing a few years ago of his experience in Chicago, and of its wasted men, Robert Hunter said : "The animalism and despicable foulness and filth made one almost despair of mankind. It is impossible to describe adequately the depths to which this submerged class descend. This lodging-house was not the only one that presented the problem of vagrancy and of unemployment ; there were a hundred others filled with men ; the police-stations were full of men ; the prisons full of men ; the poor-houses overcrowded with men ; the poor authorities rushed with applicants ; the private charities caring for thousands. More men than the inhabitants of a large city, work-less, vagrant, mendicant, drifting about from place to place, drunken, petty criminals and beggars ! These men could be of great value to

Marginal notes: *Waste in life.* — *Axiom IX.* — *A Chicago illustration.*

---

* See statistics of G. E. Hooker, Third National Housing Conference, Cincinnati, Ohio, " American Arch. Journal."

the world as producers, as employed workmen. But, as it is, not one of them gives form to a single piece of raw material. They eat, sleep, drink their idle lives into oblivion. It would be impossible to make anyone, who has not seen with his own eyes these conditions, realize the utter waste of life, as I realized it when I closed the door of this lodging-house and stepped into the cold, fresh air of that winter's night."* We who seek to apply the æsthetic synthesis to life do not think it good enough to go on building houses for rich men on such terms. We find in the condition a want of unity, a failure; the Great City—as we dream it—is, under such conditions, impossible.

The intimate connexion between waste in the Arts and human waste.

And it needs every scrap of our belief to realize the intimate connexion between the waste of the Arts and waste in men and women, between the character of "goodness" in the producer and "goodness" in the product. "The ἀπολις, the man who does not carry his city within his heart," says the Glasgow idealist, "is a spiritual starveling. The measure of manhood is the fullness and generosity of its interests." And why should not character in the producer be the test of the product? In the end the truth holds good, and the artist, even as the philosopher, pleads for such a test. Speaking of the waste of human qualities, and of how in the modern State men are being "scrapped like old iron," he goes on to say: "The more enlightened modern States are striving to improve the conditions of labour; but so far they have not seen their way clear to prohibit much of the labour which dehumanizes men. It is recognized in a theoretic and academic way, that, even from the point of view of political economy, which is one of the most inadequate points of view for considering *man*, the waste of human qualities is the greatest of all waste."†

The waste we suffer in England is but a type of Industrial waste everywhere. As we artists see it, the key to order lies in the Arts, and the control of Mechanism through the Arts. To mitigate and do away with this waste is the problem of Industrial Democracy all the world over.

* R. Hunter, "Poverty," 1905, p. 119.
† Prof. H. A. Jones, "Idealism as a Practical Creed," 1909.

94

CHAPTER I.—Co-ordination in the City as against Competition.

Our seventh axiom laid it down that when we had learned to Axiom VII. readjust mechanical conditions it was through the city that we should again focus civilization. The axiom contains two statements : First, that a change is needed in our use of and attitude towards mechanical power ; second, that it is through the city that this change will come about. The younger generation of Artists, in sympathy with whom this book is written, look at things differently from their fathers. We no longer believe with Karl Marx in the Class War, nor with Morris in rebellion to overturn Society as a whole on behalf of the Arts. We aim at a gradual ordering ; we demand intelligent co-ordination.

I spoke before of the city of Internationalism as distinct from the The comparative survey of cities. autonomous city and the national city. A comparative survey of the English-speaking cities throughout the world, especially of the American cities, is a fascinating study. It grows in interest as we compare them with the autonomous cities of Mediæval or Renaissance Europe, or with the cities of Hellas. The civic movement of the last ten years in the United States is one of the most significant of our time. To the American himself it appears as "reform politics"; to the Englishman, and the student of cities, looking on from outside, it is altogether greater than that. It is ethical, and it has in it the first elements of the æsthetic synthesis. Also, it is European, but freed from the trammels of Europe ; the Latin, the Teuton, the Slav, each has his part in it.

"You, sir," said one American to another, "come from the worst-managed city in the Union."

"I know it," said the other ; "but how did you know what city I came from ? "

"I don't know," was the reply.

The conscience is beginning to prick. The new link that is binding these cities together is not politics, nor nationality, nor religion ; rather is it a sense that something is wrong with life, that a community having finer ideals must be built up on a proper understanding of mechanical power.

It would be possible to make out of these hundreds of American cities one composite city, as they make composite portraits of criminals. The resultant city of Democracy would be an almost

95

CO-ORDINATION AS AGAINST COMPETITION

perfect type. We should find in one city a model milk supply—as in Rochester, N.Y.; in another an ideal market—as at Indianapolis; here a superb park system—as in Kansas City, Mo. (see No. 62); there a splendid library organization—as in Portland, Oregon (see Nos. 120, 121); here, as in the ugly little agricultural city of Fargo, North Dakota, a live network of village theatres for the encouragement of Drama as a force in rural life. One city might give us for a moment, as in Los Angeles, the finest normal school; another a perfect dental clinic; here we should find a system of street scavenging splendidly organized on military principles—as are the White Angels of New York; there a Board of Public Welfare—as in Kansas City, Mo.—beyond the dreams of the Minority Commissioners of English Poor Law Reform. Indeed, we should find everything to the minutest detail—even to a "municipal Bat roost" for mosquitoes in San Antonio, and, as in Redlands, California, a municipal "fly-catcher"—a picturesque and perfect gentleman, reminiscent of the pied piper of Hamelin. There is no end to the specialization, and invariably there are keen and burning spirits behind, the music of whose pipe is all-compelling. But, as in Hamelin, the city as a whole is often "wanting." The need is synthesis: every city could have what every city has.*

Over-
specializa-
tion.

We get in our survey the same impression as we have in talking with the faculty of an American college; that of an immense variety of detailed and special knowledge, but little or no co-ordination—the human being is so often incomplete. The analogy could be carried farther; over-specialization is the antithesis to a wise co-ordination in the city. A community too engrossed in the petty affairs of business is not using the best of its brain force; vital energy is being misapplied, going to waste. We see how this works in many ways. The fierce competition throws a number of men and women out of the running; they have given of their best to certain specialized work, and now there is nothing further for them to do. We see it in the absence of leisured "parerga"; young folk have few intelligent recreations. It is here that the Arts help to correct the atrophy that we meet in every rank of life. Men use their legs only, or their arms, or their eyes. These thousand and one "specialists," what dull dogs they are—each his speciality, and so ill-educated! Too much concen-

---

* For an admirable study of these various civic functions, see Zueblin, "American Municipal Progress," 1916.

tration weakens the rest of our power—it does not give us all-round, hard-headed, warm-hearted human beings with the needful resistance and sympathy. Not unlike the concentrated force of great battleships, it may be good for the destruction of certain points, but of doubtful service in the slow and silent process of creating the finer life at which we aim, and rather helpless against attack from below the water or from other planes beyond their range.

This new, co-ordinated, as against the old competitive way of life *The new* means a new method in civics—it means the æsthetic synthesis. We *method in* have now to consider all the scientific data, all the inventions of the *civics.* Industrial era, test them, and re-apply them to the life of man as a citizen ; and "citizen" in the Latin and American rather than "subject" in the English or German sense : there is often virtue in a mere word. The Arts in the city indeed fulfil somewhat the function of the belly in the fable of Coriolanus.

> "True is it, my incorporate friends," quoth he,
> "That I receive the general food at first,
> Which you do live upon   .   .   .
>   .   .   .   But if you do remember,
> I send it through the rivers of your blood,
> Even to the court, the heart, to the seat o' the brain,
> And through the cranks and offices of man :
> The strongest nerves, and small inferior veins,
> From me receive that natural competency
> Whereby they live : And though that all at once,
>   .   .   .   cannot
> See what I do deliver out to each ;
> Yet I can make my audit up, that all
> From me do back receive the flour of all."

Our new community will take into the audit what we now *Syndicalism* neglect, but what should be complementary to the mechanical order : *re-applied.* Agriculture, the Arts, the Home. "The Socialism of Robert Owen," says Graham Wallas in his analysis of Syndicalism, "Louis Blanc's plan for the organization of labour in 1848, and even many of the ideas of Lassalle, and Marx, and William Morris, were syndicalist, in the sense that they proposed to create a community the industrial or political basis of which should be the 'self-governed' workshop of the self-governed 'craft.'" We later Artists wish rather to create a community the basis of which shall be the reconstructed city life—a life in which, because mechanism has been mastered, the Arts once more take their proper place, and in which, as I shall show later

(Chapter XXX), town and country are rightly related to each other. The method and order of Syndicalism is needful for us Artists. We cannot become effective unless we organize. And, because we are here to check mechanism, our influence upon life, if we were organized, would be much greater than ever was that of any ancient Guild. "The history of the late Mediæval Guilds shows both the strength and the weakness of the syndicalist form of Will-organization. The Guild brother, whether painter, or weaver, or lawyer, lived a vigorous and interesting life, and his close association with his fellows tended to maintain a high technical standard in the use, and sometimes, perhaps, the development, of traditional methods."

Wallas then points to the breakdown of the autonomous city as the result of Guild Syndicalism, much as we might—in the War—point to the breakdown of the Industrial system as the result of a city life improperly co-ordinated, or built up without regard to the Home, to the Arts, or to Agriculture. "Cities which could enter into no binding agreement that did not bear the seals of twenty jealous Guilds, and which could not keep order in their own streets during a trade dispute, proved too weak to stand against the more highly organized national states which began to appear during the sixteenth and seventeenth centuries. It proved to be more important that under Syndicalism men loved each other less as citizens than that they loved each other more as Guild brothers." The weakness now is that there is no condition of life under which they love each other at all; that the Community life—at least in Europe—has broken down altogether as the result of the conflict, industrial or ideal, of two equally balanced hostile groups, each having a blind control of mechanical power, and using it for purposes of boundless destruction.

The city of Inter-
nationalism.

The new city of Internationalism—it will not be a cosmopolitan city, because of its national limitations—will have its state or imperial ties, will be master in its own house in all matters industrial, will own the land it stands on and the machinery it works with, and will build up a democratic life because other cities do the same. It will also for this reason have its ties with the other cities throughout the world, as the Greek cities had ties in the greater Hellas, or the mediæval cities in the greater Christendom. Hence a new loyalty will be demanded of the citizens towards their city, and in so far as it gives them the finer life will they give in return a little of that loyalty the Greek or mediæval citizen gave. One city in the world has alone cherished an unbroken tradition of civic loyalty—Paris; and her blindest bourgeois to this day, if he be a " vrai parisien," worships her beauty. This civic loyalty, which is at bottom a parochial quality, is part of the new teaching, and inherent in the beauty and the spiritual life of the city.*

The Vicar of a fifth-rate English town said to his churchwarden who had just returned from a holiday in the great world:

" So I understand, Mr. Binks, you didn't think much of Paris?"

" Well, you see, sir," was the reply, " I had known Maidstone."

Mr. Binks and his city were still in the Middle Ages, and had not learned to relate themselves to the larger industrial life; but he had the root of the matter in him, the parochial quality that has given Paris, or Maidstone, its character.

* Sir Laurence Gomme, the late Clerk of the London County Council, was one of these civic patriots; he more than any man had to do with giving to London and Londoners the new spirit.

CHAPTER XXII.—The Coming of the Expert.

American Commission Government.

Here are some of the forms of that " Commission Government " through which the Americans are feeling their way towards the Great City. Broadly speaking, it means freeing the city life from " business " and " boss " rule ; it means government by the expert, and by a finer intelligence.*   To attain this end without sacrificing the principle of democratic control, that is the problem. It has not yet been solved. The two illustrations (see Nos. 86, 87) show roughly the distinction between the older and the later forms of city government. No. 86 is the old Republican mediæval plan, with the Mayor having somewhat the functions of a constitutional monarch. In No. 87 he is replaced by the highly paid expert, appointing his heads of departments, who are supposed not to be subject to political pressure, as in No. 86, where they are appointed by the Aldermen and Council.

Such diagrams are but optical generalizations, and do not take us very far. At any moment the Electorate may have lost the fact of democratic control and slipped on again the noose of privilege. "Rome did not appreciate that her liberties had vanished," wrote one of the American reformers a few years ago,† "so long as the senatorial oligarchy observed the cherished forms of the Republic. The Italian despots of a later age were sedulously faithful to the prejudices of Democracy, and the constitution of the City republics which they governed. England does not resent the domination of the landed aristocracy, so long as manhood suffrage, the right of petition, trial by jury, and Magna Charta are secure. And history has been slow in discerning that slavery had woven itself into the warp and woof of the government, until it became a system of government as well as an organized privilege prior to the American Civil War. A similar condition had been developed within the past decade in the Northern States of the Union. It has possessed itself of the patronage of City, County, and State."

But the situation is changing rapidly, just because the movement is ethical rather than political. "The City Government's

* The Metz Fund started an inquiry into Commission Government in 1911. Up to 1912 some 206 cities had adopted Commission Government.

† F. C. Howe, "The City of Democracy," p. 93.

greatest present opportunity," says another of the younger Municipal *The civic*
reformers, "is to take cognizance of the new social spirit that places *movement is*
public welfare above all other aims of human effort, in order to equip *ethical.*
itself to further the health, intelligence, and economic capacity of
its citizens . . . Honest self-analysis will bring to light a host of
unsatisfied needs. In this self-analysis we must have for every city its
own Survey. We saw in Chapter XV how the æsthetic movements
of our time brought us to that; so is the mirror held up to us.
"Public improvement departments are the dynamic centres of these
new city governments. Other municipal functions seem to assume
a position of subordination to them. . . . Each of the ten commission cities surveyed has arrived at, or is coming to, the period of
municipal development when it is customary to think of replanning,
to undo the errors of the past, to eliminate unwholesome congestion,
bad housing, and to provide adequate parks, playgrounds, and commercial facilities." We get some idea of the distance travelled in
the following: "When Milwaukee's city government (1910–1912)
studied women's wages, free legal aid, and employment agencies, it
announced the dawn in the governmental consciousness of the fact
that the people do not live by asphalt and pure water alone." And
it is the far-reaching influence of the Survey within the city that is
so significant. "Few city departments will remain as they are if
commissioners or directors will have existing organizations diagrammed,
functions listed in detail, and actual duties described."* If, that is
to say, the expert is in his right place and not wasted. Perhaps we
might add, in the pithy phrase of "Æ," he should not be "on top,"
but "on tap."

Expert knowledge and co-ordination go hand in hand. Another
writer on the new civics compares American and European conditions:
"German cities have both the form and the fact of administration
by paid experts; the cities of England and France have the fact but
not the form. Indeed, it may very well be doubted whether the German
expert has a whit more of actual influence in the determination of
civic policy than have his prototypes in the other two countries.
In all three lands the most potent factor in securing efficient and
economical administration for the municipalities is the plain fact that,
whatever the external forms of local government may be, the actual
conduct of affairs is entrusted very largely to professional officials who

* H. Bruyère, "The New City Government."

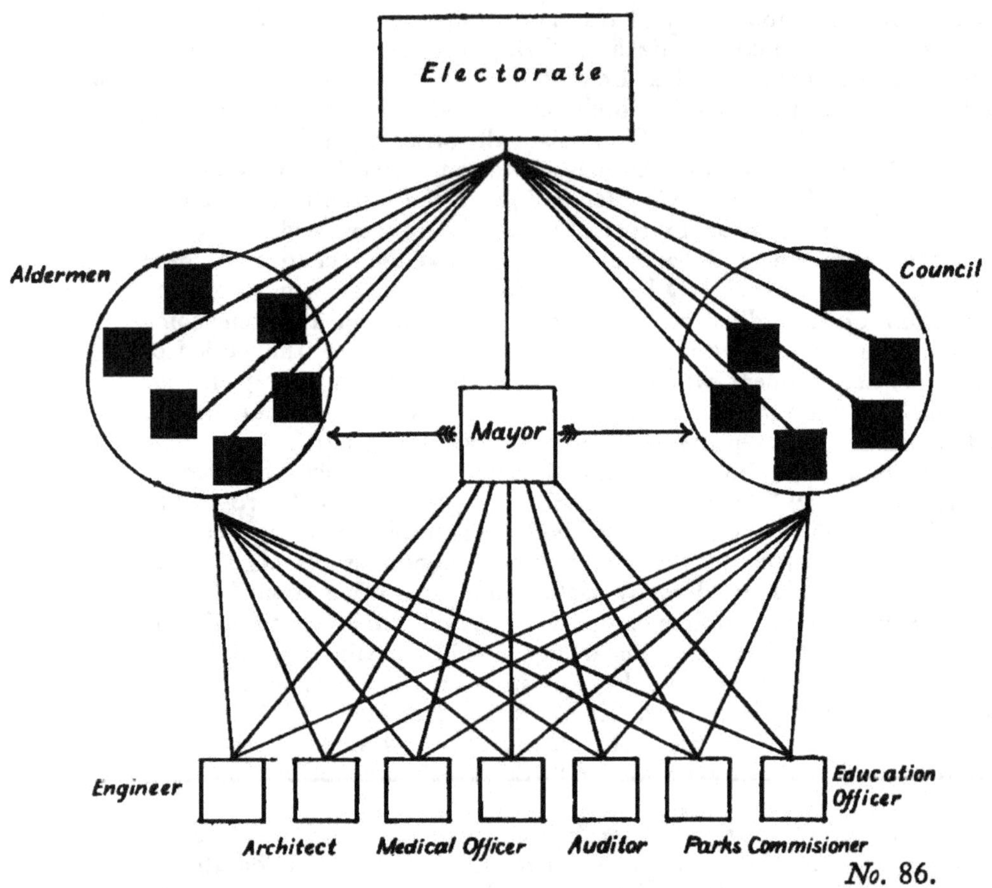

No. 86.

hold office for long terms." * If this be true, and I believe it is, in most progressive cities, we have now to educate those officials not only in their own special "science," but in the meaning of the æsthetic synthesis—how to put the whole thing together nobly.

It was two great disasters in the United States—the Galveston wave and the Dayton flood—that led to the new form of commission government in American cities. The greater disaster of the European War may bring all the cities of the world to a clearer vision in the

* W. B. Monro, "Government of European Cities."

102

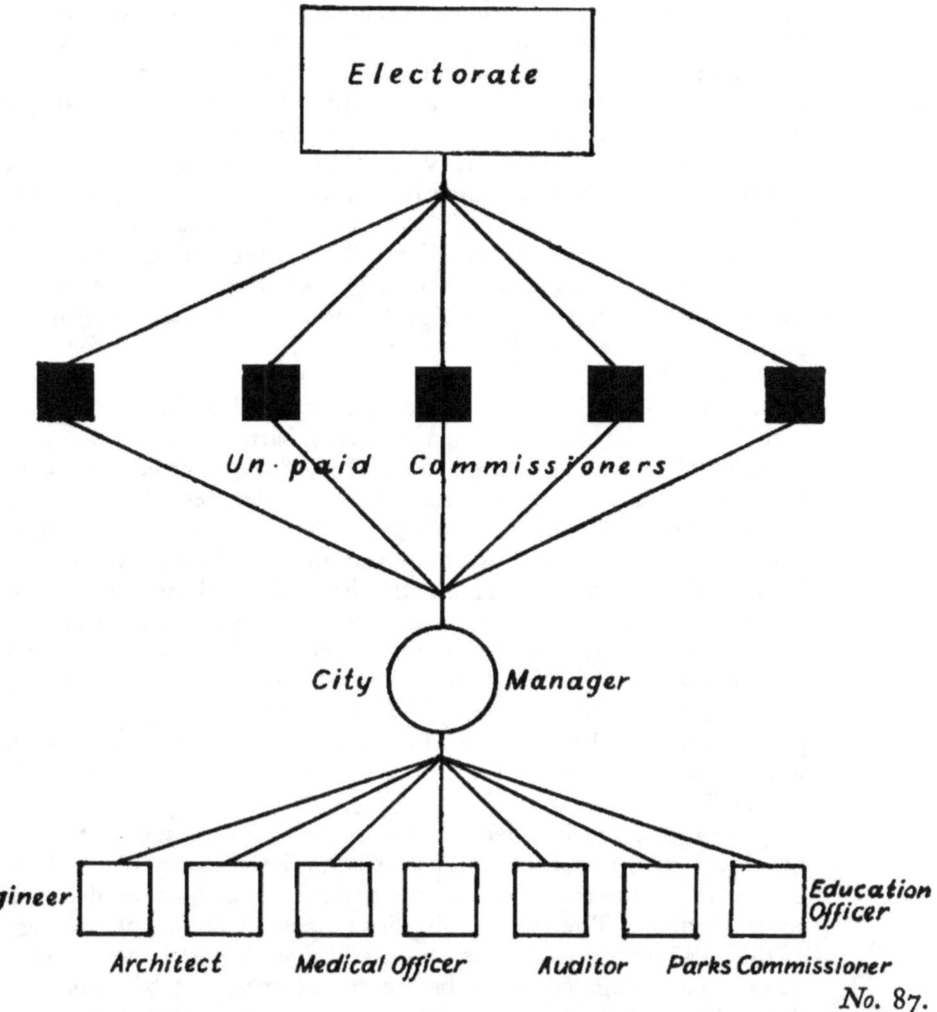

No. 87.

management of their affairs. We can be governed unintelligently
no longer, whether by soldiers, or county gentry, or business "bosses,"
or rabble.

What the cities need is union, some international give and take
of civic intelligence. The formula is still to find. By some curious
irony of fate the last piece of design in metalwork that I completed at

103

The symbol of the Boston " Peace Cup."

the workshops of the Guild of Handicraft before the outbreak of the War was a " Peace Cup," given to the city of Boston, Massachusetts, by the delegates of the Chambers of Commerce of the British Empire. I show it here (see No. 88) less for any intrinsic interest than for some strange prevision it had. The artist interprets even when he does not understand. About the cup were engraved words from a speech of President Taft, that have since been made the charter of the American " League to enforce Peace," and within the enamelled lid was the emblem of the British Empire. This emblem had not yet been invented, so we sought it in the origins of heraldry. We set together the earliest militant and religious symbols of the English-speaking people—the first, the Lion chosen by Cœur de Lion for a sign to distinguish himself and his Englishmen from the other Crusaders ; the second, the Red Cross of St. George, which has become the cross of ambulance, or peace, to all men on every battlefield. The cup, indeed, was a symbol, and contained the prayer of the international Chambers of Commerce—voiced by the British delegates—for some greater union. The gift, curiously enough, was to the city responsible more than all others for the schism in the British Commonwealth. These leaders of business throughout the English-speaking world, all hard-headed men, experts in their own line, knew what they wanted. Even before August 1914 we were " in obscuritie of scism and wars," and their prayer was for an " international Court " to make the greater life continuous and possible. It is only within the City itself that the greater life can be evolved ; but that life must be made secure by some power without. That is a condition for the " City of Internationalism."

It is not for cobblers to lay down rules in sculpture, architecture, medicine, husbandry, housewifery. Few lessons of the War have been so convincing as that of expert control—provided we have co-ordination. The two admittedly successful factors at the beginning of the War were the German military machine and the British Navy. These were prepared years before by experts, not by cobblers. But if the War's first lesson has been that we must put the development of our cities, our Education, our Arts, into the hands of experts, it was not the only lesson. If we have to take the management of these affairs away from the cobblers, and turn them over to the people that understand and study them, we have to do this without destroying the democratic principle, or we slip out of the Anglo-American frying-pan—muddle, into the German fire—militarism.

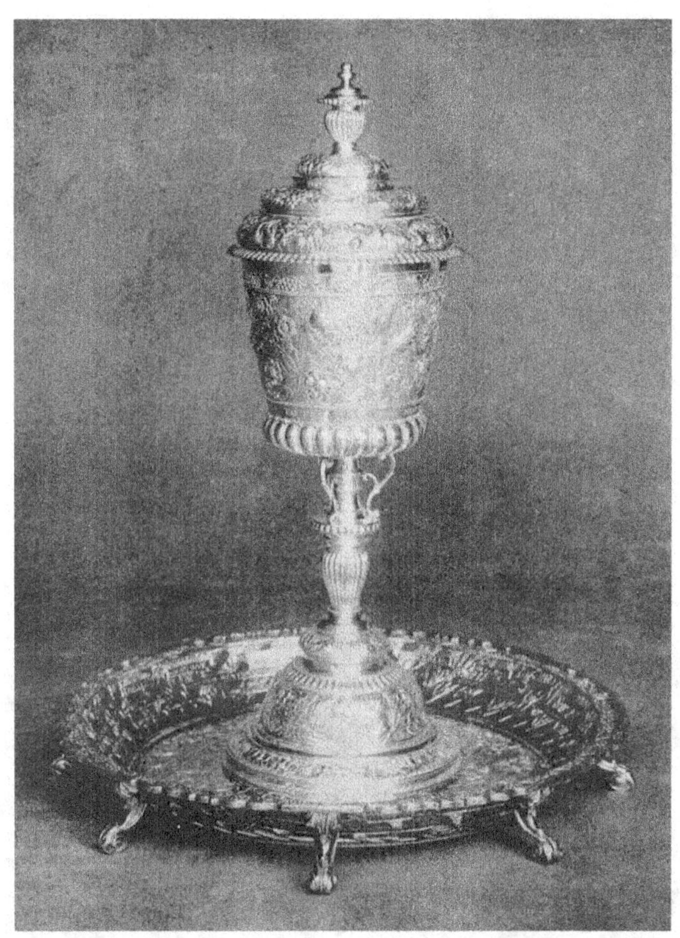

No. 88.

The " Peace Cup."
Designed by C. R. Ashbee.
Executed by George Hart and W. Mark
of the Guild of Handicraft.

The gift of the British delegates of the Associated Chambers of Commerce
to the City of Boston, Massachusetts.

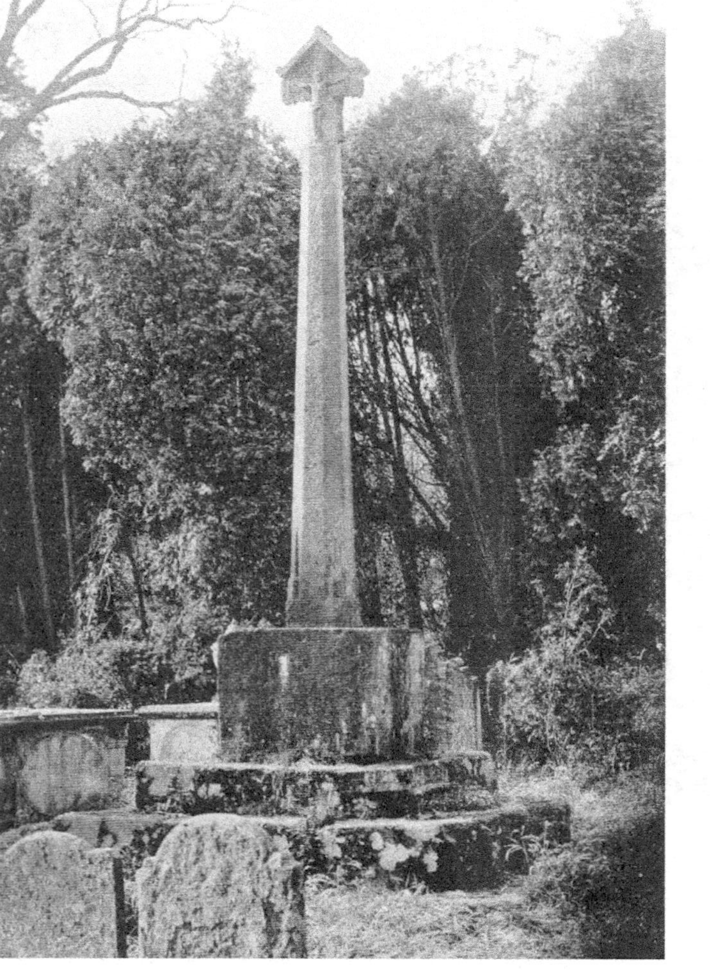

Tyberton Cross, Herefordshire. No. 89.

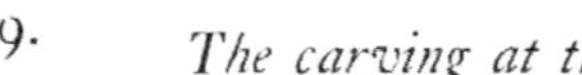

The carving at the head of the same. No. 90.

THE COMING OF THE EXPERT

My concern here is with the Arts; but if they are to fill the place we artists claim for them, we must think of them as part of the greater whole. In the Oriental story, a young man stoops down to pick up an iron ring he sees lying by the wayside ; he tries, and finds it bolted through the world.

If, then, I were asked what were the three most important The three problems ahead of Democracy, I should say first the righteous organi- problems zation of "Big business," next the finding of an economic basis for ahead of the Arts, and, last, the creation of a machinery for the policing of Democracy. the world. Only by solving these three can we protect Democratic civilization. The concern of this book is primarily with the second ; but it is impossible to ignore the other two. In the first is involved the whole question of labour unrest and social reconstruction, for I use the word "righteous" as the reverse of anti-social. But, however well we reconstruct, it is not enough. The righteous organization of Big business—our factory system, how well so ever we reconstruct it—will not fill the bill of human need, if we ignore the motive of human joy and the longing for individual creation. The third problem is in a way the most immediate, though perhaps its solution is far ahead. It will secure to the democracies of the world a means for working out the other two. Until the state of international competition—the extensive or expanding market backed by militarism—is done away with, there can be little or no intensive development, such as the Arts imply, and such as the City of internationalism demands.

One often hears the question put: "How will the War be paid The unused for ? " The answer is : "How is the War being paid for ? " We are mort- resources. gaging the future, we are discovering our unused resources in men and women and mechanism, and if we are right in doing this, clearly we must continue the process intelligently as the expert would, and reconstruct Industrial life on a basis of sound men and women, of mechanism rightly used, and no longer of mere business, or the making of cheap mechanical commodities. Another of our American reformers does not mince matters: "The business man," he cries, "has failed in politics as he has failed in citizenship. Why? Because politics is business. That's what's the matter with it. That's what's the matter with everything—art, literature, religion, journalism, law, medicine— they're all business, and all—as you see them."* Once again the pricking of the conscience. The Madison economist whom I quoted

---

* Lincoln Steffens, " The Shame of the Cities."

above puts more forcibly yet the ethical impulse that is behind the American municipal movement, and that is turning men to the new city of the expert: "The truth is law is shot through and through with conscience. The uprising against rebating, or monopoly, or fiduciary sin, registers not the self-interest of the many, but the general sense of right. To be sure, an agitation against company stores, or the two-faced practices of directors, may start as the 'We won't stand it' of a victimized class; but when it solicits general support it takes the form 'These things are wrong,' and it can triumph only when it chimes with the common conscience. In the case of child labour, night work for women, crimping and peonage, the opposition springs up among onlookers rather than among victims, and is chivalric from the beginning. The fact is, the driving force of the great sunward movement now is moral indignation."*

Mechanical power must be socialized. As John Ruskin put it to us in England half a century earlier: realize that things are wrong, and we have taken the first step towards putting them right. The second step is finding out the expert—the man who has studied the question. Mere moral indignation is not enough, and the question must be studied, not only as one of scientific detail, but of the co-ordinated city life. We have to grasp the fact that our eighth axiom is the basis of this municipal movement. In the co-ordinated city of Democracy, and only so, will it become possible to socialize mechanical power. We are nearer to the unrealized vision of Aristotle than ever the Greek imagined. All we need is intelligence. "If every tool . . . could do the work that befits it, just as the creations of Dædalus moved of themselves, or the tripods of Hephæstos went of their own accord; if the weaver's shuttles were to weave of themselves: then there would be no need of apprentices for the master-workers, or slaves for the lords."†

* Ross, "Sin and Society," page 82.
† Politics A. IV. 4.

CHAPTER XXIII.—The Guild Idea and the Idea of Competitive Militarism.

We productive artists look at the events of 1914 to 1917 from an angle of our own.   Perhaps, also, we see other things shaping that are hidden from those who only look at life with the eyes of the business man, the soldier, or the politician.   When, through history, we study the planning of the city, Hellenic, Macedonian, Roman, Hanseatic, Italian, Industrial, we find two conflicting principles at work.   I would call them the " Military " principle and the principle of the " Guild."   The best of Rome is in the one, but in the other is Athens.   The one is regular, consistent, definite ; the other is romantic, irregular, human ; it seems ever to be feeling its way.   In the one we have order for defence or aggression, the towns are part of a military system ; in the other we have imagination, the personal qualities, the city appears as the function of life.   What military order there is in the second is spontaneous, voluntary, a Guild Order of Knighthood, a levy on Mile End Waste before we go out to fight the Armada.   Shall the Military or the Guild principle dominate ?   We often see the issue presented, as in London, Paris, Florence, or the cities of Flanders, at different times in their history.   And the two principles are in conflict now on a more tremendous scale.   Shall the industrial city of the twentieth century be developed on Militarist lines or on Guild lines ?   Shall it be Imperialism or Democracy, Prussia or the Allies ?

Muddle-headed and confused though it be, there is more of the Guild principle in a Boston, Massachusetts, with its "reservations," and its pathetic efforts to preserve the amenities of Boston Common ; or in a London with its County Council, its Strand improvement and housing schemes, their failures and inconsistencies, than in the Paris of the Third Empire or the Berlin of the Sieges Allee.   The two principles often overlap.   Napoleon le Petit flatters the Democracy, Kaiser Wilhelm II is for the moment the type of what his people desire : the flashy symbol, cheap, theatrical, embodying a showy Imperialism efficient in details, but wanting in the finer life.   " Of course, it couldn't possibly go on," said one of the Generals of the Third Empire, " but it was very jolly as long as it lasted ! " and one imagines the same sentiment among the German General Staff in 1914.   Their desire was " ein frischer frölicher Krieg ! "   The imaginative forces have a way of swinging back full circle. But there is now a new factor in our considerations—Industrial machinery. Shall it be controlled by military power, or by the more human Guild system ?

At first sight industrial society lends itself more readily to organization from above, to just this efficiency in detail that a Third Empire or a Prussian Imperial bureaucracy can give. The telegraph, the telephone, the wireless message, the motor-car, and the other wonders of modern mechanism, in whom shall their power be vested ? Some of them are natural monopolies ; in the hands of despotism they strengthen it, and the greater the ignorance of the governed the greater the power they bring. It is easier, too, for cities to be planned by a single head than by the burdensome committees of Democracy. Krupp, Pullman, Lever, do these things better, or shall we say in the more efficient manner of the builder of the Pyramid of Illahûn, where was unearthed not so long ago the first example of city planning. Here was built, some two thousand years B.C., an industrial city for the employees, on the whole rather in advance of the industrial planning of the nineteenth century.

But Democracy is beginning to see things otherwise, to resent this beneficent exploiting of the individual, to say " Let us try things in our own way." The Guild principle, in other words, is at work. If with it now we can set up a finer education, a more stable condition of industrial employment, mechanism more under public control and used less for private profit than for public good ; if with it we have more of the smaller cities and the higher civilization they make possible, with committees of producers rather than committees of exploiters, we should get again something approaching the Guild cities of mediæval England, Italy, France, Flanders, and Germany. The Athens of Pericles, the Florence of Boccaccio, the London of Chaucer and Eveleigh, with their Guild ordinances, always remain the types of what, for us, cities should be. Alexander the Coppersmith and his Guild of Metalworkers, devoted to the service of Diana of Ephesus, may have done much injury to St. Paul, who admittedly interfered with their livelihood; but Ephesus was a noble city (see *Axiom VII.* No. 91). Inevitably we are brought back to our seventh Axiom : *" The new relationship of man to life which machine industry has brought with it, finds its fullest expression in the new life of our city. This implies that through the city and its proper adjustment to mechanical conditions will man realize again those finer values which the arts bring into life. Through the city we focus civilization."*

108

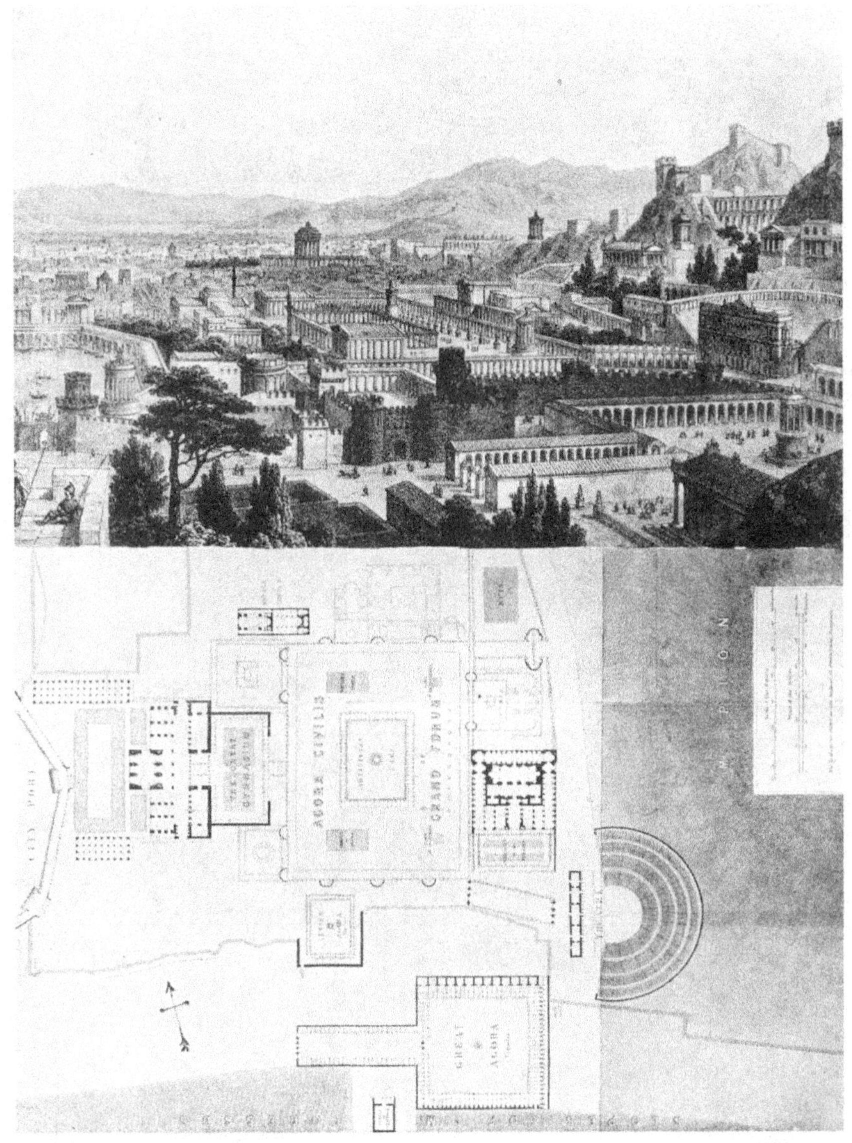

No. 91.

Reconstruction of the City of Ephesus at the time of St. Paul and the Guild of the Metalworkers.

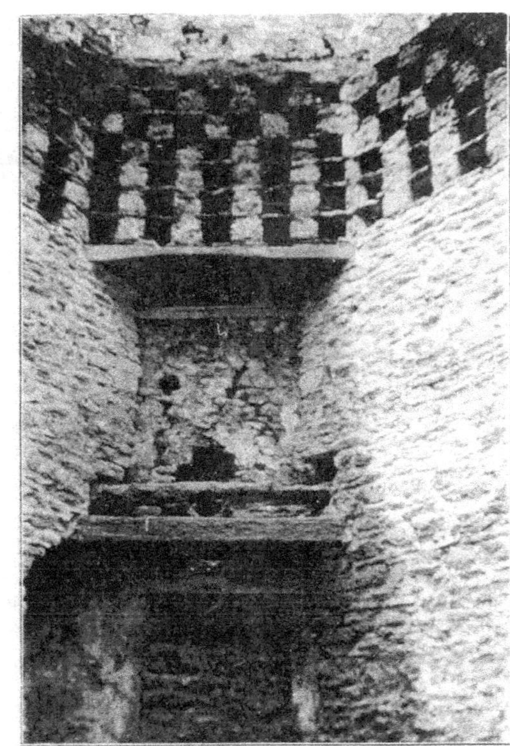

Dovecot, Bruton.
Exterior.

No. 92.

Dovecot, Bruton.
Interior.

No. 93.

THE GUILD AND COMPETITIVE MILITARISM

We dealt above (Chapter XIII) with new cities built up out of *Application* standardizable industries—cocoa, soap, railway cars ; we have yet to *of the* consider cities that have no such specialization of Industry. The *Guild idea* greater problem remains of adjusting the æsthetic enterprises to life ; *to the city.* the art schools, the art workshops, the personal and human things, to mechanical conditions. What is the formula to be ? It is at this point that the application of the Guild idea to the city has such significance. The battle-cry of the Artist craftsmen of the later nineteenth century was, as we have seen, the emancipation of the designer and the craftsman from mechanical conditions ; it was "Let us free the individual." * Notwithstanding the economic debacle of the Arts and Crafts movement as a whole, the craftsman's battle was won as far as the Arts and Crafts Society was concerned. The establishment of hundreds of little craft shops of high skill is evidence of this. But the first two decades of the twentieth century have brought an entirely fresh problem. We have now discovered that all these admirable little workshops are but drops in the ocean ; that our æsthetic individualism is out of date ; that the unit is no longer the individual, but the workshop itself. The workshop once established, the individual freed, the problem in an industrial society is to protect these workshops and their traditions of high skill from a second destruction.

How is this to be done ? If the workshop and not the individual is in future to be the unit, the answer is the Guild. It is by means of the Guild idea that we shall co-ordinate the workshops. We must devise a plan by which all these hundreds of workshops are drawn together for mutual aid. Each must continue free to perfect and develop its own skill and traditions, but all must be brought into some federated order that shall prevent their "freezing each other out," destroying each other's market, re-establishing sweated labour conditions in their respective workshops, or using mechanical power against each other. It is an ethical readjustment we need ; for greed, and selfishness, and want of understanding are always with us.

The mediæval Guild is the type of how within the great orbit *Mediæval* of Industrial Democracy this co-ordination can be brought about. *Guild* We should do well to study the old Guild ordinances against "fore- *regulations.* stalling" and "regrating," the old "rights of search," the old "limitations of apprenticeship," and above all the old morale of "standard" and "quality" in life as in production. Here, in twelve brief "points,"

---

* See Preface to Arts and Crafts Exhibition Society Catalogue, 1888.

THE GUILD AND COMPETITIVE MILITARISM

is what one of the old English Guilds lays down.* Incidentally the men who made these rules were also the builders of Westminster Hall.

1. Every Guildsman "shall be stedfast, trustye, and trewe, and upright as a judge."
2. The Guildsman "most ben at the general congregation" and "know when it shall be holden."
3. He shall "no bondeman prentys make . . . ʒet in the lodge he were y-take." You cannot create well unless you are a free man.
4. His "prentys be of lawful blood . . . and have his lymes hole." We want no bastards, and we know that lame men are no good on ladders.
5. The Guildsman is not "to take of the lord [i.e. the employer] for his prentyse, also much as his fellow." No under-cutting by boy labour.
6. He "schal no thef accept . . . lest hyt wolde turne the craft to schame."
7. "Any mon of the craft be not also perfyt he may him change." The Guildsman has power to enforce standard.
8. "No werke he undertake, but he conne both hyt end and make." There must be co-operation. And this implies collective guarantee among all the masters of the Guild. Hence
9. "There schal no mayster supplant other . . . but be as syster and brother." That is to say, there must be no competition.
10. "He schal not his fellows werke deprave . . . but hyt amende." If we are in a Guild we must pull together. Thus "style" is formed.
11. As for his apprentice he shall so teach him "That he within hys terme, of hym dyvers points may learne." Workshop "tradition" and education go hand in hand.
12. And last. "He schal do nothing that wolde turne the craft to schame." The "craft" *is* our religion, in which we live, and move, and have our being; in one word, "standard."

The War has brought us nearer to this re-interpretation of the Guild idea; it has brought that idea and the idea of competitive

* See Conder, "Records of the hole Crafte and fellowship of Masons"; also the Halliwell MS. Bib. Reg. 17 A1, and Wyatt Papworth, Trans. R.I.B.A. 1887.

militarism—that is to say, the competitive market backed by armed force—into sharp contrast. The War has drawn all men together. Competition within the two warring groups has for the moment disappeared; we are, in each group, working in concord. What for? To destroy life. When the War, and the reaction after it, are over, shall we all fall asunder again? And will the enthusiasm now used for the destruction of life be impossible for its creation? The answer is ethical. If Art is the index of life, and if it be true that "La loi interne de l'Art est de produire une émotion esthétique d'un caractère social," then the qualitative standard which the Arts demand is essential to the new order that is to succeed the War. (See Axiom IX.)

And we cannot give effect to this Guild idea without some appeal to the man's individuality, his joy in the work of his hands. Those old Guild ordinances show clearly how the desire for wages, or for clean workshops, or for shorter hours—the ordinary socialist and trade-union shibboleths—are not enough. They do not meet the human need—the need for personal creation. Only the Arts, and the various life functions they fulfil, can do this. And to do this, to give the Arts the economic stability they demand, there must be curtailment of the mechanical product. A great English employer of labour was lamenting to me the complete cessation of his output as the result of the War.

"So all your 'necessities'," said I, "are now as futile as our 'Arts and Crafts.'"

"But men must have soap, men must have corrugated iron."

Quite so. I will not say which was his own speciality.

"But, sir, does it not occur to you that if our cities were cleaner, and our buildings less ephemeral, we could dispense with three-quarters of our output in both of these 'necessities'?"

His was the old fallacy of the circulating sixpence. A beggar *The fallacy* begged a sixpence of everybody in the world, and so got fabulous *of the* wealth. He said it was his energy and ability that did it, said that *circulating* he rendered some service. Another beggar followed his example, he *sixpence.* also grew rich, he also used the same arguments. The idea took on. All the world started doing likewise. And what was the result? Nobody grew rich any more, it merely circulated the sixpences. So it is with soap, or corrugated iron, or any other commodity. There is a limit to their serviceableness. That limit is to be found not in their power of bringing wealth to individuals, nor in any law of "supply and demand"; it is in the communal need, and that is a matter

THE GUILD AND COMPETITIVE MILITARISM

of ethics. The Guild idea, based upon unity and brotherhood, necessarily has this limitation behind it—limitation for common service, limitation of individual freedom in the common interest.

Cromwell's army again. The three million men in England and the Empire who volunteered in 1915 offered their lives less to fight the Germans than for some obscure ethical call. Cromwell's army has not been called into life again for nought. But the winning of a war does not determine its issue. Either side vanquished may yet lead captivity captive. It is after the War that the real problems will be—in the twenty or fifty years of reaction or attempted reconstruction. It is often harder to live and make life than to die gloriously, as Cromwell's Major-Generals found to their cost when they sought to reconstruct England after the Civil War. The English spewed out Militarism then, and for two hundred years it became unfashionable, until Carlyle started again a cult of Cromwell and of Prussia. When we contemplate the possibility of the "servile state" under militarist control it is well to remind ourselves of Cromwell's army, and perhaps also of the witticism attributed to Arthur Balfour: "Thank God we are not a militarist people, and so still can fight!"

How, then, shall we apply the Guild idea to the Arts of the City? What, under conditions of Industrial Democracy, is the formula to be?

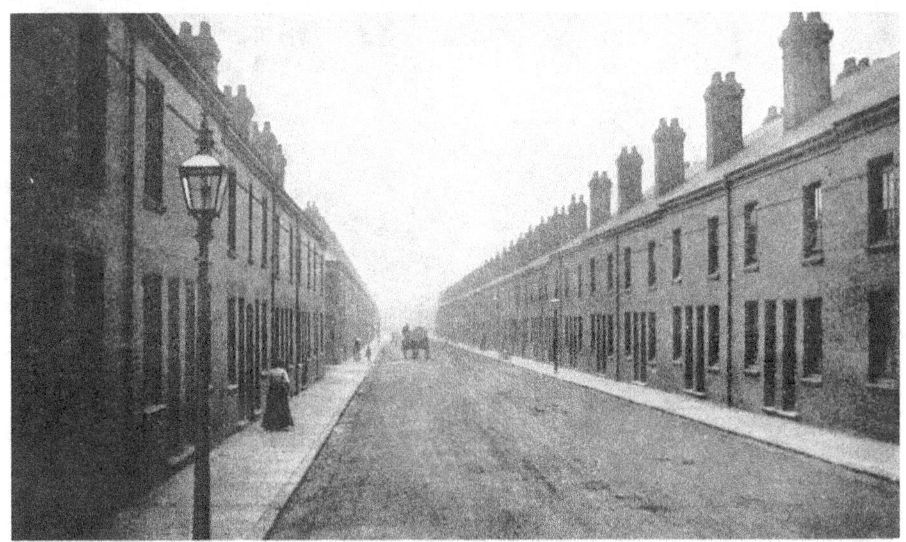

A dismal street in Coventry.

No. 94.

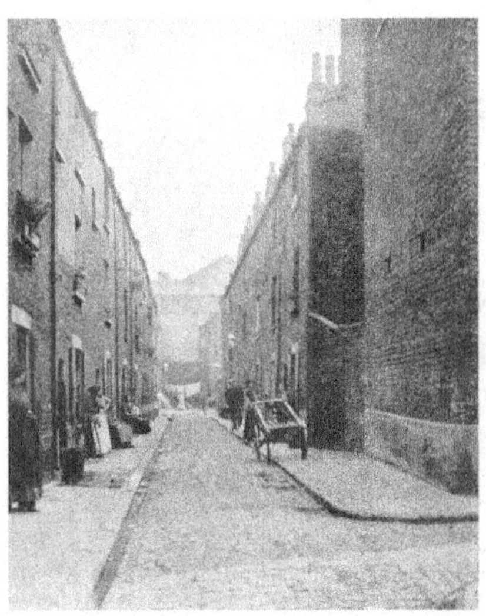

No. 95.

A newly built slum in East
London, 14 ft. 6 in. wide.

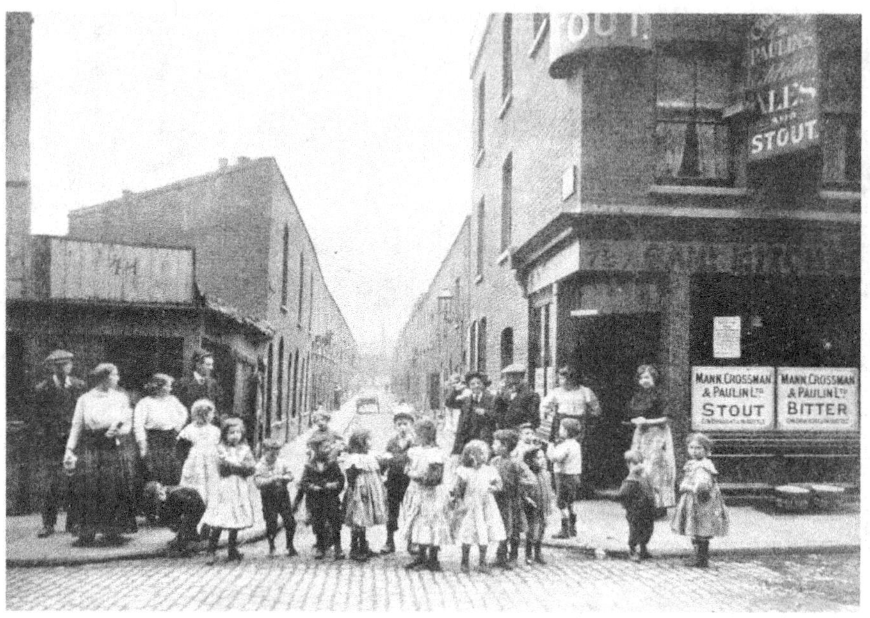

Everard Street, St. George's in the East, 13 ft. 6 in. wide.   No. 96.

A typical London slum buttressed by the brewer.

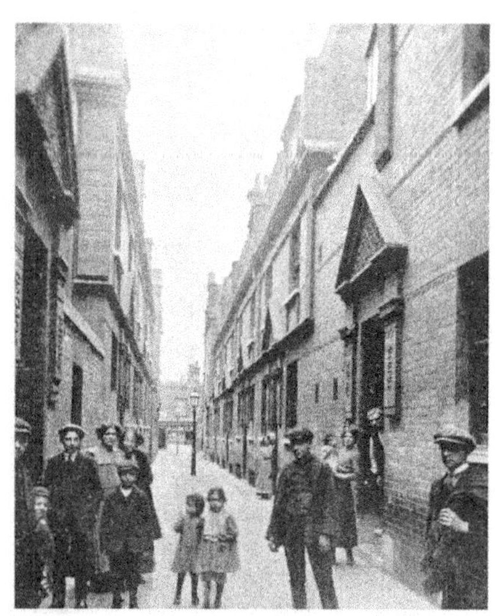

A newly built London slum,   No. 97.
11 ft. wide.

Put up on the site of two-story cottages.

CHAPTER XXIV.—How the Arts Might Be Maintained.

I submit that the right way of finding the formula is to create within our cities new groups—live organizations in each city or in suitable country districts—of individuals engaged in the Arts. These groups must be given an economic independence, they must be freed from the disintegrating control of mechanical power. How in our Industrial Democracy is this to be done? How are the Arts to be maintained? We have now to give practical effect to Axioms I, II, and III. We have considered the city and the civic centre, the zones and parks, we have discussed noise, dirt, the evils of mechanism; however much we improve them our cities are but empty shells unless they hold some live creative enterprise, unless in every city there are men inventing, dreaming, finding the city its soul.

Why is there so little character in the average Industrial city? Look at these streets I show in Nos. 94–97, built within the last ten years, the fœtus of new slums, the triumph of unintelligence, of thoughtlessness. And why are all Industrial cities so deadly alike? These questions, often asked, contain a paradox. In the "alikeness" is their strength, for it means the final displacement of the small, thinking, inventing craftsman by the great factory. It means the triumph of standardization. But it also means the new possibility. The cities are alike because everything is made to specific patterns, and the ideal up till now has been to make everything to specific patterns. The more this can be done the greater and more powerful the city can become. See Axiom I: "*Modern civilization rests on machinery, and no system for the encouragement, or the endowment, or the teaching of the arts can be sound that does not recognize this.*"

Yet this very triumph of standardization which makes the modern city, also makes possible the greater city within. For all the while the desire is there, the rebellion alive within us, everlasting in the human being, the need for self-expression. He must leave his stamp on the material, his mark on something. This rebellion against mechanism is never-ending, for it demands the live work of art— "something made for a human being by a human being."

I was asked a short while ago, in one of the great American cities of the Middle West, where a fine site and a large sum of money had been given for the founding of an Art Institute, or as in England it is sometimes called, a Craft Museum, to advise how this might be done.

HOW THE ARTS MIGHT BE MAINTAINED

The obvious reply to the men and women who had the disposal of the endowment was, " What is your aim ? " But they had no aim. They were bewildered at the responsibility thrust upon them. I want now to give some answer to this question, to suggest how in a new democratic city the Arts might be maintained. I want to crystallize *Axiom VII.* my seventh Axiom : " *The new relationship of man to life which machine industry has brought with it, finds its fullest expression in the new life of our city. This implies that through the city and its proper adjustment to mechanical conditions will man realize again those finer values which the arts bring into life. Through the city we focus civilization.* "

The new "Art centre ": its first object to create.
     What is a " Craft Museum " or an " Art Institute " ? What ought it to be ? I know hundreds in England and America, and they none of them appear to be fulfilling a very useful function in the social life of the community. They are either dead places where the works of dead artists are stored, like mummies, or, where they are definitely educational, they are places for teaching painters to teach painters to teach painters, a sort of recurring decimal process in futility, ·999999999. We do not progress that way ; we only go round the nines. I do not object to the collection of good pictures and statuary within reason, though no good pictures are ever painted with the object of being housed in galleries ; nor do I object to the teaching of the craft of painting by the painters themselves ; but I do object to the false theory that these are the two ends of an Art Institute. Indeed, I hold that an Art Institute may become a great social force in proportion as it puts this falsehood behind it.

How, then, should we plan and endow it ? Its guiding principles should be these : It should first be productive. It should be devoted not primarily to exhibition or display, but to creative work. Hence it should be educational only through its productions. In the next place it should be productive in all those things that admit of the application of Art, or let us rather say Beauty : those things especially that have been injured by or that get no proper chance under industrial conditions. Our new Institute or Museum should be a guide, but also a protest, to Industrialism. Its real object is to determine the ethical question : What shall and what shall not be made by mechanical power ? What is and what is not standardizable in the interests, not of the individual, but of the whole community ? The current theory that everything is standardizable is false.

If, then, we are to build and endow an Art Institute or Craft Museum on these lines, we must group around, and as part of it,

114

a number of small productive workshops, somewhat as shown in diagram No. 98. The object of these small workshops shall be to turn out good hand-made commodities, irrespective of whether they are being standardized by machinery. The continuous aim is to be freshness and invention, as well as traditional workmanship. We might express the theory of our new Art Institute in its relation to life by a further diagram, No. 99, showing how these workshops should be grouped into four main divisions having reference to—

    (*a*) The beauty of the home.
    (*b*) The beauty of the person.
    (*c*) The beauty of the book.
    (*d*) The beauty of life and deportment.

I suggest this division for economic reasons, and the endowment of each school or group will vary accordingly.

(*a*) will have to do with architecture, building, furniture, and will embrace such arts and crafts as cabinet-making, joinery, carving, plasterwork, blacksmithing, decorative painting, stained glass, carpet weaving, table service, pottery, etc.

(*b*) will have to do with weaving, textiles, dressmaking, lace-making, jewellery ; also the mother and children crafts. Possibly, as in the Margaret Morrison Hall at Pittsburg, a school of housewifery could be incorporated with this.

(*c*) will comprise a printing press, a bindery, and the different crafts that have to do with books and printing, block-drawing and cutting, and with journalism understood as an art and not as a matter of commercialism and advertisement. Here also will be grouped the crafts of lithography, etching, colour printing, illumination, and calligraphy.

(*d*) will comprise a school of drama, elocution, and music. It will have its little theatre, its orchestra, its costume rooms, its masques and plays. Here will be studied eurhythmics, singing, folk-song, language, and dancing. I do not include athletics, as these are already provided for in modern life; but the object of the school would perhaps be to humanize them somewhat, as in the Greek and Elizabethan manner—make them less barbarous.

HOW THE ARTS MIGHT BE MAINTAINED

The secondary function of the Art Institute will be its work in Education, but this will only be done through the craft workers, who will not be allowed to teach unless they produce. They will be organized in some form of Guild, and will be expected to take, whenever necessary, apprentices, bound under proper indentures, and

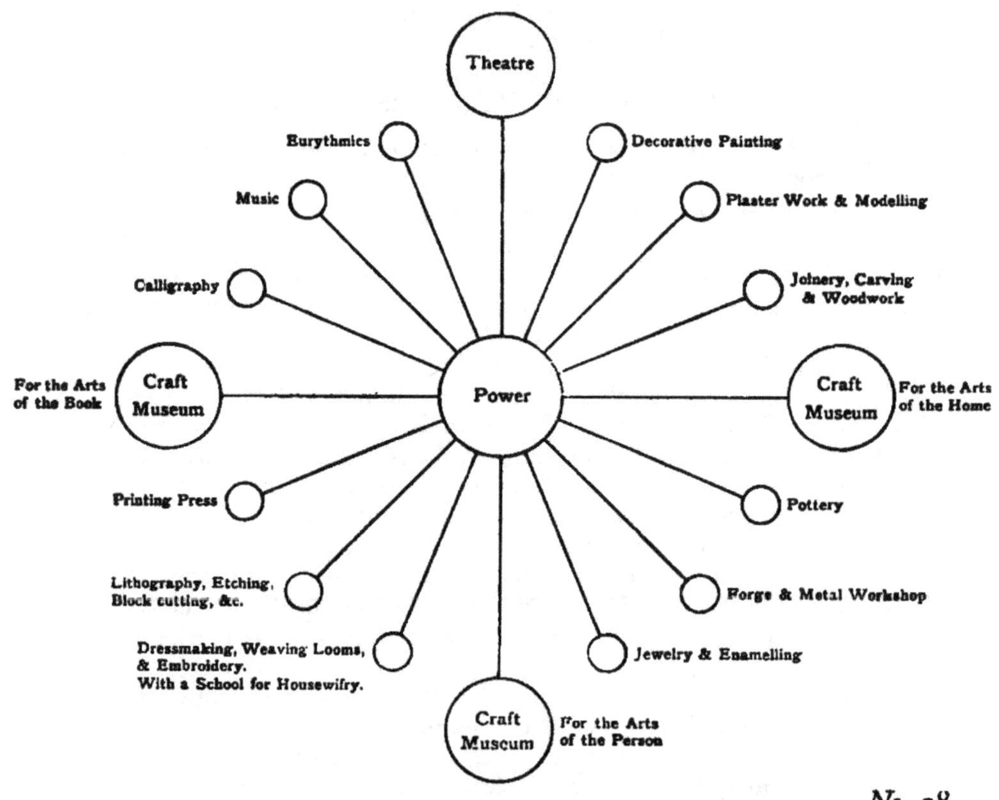

No. 98.

for a period of years. This process of apprenticeship shall be linked up with the educational work—the schools in the city. There might be a certain amount of class-work teaching, but it will be of a tertiary nature, and only in certain specified directions—e.g. drawing, manual work in wood or metal—and for this purpose small lecture-halls or class-rooms would have to be provided.

The craftworkers, men and women, thus formed into a body of *Guild or-* Guildsmen, will make their own regulations for such co-operative life *ganization.* as may seem to them advisable, for the maintenance of the standard of

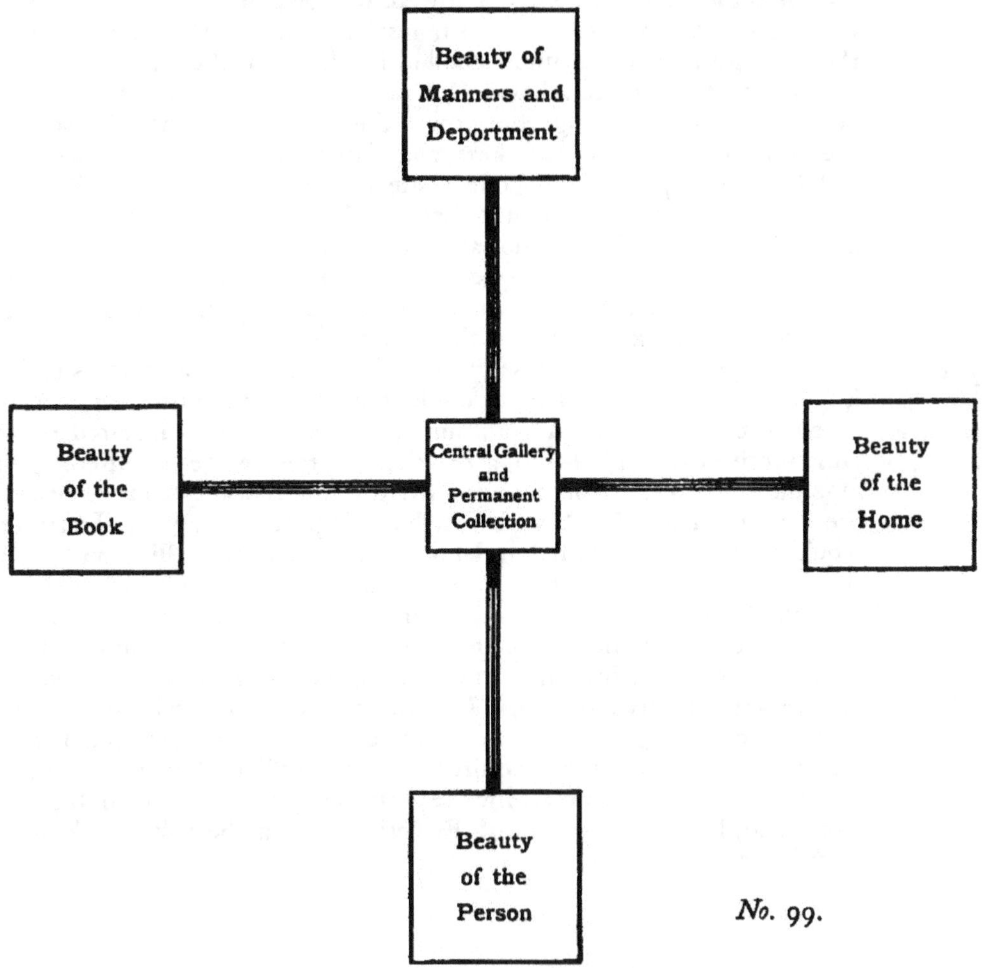

No. 99.

their work, and for the combined use of such mechanical power as shall be proven to be beneficial to, and not destructive of, the work- shop life and standard of quality in the crafts they practise. The

117

HOW THE ARTS MIGHT BE MAINTAINED

English Arts and Crafts movement has already proved certain machines to be beneficial, and others harmful, to the social organism. Our new Institute is to work this process out scientifically—it is a social and ethical problem.

The craftworkers, except in the case of (*d*), the theatre, which will be somewhat differently endowed, will be paid a retaining fee sufficient to make life possible. I suggest that ultimately the principle of the minimum wage—as understood in England—is the right one to aim at. Given their material and the essential tools, the minor and more personal tools remaining their own, their work will then be sold for the joint benefit of craftworkers and Institute. I suggest that a half and half sharing of the labour value would be proper : e.g. if a man puts ten dollars or ten pounds' worth of labour into a commodity, and it realizes twenty, this should, after deducting the cost of material, be divided into equal shares between him and the Institute. The actual value of the man's labour would, of course, vary in accordance with the craft, the market rate, and the man's personal skill.

Application of the minimum wage principle. I have used the phrase "the minimum wage as understood in England." In America and elsewhere the minimum wage has a different meaning. In a community where labour is inspired by the same motives as capital—to grow rich, or raise wages at all costs, and regardless of standard of quality—the minimum wage tends to become the maximum wage. My plea is that our productive "Art Institute" would set another ideal before labour. It would crystallize within our whole Industrial Democracy a new condition of life, and do what the Arts and Crafts movement has done in its little aristocratic environment in England. It would set up the new ideal of quality—doing the thing well. It would bring into practical operation that other economic motive—the motive of joy. I have in my own workshops proved that this can be done, that the motive of the artist craftsman is not the motive of the mere acquirer of "wealth" or "wages." He is prepared to live a simpler life because he groweth wise in his own work, and, like the artificer of Ecclesiasticus, in the handiwork of his craft is his prayer.

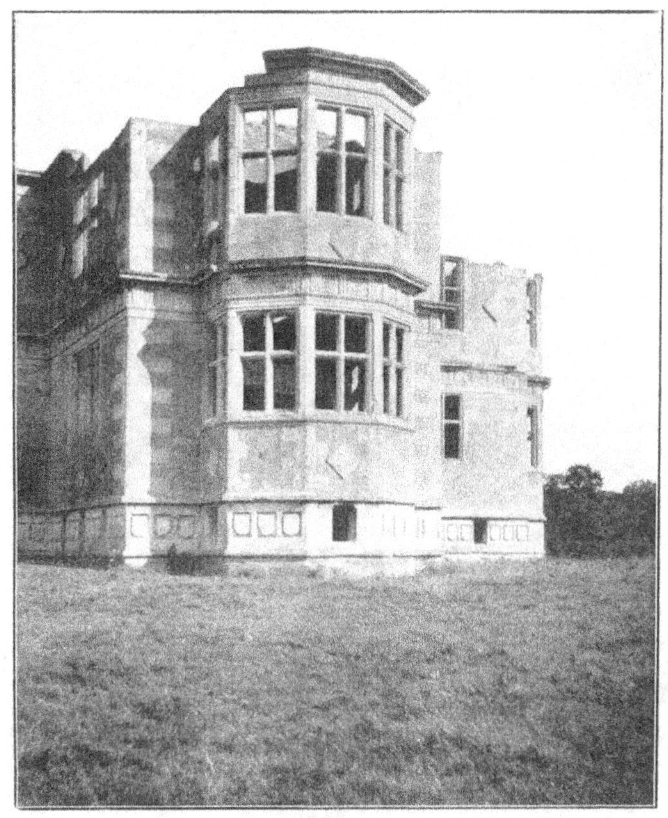

Lyveden New Building. No. 100.

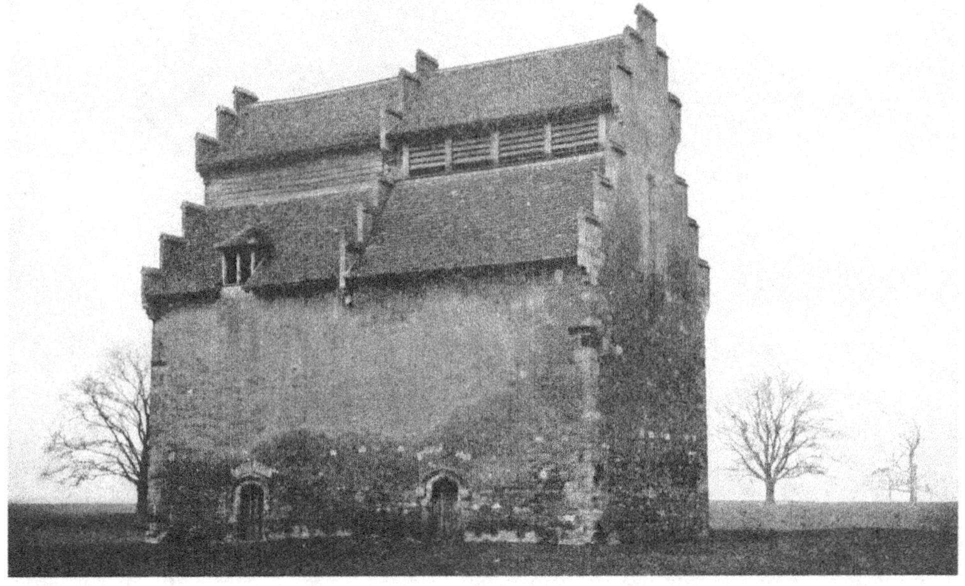

Willington Dovecot. No. 101.

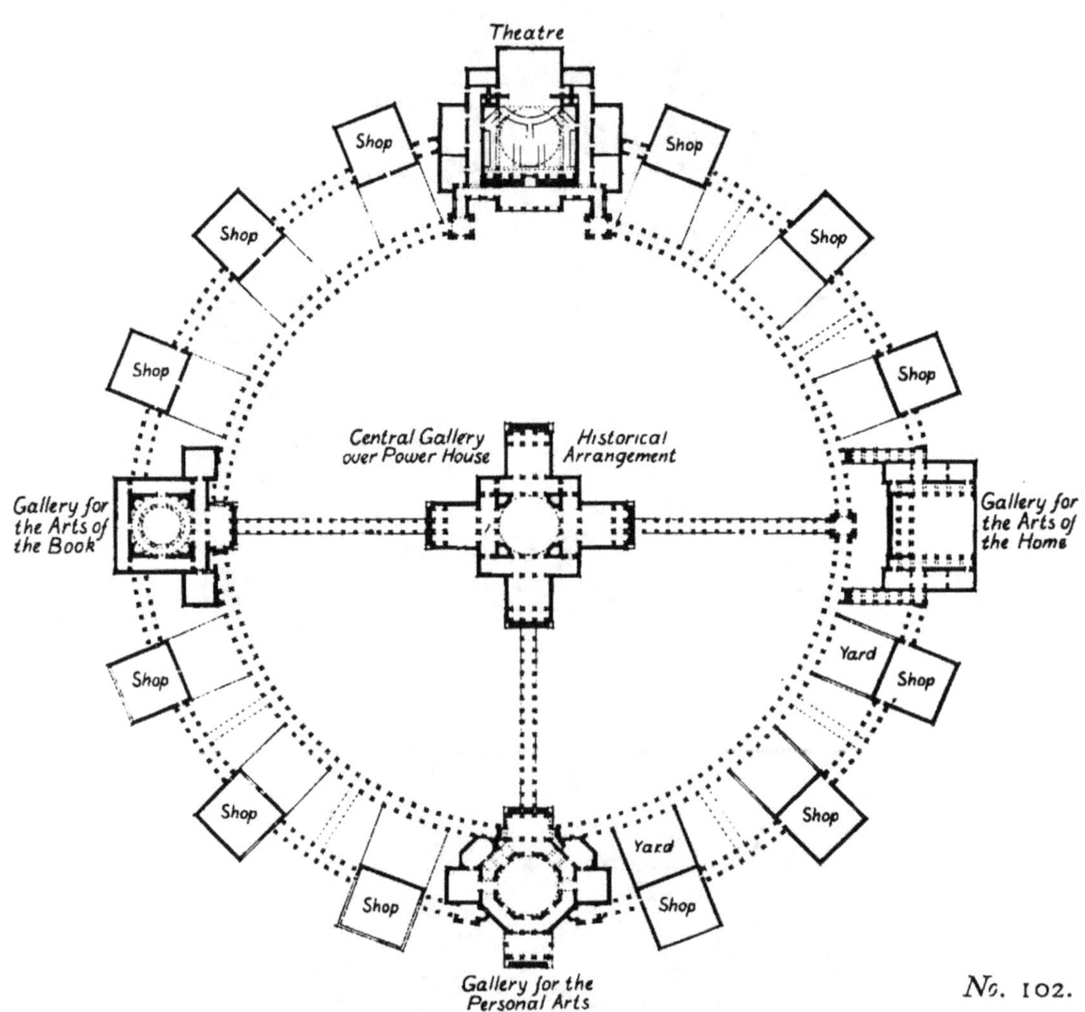

Plan to show the architectural treatment of the grouping of the " Craft Museum " or " Art Institute " with the Creative Guild.

CHAPTER XXV.—Exhibition and Endowment in the Arts.

Passing now to the method of exhibition. I would have exhibitions of two sorts : permanent and temporary. But all exhibits should be good models, works of high standard in the different arts and crafts practised in the workshops. They should embody the central idea of the Institute—the maintenance of the qualitative standard as a protest against, and as a guide to, the mechanical and quantitative standard of modern Industry. I would not rule out easel paintings, and if good pictures or sculpture were offered as gifts I would accept them, but I would not buy them. Indeed, I would leave the assembling of the permanent gifts to the good sense and public spirit of the citizens. There will always be men and women of taste who are collectors of beautiful things ; they cannot take these things with them when they die, and so will leave them to the Institute. But I would earmark an annual sum—it need not be large—for the purchase of good models bearing upon all the productive arts practised by the Institute ; and I would have the interior of the rooms and exhibition halls so arranged that these objects are placed to the best advantage. This is an important point, and closely affects architectural plan ; e.g. the planning of a regulation picture gallery with top lighting, etc., is a very different matter from the planning of a building with cross lights for the display of all the arts of life, and the surprise, the enjoyment, the variety, and the beauty these arts bring with them. *Permanent and temporary exhibitions.*

The interpretation of the idea rests with the architect selected to carry it out ; but it might take some such form as shown in the architectural plan I give here (see No. 102). There would be a central building with a power-house in the basement, from which the heating, lighting, etc., of the different group buildings would be carried. Above this, on the ground floor, would be administrative offices, secretarial and committee rooms, and above them would be the large gallery and exhibition halls for permanent exhibits, loan collections, and objects of art and craft given to the city. Linked up by covered corridors leading north, south, east, and west, would be the theatre and school of music to the north, and the three minor halls, class or assembly rooms, that have to do with the commodities or exhibits produced by the grouped workshops. The workshops themselves would be grouped in between as shown. They should all be low one-story buildings, well lighted, and standing free of each other to avoid danger *The architectural interpretation of the idea.*

from fire. Further, this segregation is necessary in view of noise and dust. For example, music is incompatible with cabinet-making, so also are the dirty crafts of plasterwork and blacksmithing with the scrupulously clean crafts of the needle or the making of the book. The architectural plan need not necessarily be cruciform; it might even be seven-sided, as was Rabelais's great educational plan of the building of Thelema; but it must radiate outwards from the power centre, and the workshops must lie clear of the exhibition halls. Once given the idea, the architect should be left free to interpret it in stone.

Endowment. An endowment fund will, of course, be required. But this need not be much greater than that of the ordinary Art Institute or Museum, having its well-paid director, staff, and quasi-educational or expert officers. My scheme postulates a certain annual revenue after the first initial years. This revenue will be drawn from the sale of the good work produced by the Institute, the proceeds of which will be divided between the Institute and the individual craftworkers. What the revenue will be will depend upon conditions which cannot be forecast, and it would vary with the purchasing power of the public. But the object of the Institute should be to " democratize " the arts, to make them wanted in the city; and so I would arrange to reprice all the saleable commodities every year, " writing them down," so to speak, as the draper does, and after a certain period selling them by auction in the Institute itself. It is not good for the producing craftsmen to have their works loaded up in museums, shelves, and storehouses. Good work should be used and enjoyed. The craftsman calls this unused work " cold pig," and it spoils his inspiration for fresh and spontaneous work. The method of sale and distribution, and the taking of orders, would vary in the different branches of the work; and a special secretary, with a sales office, who is not himself a producer, must be provided. Statistics in English arts and crafts workshops of high standing show that under existing economic conditions capital invested in fine craftsmanship tends to destroy itself in a period of ten years. If the capital so used is to be kept intact, we must arrange that such of the revenue as is to be laid out in productive enterprise shall be returned within a period of, say, ten years. We might figure it out thus: Assume we have an annual endowment of £2,000; £1,000 might be devoted to permanent maintenance, and would be used up every year, but the other £1,000 would be put to productive enterprise. Under ordinary trade conditions, calculating over a period of ten years, the £10,000 would be written off in that period. In our Institute we should therefore assume that at the close of the tenth year it would no longer exist. As a matter of fact it will still exist in the form of beautiful things created in our different Guild workshops, and a good deal, possibly fifty per cent, possibly more, would come back to the Institute in the form of revenue from sales to the public. And all this would be exclusive of the enormous educational work meantime accomplished.

It will be seen that what I propose is not a commercial enterprise that can be carried on under the ordinary conditions of trade, where profit and interest on capital are postulated. Both these factors are abolished at the outset. Nor is it an Art Institute or Gallery of the ordinary type, petted by wealthy collectors, and housing the work of dead artists, who may have been left to starve in their day. It is a productive Guild enterprise, where, as in the manner of the mediæval Guild workshops, the qualitative standard of life is first considered, and hence the livelihood of the producer first secured. He is then rewarded for the excellence of his work. I would set no limit to this reward, but I would, as above suggested, share it with the Institute. The only difference between my plan of endowment and mediæval conditions is that the latter depended on monastic institutions, or on the " closed-in " city with its Craft Guilds, or on the King's bounty ; whereas mine is democratic and accepts the conditions of Mechanical Industry as the fundamental fact of modern life (see Axiom I). The maintenance of the qualitative standard in the workshop is the same in either case. In that fact lies the new ideal.

It is a little University of the Arts in every city at which this *A University* plan of mine aims, and in each case the object is the same: to free *of the Arts* the Arts from mechanical servitude. It is not only the plastic arts *and Crafts.* that are enthralled by the Machine. The cinema, the gramophone, the typewriter, the telephone, valuable as they are if rightly used, have each in their way as much to answer for as the circular saw, the spinning chuck, or the carving machine (see Axiom V). Our Art *Axiom V.* Institute would deal with the problems that they have introduced into life. " Canned music " would be checked by the use of the real living instruments again, the " upholstered drama " by the live theatre. Our centre for the Arts would be a place for plays and masques, such as Percy Mackaye conceives them, or as I have seen them played in the Carnegie Institute at Pittsburg ; amateurish if you will, but alive, because performed by the people themselves. A living drama might well grow up as the result of the placing of our theatre in the crowning point of our synthetic scheme. Commercial writing, the dreadful "hand" of our schools and counting-houses, would be checked by the reed pen; and commercial printing, with its elongated type, by the book produced at leisure, and without reference to trade requirements. We should have "standard," good example, in our midst. Manners, deportment, costume, would be alike influenced. Above all, the voice, and manner of speech, now in such danger of degradation from mechanical appliances, telephones, gramophones, cash registers, automatic appliances, hooters, and the appalling noises of our streets, would be given a chance again of freedom and repose. Every Art would be helped by every other, and they would be acting in concert to check and control the Machine that is now destroying them piecemeal. I write as an architect, and when I think of Art it is first in terms of my own art. But I cannot do this without thinking also of Music, Drama, Poetry, and the joy of sound, movement, language. To practise my own art I have to live and enjoy the other also. Not to enjoy Art as a whole sterilizes the Arts we practise. If we specialize in one, we cannot but be amateurs in all. That is the lesson our Art Institute would be teaching, not merely to its working guildsmen, but to the city as a whole. And here we touch the Humanities.

CHAPTER XXVI.—WHAT AN ART GALLERY SHOULD BE.

Every modern Industrial city should have some human and creative *The* centre of life as above described.   In the larger cities there is room for *Humanities.* many.   In new countries new endowments should be created to build them up; in old countries existing endowments for teaching art should be re-applied.   In England I would utilize the "art grants" for this purpose, decentralize the existing "Art Schools," and turn them into endowed, creative Guilds.   Around these centres all the Arts should be grouped.   We should have no more Art Schools that teach without reference to life, no more Art Galleries to impart antiquarianism. Now, the vital significance of our new synthetic plan is that we bring the Humanities into life again by another road, and that road is through the hearts of men and women in our re-created Guild order. It is through the Guild—the grouping of small non-mechanical work-shops throughout the country—that we shall break loose from the present futilities of our educational system, with its narrow competitive bias, its petty book learning, its mean industrial outlook, its grasping at immediate results, its want of any sense of the qualitative standard. The War has brought home to us more vividly than ever this old fight for the Humanities.   Once again the men of Science, and the men of Scholarship, are belabouring each other in the newspapers, the dry bones of the Renaissance are being dragged forth, and each side the while is blind to the fact that it is mechanical conditions which are the real danger to Science and to the Humanities alike.   The whole question must be looked at in a new way.   We need the Humanities as a check to Mechanism, but the way to safeguard them is through the Arts, co-ordinated and applied to the needs of the City.

And here there is yet another point to observe.   If our Art *The origin* teaching is to come alive, we must change entirely our point of view *of the* in regard to the great Collections we already have.   Henceforth we *modern Art* are concerned with Democracy; and a Picture Gallery or Art *Gallery.* Museum for Democracy is a misnomer.   Rather should it be called a Mausoleum for easel pictures, or the dead Arts.   What is its origin, and how has it come to be the lifeless unreality it is?   All the great galleries were once the houses of kings and noblemen, or based upon their collections;   the Louvre, the British Museum—out of which grew the South Kensington Museum—the Dresden Gallery, the

WHAT AN ART GALLERY SHOULD BE

Uffizi, most of them were centres of Court life. The hanging of pictures on their walls was an incident in their furnishing. They represented quality and standard in everything that was desirable in the cultured life of their time, that organic society of which the King of France, the Elector of Saxony, the Florentine Grand Duke, was the centre. When Endymion Porter, on his diplomatic missions, bought Mantegnas for Charles I, he was thinking of the new palace of Whitehall that Inigo Jones was planning for the Court ; he was not collecting bric-à-brac for museums, but live work by live men for live conditions. The famous Cavalier song, written a few years later, in the sorrow of the Civil War, "When the king enjoys his own again," puts it quite plainly :

> Though for a time you may see Whitehall
> With cobwebs hanging over the wall ;
> Instead of silk and silver brave,
> As formerly it used to have ;
> And in every room
> The sweet perfume,
>   Delightful for that princely train :
> The which you shall see
> When the time it shall be
>   That the king enjoys his own again.

The Art Gallery reconstructed for Democracy. Our preoccupation is with the cobwebs, but it was Court ritual that these men were thinking of—silks, music, colour, life, and the administration of life; not "collecting." The lesser houses imitated the greater, and the "Court House," of which now often the administrative function alone remains, was the centre for the distribution also of culture and beauty in life. After a while, when the great man had collected more "works of art" than he could house, he would either, as did Samuel Pepys with his books, weed out and give them away, or he would build a larger gallery to house them. Some such plan, perhaps, an intelligent Democracy will also devise, that has learned to live. It will weed out its less important works of art, and lend them to the individual homes of its citizens, as it now lends books, where they will be well taken care of, properly contemplated and enjoyed. It is much better to see a De Wint water-colour, or a Whistler nocturne, or a Sandys drawing, or a Morland lithograph in a private room where a few can enjoy it as a gem, than in Room Number 365 of an Art Institute, where thousands shuffle daily through the turnstile, gaping at ten pictures at once. If the picture could only speak, it would feel less shame thus, conscious of the human appeal.

124

WHAT AN ART GALLERY SHOULD BE

So if I were planning an Art Gallery it would be on historical lines, but synthetic. Its purpose would be to reveal the beauty of life as men in the past understood it. To strip the altar-pieces and the sculptured saints from their church walls and niches, is as monstrous a want of taste as jumbling all the schools of painting together in a great modern " Museum." We might have a few choice paintings, but only in their appropriate settings and with the furniture of their time : Rembrandt, Franz Hals, Teniers, in a Dutch surrounding ; Van Eyck and Memling, with a Van Orley tapestry, in some fifteenth-century Flemish chamber ; Boucher, Watteau, Fragonard, carefully set in the atmosphere of the Ancien Régime ; Turner, Opie, Etty, in an Early Victorian room, and so on. We might even have a pseudo eighteenth-century apartment in which to put our own revivalists, the duplicating machine, and the Jew dealer. The purpose of my whole gallery would be no longer vulgarly to collect, but to teach, through history, fitness and beauty in life. And even history is a detail, for the objective is to live, to imagine, to create. Our "Art Gallery" should be but an incident in the life of our Creative Guild, for it is in the present that we live, and should live. My plan (see Nos. 98, 102) shows how it is set in the centre of a circle ; but the circumference is more important than the centre, and it will radiate ever outwards, penetrating the city life.

This demand we artists make is not merely an English demand ; they have made it in France, in Germany, perhaps most clearly in the little countries, e.g. in Sweden. The " Art Proletariat " is shot through all society ; it has no patriotism, it is not national, and though for the moment it may be swept up in the great blind movement of the peoples, it retains its force, it is democratic, even as it is parochial. Our protest is against mechanism, our plea is for a policy in the æsthetic economy of life. We want, as a Swedish painter put it, " the socialization of Art." " Everywhere we travel and enter a great museum, the same impression . . . Rooms with walls filled with pictures . . . pictures in long rows, in rows over and under each other . . . room after room without end . . . floor after floor . . . In long lines, in double aisles, in niches, on pillars, in window corners, in cabinets and show-cases, stand busts and statuettes, hang reliefs and medallions, in bronze and marble, plaster of paris and terra-cotta . . .! Compiled according to technical methods . . . historically, chronologically, alphabetically . . . the whole conception of an Art Museum becomes an anomaly, where no deliverance is possible, except in a radical change of the

The painters' mausoleum and the need for change.

entire system for the care of the State art treasures.   I will, at once, in order to be clearly understood, state my opinion, that the '*reformation of the Art Museum into a work of art*' can only be brought about on a synthetic foundation."* And what is the foundation to be ?   As many of us in England see it, it must be some new ordering of life, in city and country, on a basis of the revival of the small workshops of high standard, the machine under control, and these workshops co-ordinated into the Guild.   And so it might be in America also.   The best " Art Institute " or " Craft Museum " I know there, with the exception of the Metropolitan, is that of the University of Pennsylvania (see Nos. 103, 104).   But, like the rest of them, it is dead, but for its curators and such tender reflections of civilized antiquity as its cases irradiate.   Some day, perhaps, when life is better understood, the youth of Philadelphia may build up around it some such circle of productive workshops as I have outlined, where men will again be working with their hands to the glory of the city.

Decentralization of the Art Gallery and decentralization of the Art School go together.

It is clear, then, that the question of the Art Gallery and the reconstruction of the workshop life hinge upon one another ; the decentralization of the Art Gallery follows upon the decentralization of the Art School.   If, as I would see them, the Art Schools throughout the country are made the centres of Creative Guilds, the Guild buildings will *ipso facto* become the places for housing the surplus works of art that now crowd the walls of our great " cacoplastic " galleries.   We need the æsthetic synthesis here as in all things.   " I do not understand," said Puvis de Chavannes, " the purpose of painting that is not decorative.   Either it must be somewhere on a wall—painted for a particular place—or I must be able to hold it in my hand."   If that is true, the great Art Gallery has no *raison d'être*.

We come back, then, to the point where our study of civics brought us in Chapters VI and XV.   What have the Art movements of our time taught us ?   What was the synthesis we made of them ?   Just this : that their combined appeal is for the emancipation of the Artist producer, and for a fellowship in the plastic Arts.   But the freeing of the Arts implies also the freeing of the individual from the Machine.   Here, then, is the new Humanism in Democracy ; and our Museum, if we give up merely filling cases and collecting mummies, may become a real " Mouseion," or seat of the Muses.   Thus shall we bring the Humanities into Industrial life by another road.

* Georg Pauli, " The Socialization of Art," trans. Carl Eric Lindin, 1916.

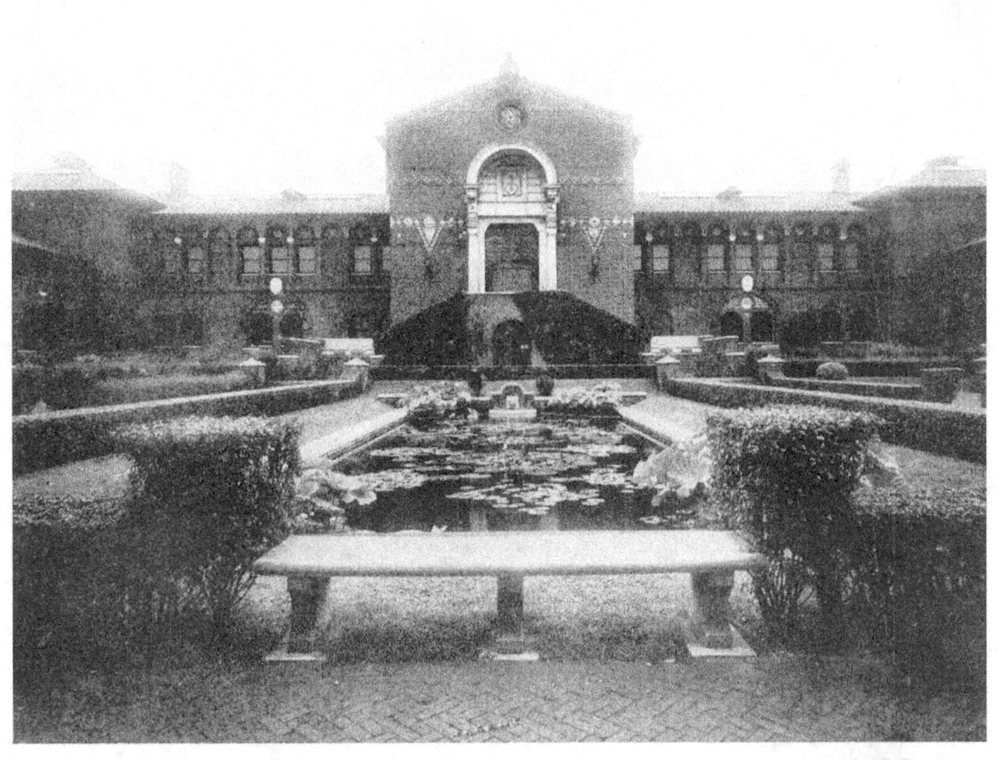

No. 103.

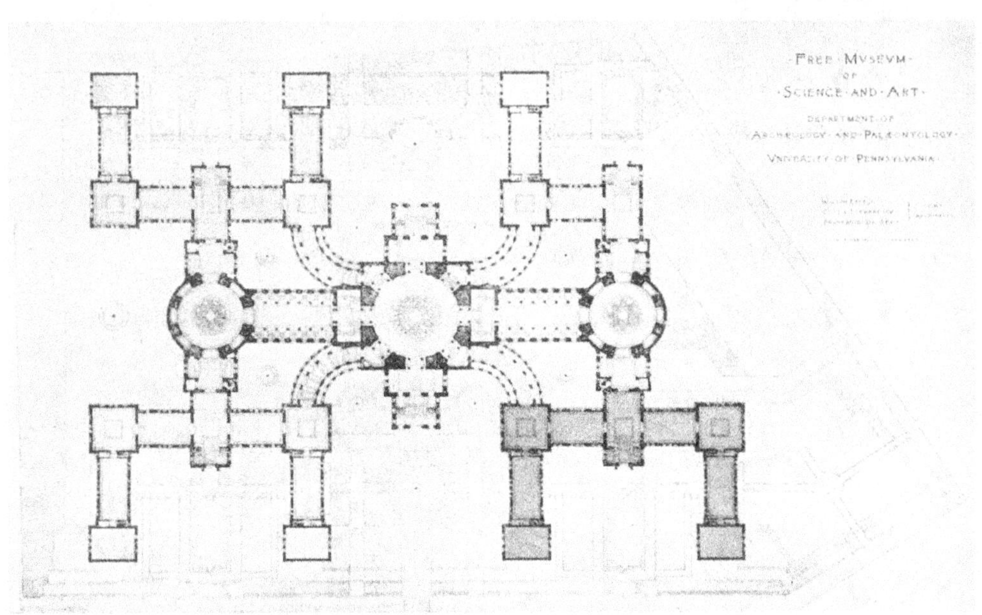

No. 104.

Museum of Science and Art, Pennsylvania University.
Architects: Messrs. Wilson Eyre, Cope & Stewardson, and Frank Miles Day & Bros.

The shaded portion shows the part built.

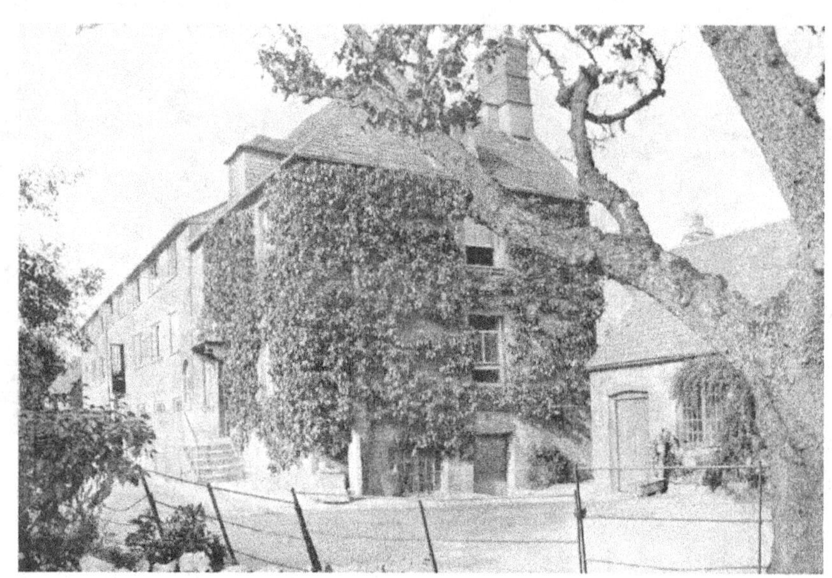

No. 105.

*The Workshops of the Guild of Handicraft at
Chipping Campden, Gloucestershire, from* 1902 *to* 1914.

*This building was once an old silk mill. Observe the eighteenth-century
house of the employer of labour, on to which is built a small " factory
annex "—the domestic industry in process of development out of the
home craft.*

*The experience of the Guild of Handicraft, over twenty-five years,
has shown :—*

(a) *That to carry on craftsmanship by factory methods is impossible.*
(b) *That for a federation of craft workshops a distribution of these
workshops is desirable. It is better for them to be near to one
another, but not under one roof.*

CHAPTER XXVII.—STANDARDIZATION AND STANDARD.

The educational and human influence of one such productive *The plan* "Art Institute," or Guild, in lieu of an "Art School" and a dead *tested experi-* Museum, working quietly and consistently for, say, a period of ten *mentally.* years in one Industrial city, would be enormous. I know this because I have proved it in England.* If every city of over 5,000 inhabitants had its endowed Guild working thus at the problems of the qualitative standard, it would revolutionize life. For it would mean that we should, in educating ourselves, be disentangling the mechanical problems with which we are now struggling blindly—these problems of waste, poverty, noise, dirt, or that result from power at present out of our control. Furthermore, it would help the factory order, and the quantitative standard, because it would circumscribe and limit it. It would force us to give up the assumption, the lie we still believe, that everything can be better done by factory processes, and every-thing purchased by money resulting from factory processes. Above all, we should be free of the fatalism which our competitive Industry has brought us, and which also underlies the socialist hypothesis that things must go their course and quality be destroyed by quantity when-ever the two conflict.

Further, as "big business," which is essentially quantitative, was *Quantitative* being more and more worked in the public interest, we should be *"big busi-* able to endow our productive qualitative Guilds with such commodities *ness" and* as tools, plant, raw or partially prepared material, domestic appliances *qualitative* —all the things for which the working craftsman is now bled. He *Guilds.* could have them at cost price or even free. This would be a fair form of endowment in return for the good stuff the community was receiving from him. It would be payment "in kind," much as such payment was made of old by monks and kings. It would have the effect of helping to cheapen and "democratize" the good work.

It is very necessary to keep clearly in mind the two principles contained in the words "standardization" and "standard." At times they conflict. Let us recall our third Axiom: "*The purpose of the Axiom III. Arts and Crafts (understood as an æsthetic movement) is to "individualize,"*

* From about 1896 to 1908, the twelve most productive years of its life, the Guild of Handicraft performed much such a function in England, handicapped though it was by the constant drive of its moneyed interest, which sought, and rightly according to commercial principles, to make "standard" conform to market demand, in order to pay dividends.

to set a standard of excellence in all commodities in which the element of beauty enters. The tendency of machine industry is to " standardize "— that is to say, to create as many pieces of any commodity to a given type as is economically possible."

When the maker of the Ford motor-car was asked what was the secret of its success, he answered, " One model"; and this, so profoundly true of all mechanism, is the antithesis of our Arts and Crafts. In most of the necessary mechanical functions of life the two principles contained in "standardization" and "standard" move concurrently: in most of the æsthetic functions they diverge. Wherever the attempt is made to develop the one by means suitable to the production of the other, the result is disaster. The diagram here given (No. 106) shows how the individual product is handicapped in its race with the standardized product. The two start carrying an even burden, but as they go the standardized product shares its weight of dead expenses with a thousand of its reduplicated brethren, while the individual product has to carry all of its own. Next, as quantitative conditions in life develop, the burden on the qualitative product increases—it is more and more difficult to buy raw material cheaply; high skill demands higher wages, and so forth. Then there enters the element of time. The burden of the standardized product is still more distributed, as in the Ford motor-car; the burden on the individual piece is proportionally increased. In fine, at the end of Stage 3 the individual or qualitative product is crushed: Gresham's Law, as we saw in

Axiom IV. Axiom IV, has taken effect. *" There is a Gresham's Law in the industrial arts as there is in coinage. In the latter the bad coin tends to drive out the good. In the former the bad product tends to drive out the good product, the unskilled workman and the machine tend to drive out the skilled craftsman."*

The development of standardization. Meantime the countless processes of standardization continue. "Owing to the growth of psychological science," says Graham Wallas, "those characteristics of the Great Industry against which Morris and Tolstoi specially protested will be enormously increased." And then, with fine insight, he puts his finger on the weak spot of the teaching of the American advocates of Scientific Management. "Their thinking is based on conditions which we are beginning to take for granted, but which, in fact, have only come into existence during the last generation. They assume that a large body of workmen are dealing with material—iron, cotton, etc.— so exactly assimilated or graded that any portion of it labelled in a

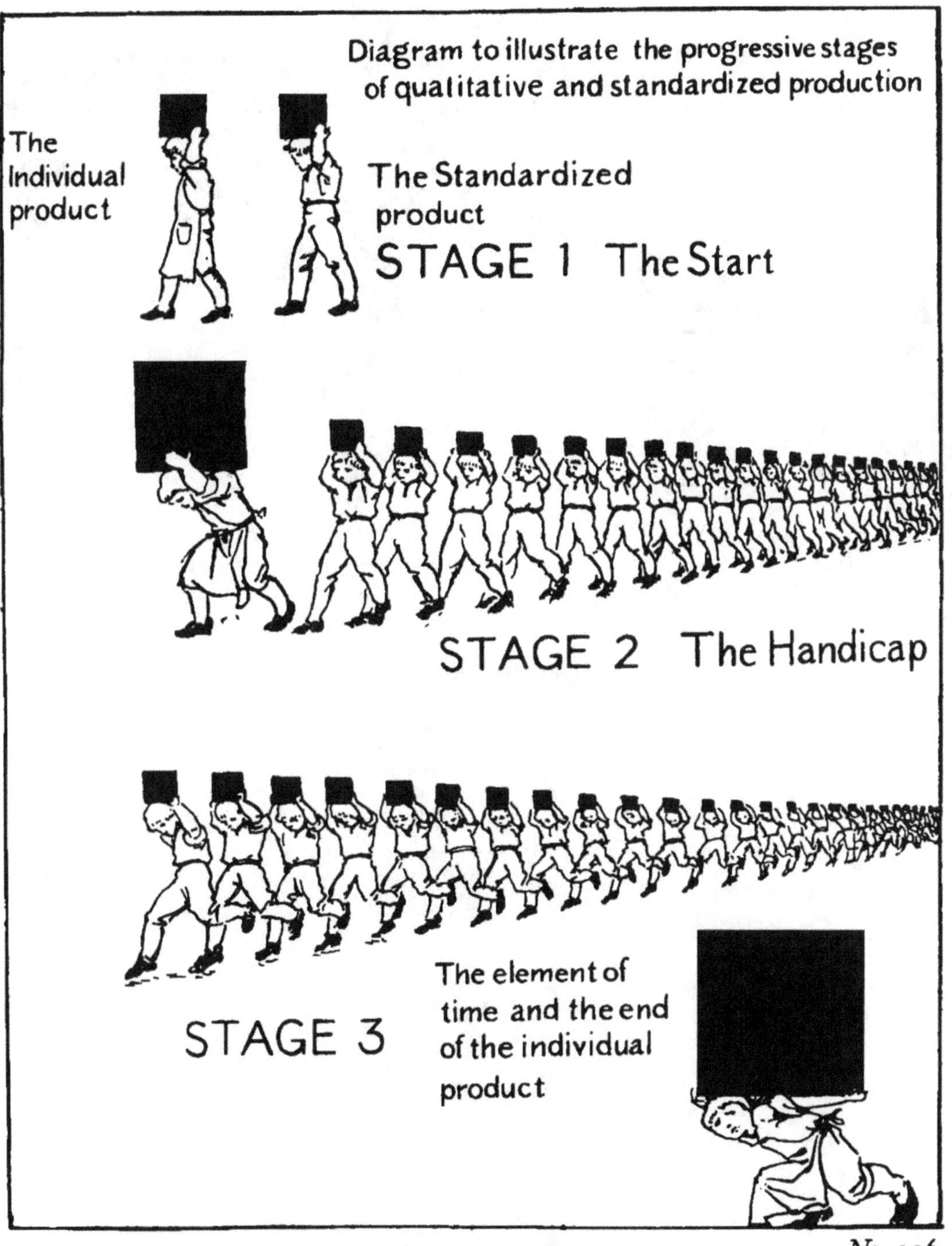

Diagram, drawn by A. Miller, to illustrate the progressive stages of qualitative and quantitative or standardized production.

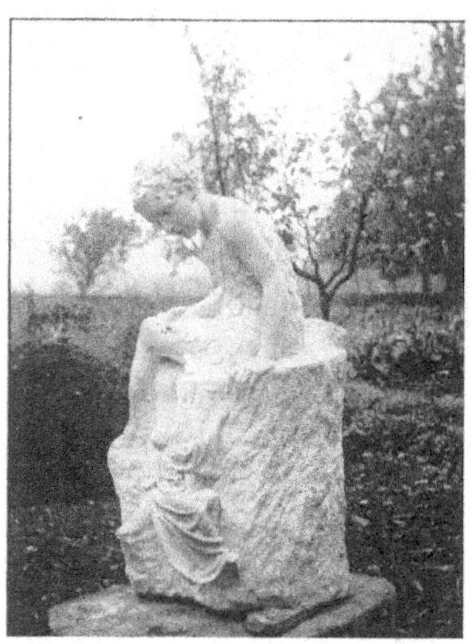

Garden Statue in portland stone, " Peter Pan." No. 107.

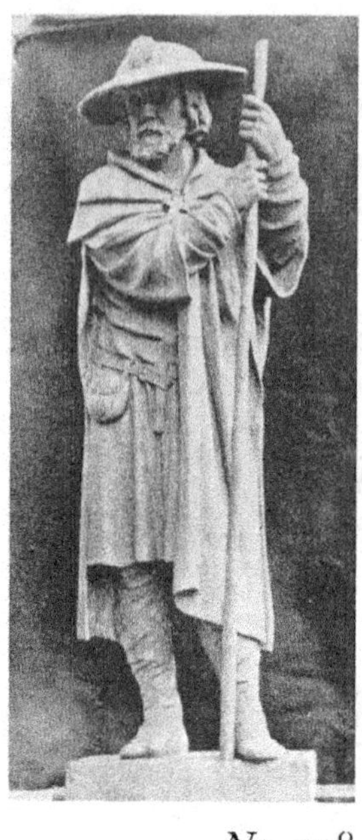

Part of a Rood No. 108. Screen, Urswick Church, Lancs.

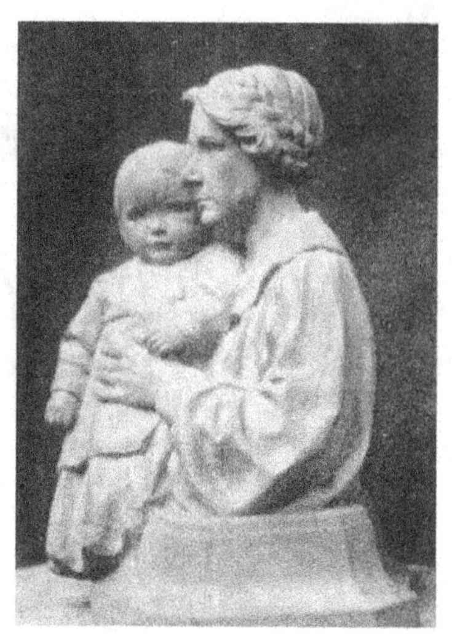

Portrait Group in pearwood. No. 109.

Examples of Carving designed and executed by A. Miller.

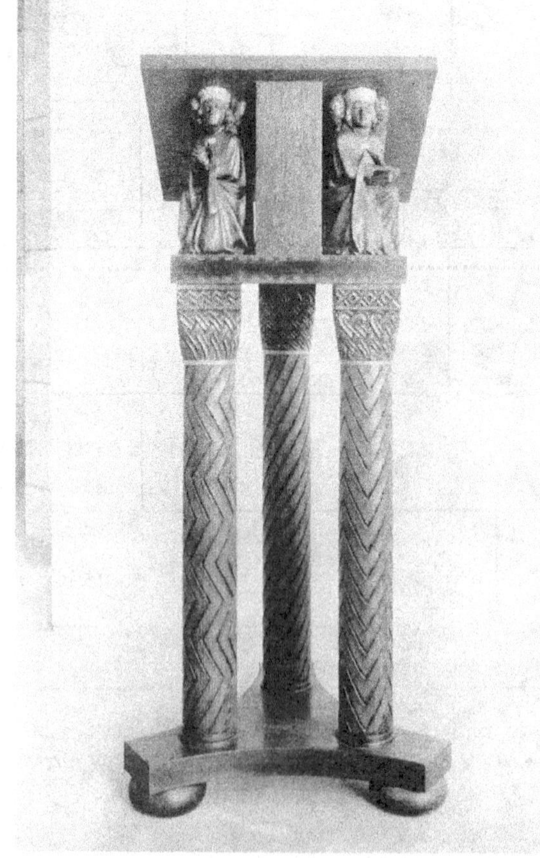

From the workshops at Campden, Gloucestershire.

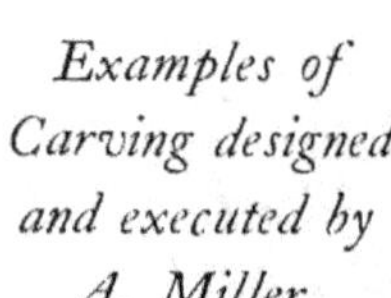

Lectern in oak for King Edward VII Sanatorium. No. 110.

particular way is equivalent to any other portion so labelled. They also assume that it is easy to make large numbers of tools and machines which, however complicated, are exactly identical with each other. The workmen cannot be so assimilated. . . ."[*]

Unless, indeed, human considerations, "the quality of joy" as Morris called it, are taken into account, or as Wallas would say, "the happiness as well as the efficiency of the workman,"[†] it is difficult to avoid the conclusion arrived at by Anatole France in the "Isle des Pengouins," when he forecasts the downfall of Syndicalist society. But what gives the greatest hope for this revival of the individual product, and the closer relationship of man to his labour that comes with it, is the rapid growth of mechanical Industry itself. This growth is so vast that it is passing out of the competitive form. "The real news about business," says one of the younger American writers, "is the fact that it is being administered by men who are not profiteers. The managers are on salary divorced from ownership and from bargaining. They represent this revolution in business incentives at its very heart. For they conduct gigantic enterprises, and they stand outside the higgling of the market, outside the shrewdness and strategy of competition."[‡]

For the Arts there are few greater pieces of news than this. "What has happened to the railroads is merely a demonstration of what is likely to happen to the other great Industries—steel, oil, lumber, coal, and all the others which are adapted to large-scale production. Private property will melt away ; its functions will be taken over by the salaried men who direct them, by Government Commissioners, by developing labour unions. The stockholders, deprived of their property rights, are being transformed into money-lenders."[§]

The prophecy carries with it the possibilities of that finer æsthetic life at which we artists aim, and, above all, the life of the "Great City." We can trace the processes of standardization elsewhere. The two fundamental contributions of the United States to civilization have been the standardization of travel and the standardization of the newspaper. The significance of this has not yet been fully realized, least of all by the Americans themselves ; perhaps because they have only just begun to put the first to proper service, and have degraded the second to base uses. But the City as we here conceive it, the

The quality of joy.

The tendency of "big business."

---

[*] "The Great Society," page 327.   [†] Ibid. page 332.
[‡] Walter Lipman, "Drift and Mastery," page 46.   [§] Ibid. page 61.

City of Industrial Democracy, is only possible as the result of transcontinental travel and the five-cent car. As for the daily paper, "the staple of news," it has been destroyed by advertisement; its redemption lies in the education of the woman, for it is based fundamentally on the desire for the petty bargain. "The commercial success of the Pacific Coast papers," said one of the editors to me, "is the result of a study of female psychology."

And so it is with the other great standardizable Industries. Their significance is gradually growing clearer. I have been many times to Pittsburg, and have always felt it to be a dreadful city; but latterly has come a change, and I see the beginning of a spiritual revolution. In that wonderful book, "The Pittsburg Survey," it is said of the steel-workers, "they are not highly paid. But even if their earnings were very high, it would be folly to claim that they are compensated for their lack of opportunity to live the lives of normal men who work a normal day and rest at night, or for their lost privileges of free speech, or for their stolen political rights. These are things for which you cannot pay a man."* And then the writer makes a forecast—much as Morris once in my hearing forecast the cataclysm that came upon us in 1914, the revolution that was to change the face of England— a forecast without reference to time. "Revolutions . . . do not necessarily involve violence. And through either the Trade Union or the political movement, or through some other means, there is bound to be a revolution ere long that shall have as its goal the restoration of democracy to the steel-workers."

" Sachons connaître." Through a clearer knowledge of what is implied in "Standard" and "Standardization," we shall learn to build up the newer life, whether in large-scale production on the one hand, carried on for the public benefit, or in the small Guild-grouped workshops of the individual producers on the other. It is new organizations we need. In the former case they are finding themselves, in the latter they are still to find. At present there are few agencies in life that make possible any venture that is not out for profit; it is our only present gauge of success. Until we have educated our community to want or re-create them, we are thrown back upon the capricious and often contemptuous charity of "wealthy men who care not when they give"; and such giving, since it is without sacrifice, often defeats the charity it seeks to contain. Such organization the Middle Ages had in Church or Guild;

* "The Pittsburg Survey," J. A. Fitch : The Steel-Workers, 1910, p. 242.

Hellas had it in the City State ; within our Industrial life, the order of Mechanism, it has still to be created.

But we shall not create it till we discover our objective to be *men,* not *things.* There we have the secret of the Hellenic city as of the Mediæval Guild, the Platonic State as of the Christian Church. "Blessed of old are the sons of Erechtheus . . . moving luminously through the brightest air, where once, they say, golden-haired Harmony brought forth the nine chaste Muses of Pieria." It is the "desired thing," the Abbey of Thelema. Not mechanism nor the endless making of things will bring it ; it can only be attained through men, quality, standard.

The failure of things as against men has never been more clearly witnessed than in our age. Of what good has been all this hurling to and fro of high explosives ? It has not deterred brave men. Of what use the German theory of terrorization by Zeppelin, submarine, and bomb ? It took no account of free men and how they felt. As Will Dyson's cartoon has it from the lips of the War Materialists: "Ah, if the creator of our cannon-fodder were only as efficient as the creator of our cannon ! " The war has revealed the breakdown of the Industrial system, because it has shown us that men are more important than things. And in America the debacle was as complete as in Europe, for there also men were blind to it, and still believed that "things," or their token, dollars, could accomplish the vital need. They who believed in things rather than men, the Morgans, Fricks, Freers, Carnegies, Fords—of what use was all their wealth ? The accumulation of things did not help. The "Carnegie Palace" at the Hague," the "Ford Peace Ship," the "Morgan collections"—how did these things aid the world in the hour of need ? To each the same answer : "He walketh in a vain show : he heapeth up riches, and knoweth not who shall gather them."

Our objective must be "men," not "things."

CHAPTER XXVIII.—SHOULD MEN MAKE "PROFIT" OUT OF THE ARTS?

" Big busi-
ness" and
the Arts
touch on the
point of
profit.

We have been brought, then, to the question of profit in the Arts. What is its justification? What contribution have our small creative workshops of high standard to offer towards solving the question of its justification in the larger life of the State? If the American thesis is sound that private property will melt away as the result of the evolution of Big Business, and its functions gradually be taken over by the salaried official, then Big Business and the Arts have an immediate point of contact. They meet on the question of profit. The process of the Industrial Revolution has, during 150 years, partially completed itself; the workshop of the standardizable product has grown bigger and bigger until it has become a Trust or State monopoly, the workshop of the non-standardizable product smaller and smaller till it has withered down to one man—the artist craftsman, working unaided and alone. That this man shall be able to go on working postulates a spiritual revival; that Big Business shall be conducted in the interest of the whole community postulates a like revival. In both cases we eliminate profit, for profit is the surplus product of industry, after deducting wages, cost of raw materials, rent, and charges. Neither in the State-controlled Trust nor in the small human workshop is there any room for it.

"When one looks back with dispassionate eye over the last fifteen years," writes another student of American Big Business, "fifteen years of unparalleled financial turmoil and upheaval, the conclusion is inevitable that whatever there has been of progress in the world of trade and industry toward higher ideals, toward franker and more straightforward methods, has been due directly or indirectly to the development and operations of the so-called 'Trusts.' They devised nothing new in 'brutal' trade methods, but they have done things on such a large scale that the public begins to see and understand the unfairness, the oppressiveness, of common, everyday trade customs. The large corporation has been a wonderful magnifying mirror in which the people for the first time see *themselves;* it has set the entire legislative, executive, and judicial world groping for remedies for economic ills that have their root in the selfishness of the individual."*

* A. J. Eddy, " The New Competition," p. 63.

SHOULD MEN MAKE "PROFIT" OUT OF THE ARTS?

The writer reduces the whole question to ethical principles; he *The issue is* brings us back to the individual. When he goes to the root of his *ethical.* subject he as good as speaks in the terms of my Axioms III, IV, IX. *Axioms III,* But he is speaking for Big Business: I am speaking for the Arts. *IV, IX.* Both speak for the Great City. "The effort to produce quantity leads inevitably to the organization of industry, to the factory system, the large corporation, the trust—a break-neck pace in which to halt is to fall. The effort to produce quality means a reversal of these steps, the disintegration of the factors of wholesale and indiscriminate production until the individual is permitted to emerge and impress his personality upon his work."*

We are therefore ready, as the result of the action of the great Trusts, for a new condition of life in which the individual is to have his chance. The new condition, as far as the qualitative standard and the Arts are concerned, is the Guild.

We artists also have had the mirror held up to us; we have dis- *What the* covered in our work "the franker and more straightforward methods," *small work-* and we find them to be these: That artists must not *deal* in each other's *shops teach.* work; that their concern is their own production, its standard, not how much they can make out of the productions of their colleagues; that profit on the other fellow's work is unjustifiable; that in so far as he takes it the artist weakens his own productive power, drops the artist, and becomes the dealer. It took us a long time to discover this, and we found it out in the failure of the Arts and Crafts movement, which was a failure in organization, and in the failure of the Art Schools and Galleries, which have sterilized the Arts instead of bringing them into life. They have been concerned with commercial values and "collecting" things, not with standard of quality in life and work.

In the five and twenty years' experiment of the Guild of Handicraft, with its affiliated Educational work, much of what I have pleaded for was carried out *in petto*, its practical effectiveness proved, and its limitations tested.† It was the dual nature of the work, productive as well as educational, that was so valuable. The educational part was carried on without endowment, and without resources, unless the trifling pittance of the State grant, jealously guarded and often

---

* Ibid. p. 43.

† See "Craftsmanship in Competitive Industry," 1906, and "The Trust Deed of the Guild of Handicraft," 1910; while for the Educational side of the work, see the Reports of the Campden School of Arts and Crafts, from 1903 to 1914.

paid over for the sham rather than the real education, be called endowment. It may be urged that little remains either of the Guild, or the educational work it initiated, and that the War, or rather the obscurantism of a Local Education Authority, panic-stricken by the War, swept away what was most valuable of the latter. The future must decide. It is the human results alone with which I am concerned. These justified themselves. The success of the Guild as an idea was as conspicuous as its failure to make the necessary "profit" to pay dividend to non-workers. Hundreds of illustrations could be given of the success of the idea, not only in England, but in Europe and America; not only in the many ventures of new organization, but in the splendid fights of individuals—those who have now "given themselves in the War." Not least among the truths the Guild of Handicraft proved has been that standard of work and standard of character in individuals go together, that organization is effective according as men willingly subject themselves to it, and that a Guild system postulates an organization based upon the character and honour of the individual, and where the element of profit will no longer exist.

In a Guild order profit is incidental, not essential. "Profit from our industrial operations," said Samuel Chapman Armstrong of his great venture at Hampton, Virginia, one of the noblest pieces of educational work in the world, "is incidental, not essential. Only getting back cost of material and of students' labour is essential. But a dollar earned is better than a dollar given. Man-making is first, money-making is second. But the skill and the drill that make money may be good for men." The Guild idea rules out the element of profit, and when once it is accepted as a part of our educational system we shall create endowment by the sale of good standard work—pupils' or not, as the case may be, much as Armstrong did at Hampton, only on a grander scale. To incorporate the Guild idea into the structure of English education would revolutionize life.

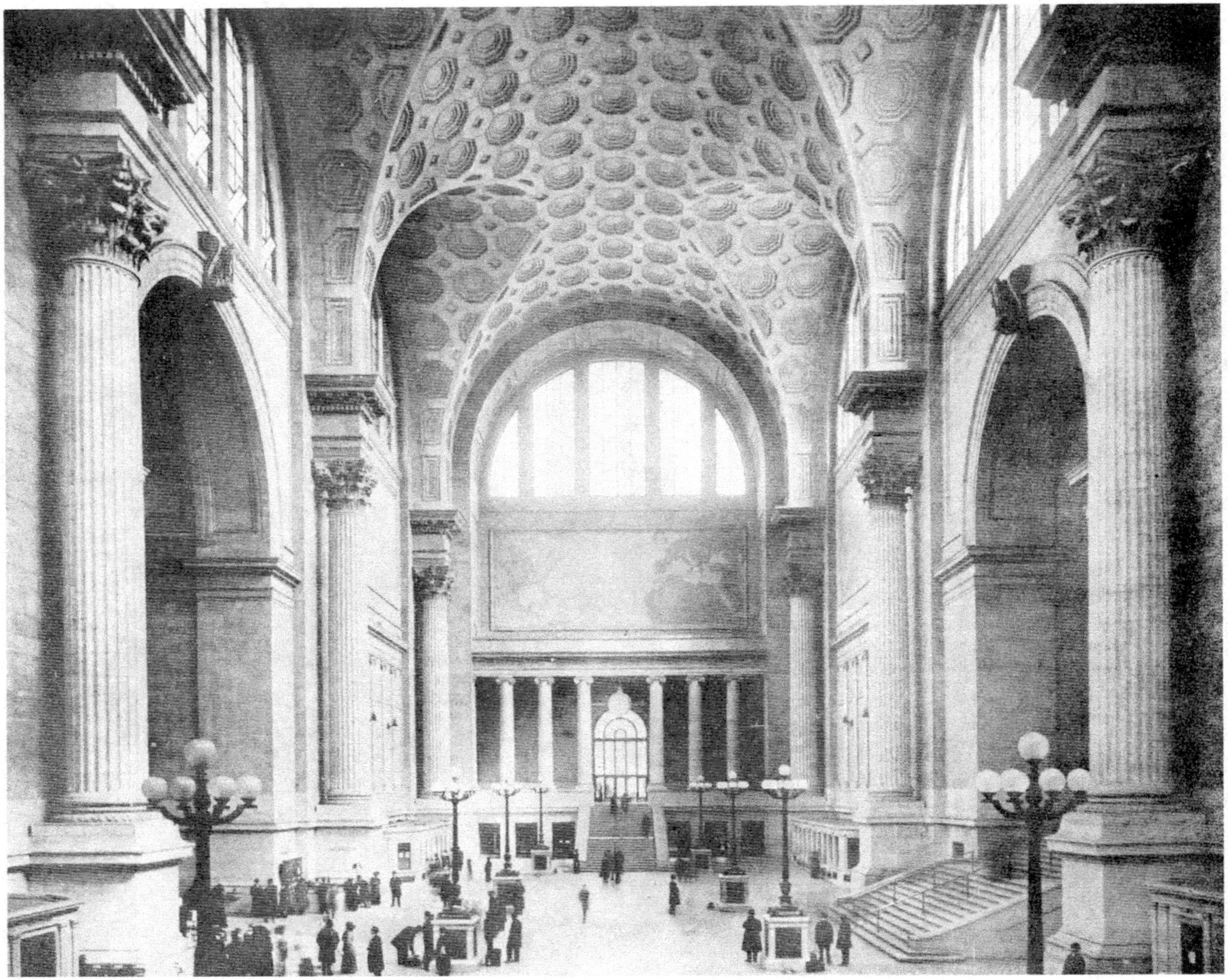

The Great Hall, Pennsylvania Railroad, New York.

No. 111.

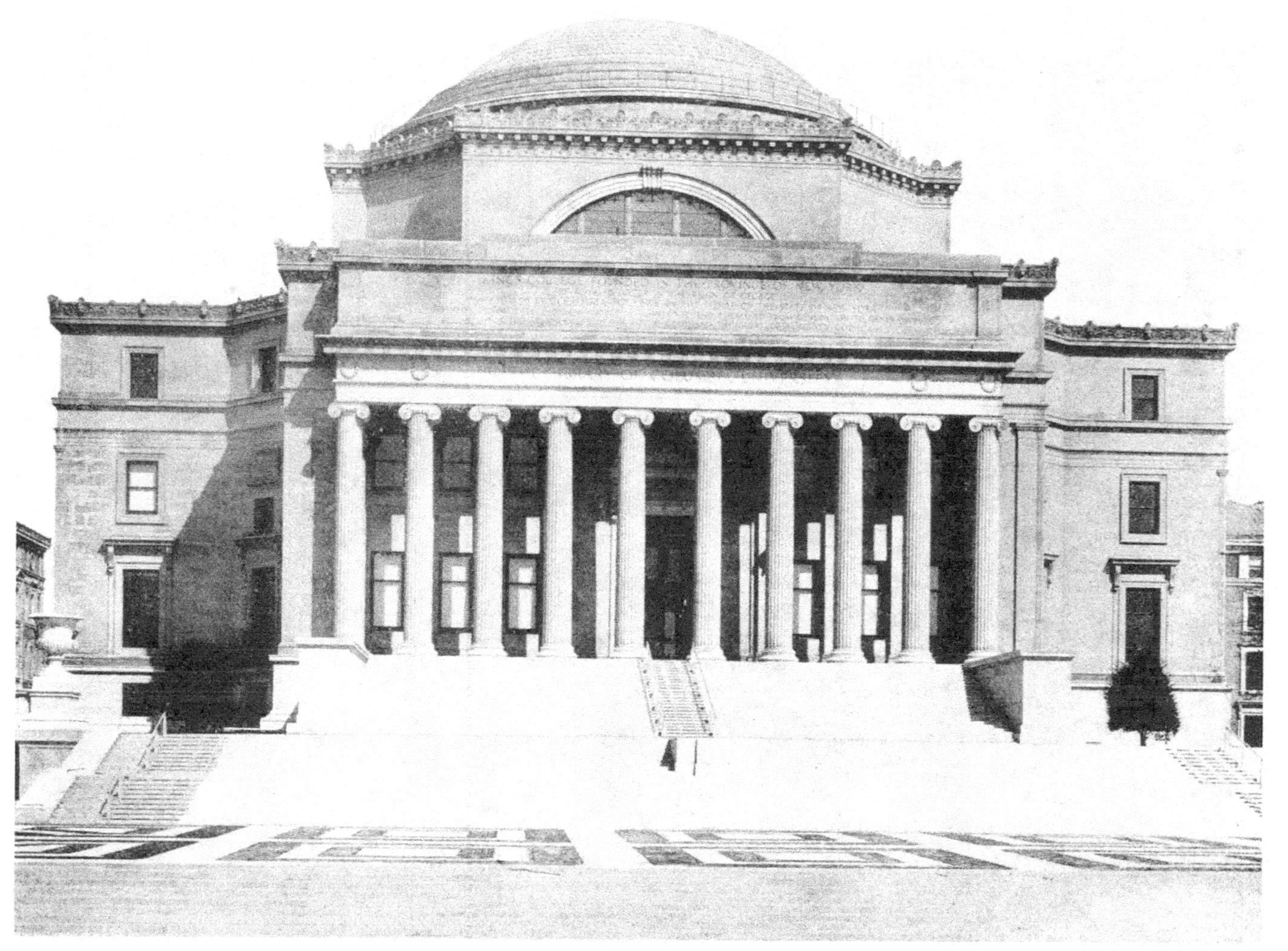

The Library, Columbia University, New York.
Messrs. McKim, Mead, & White, Architects.

No. 112.

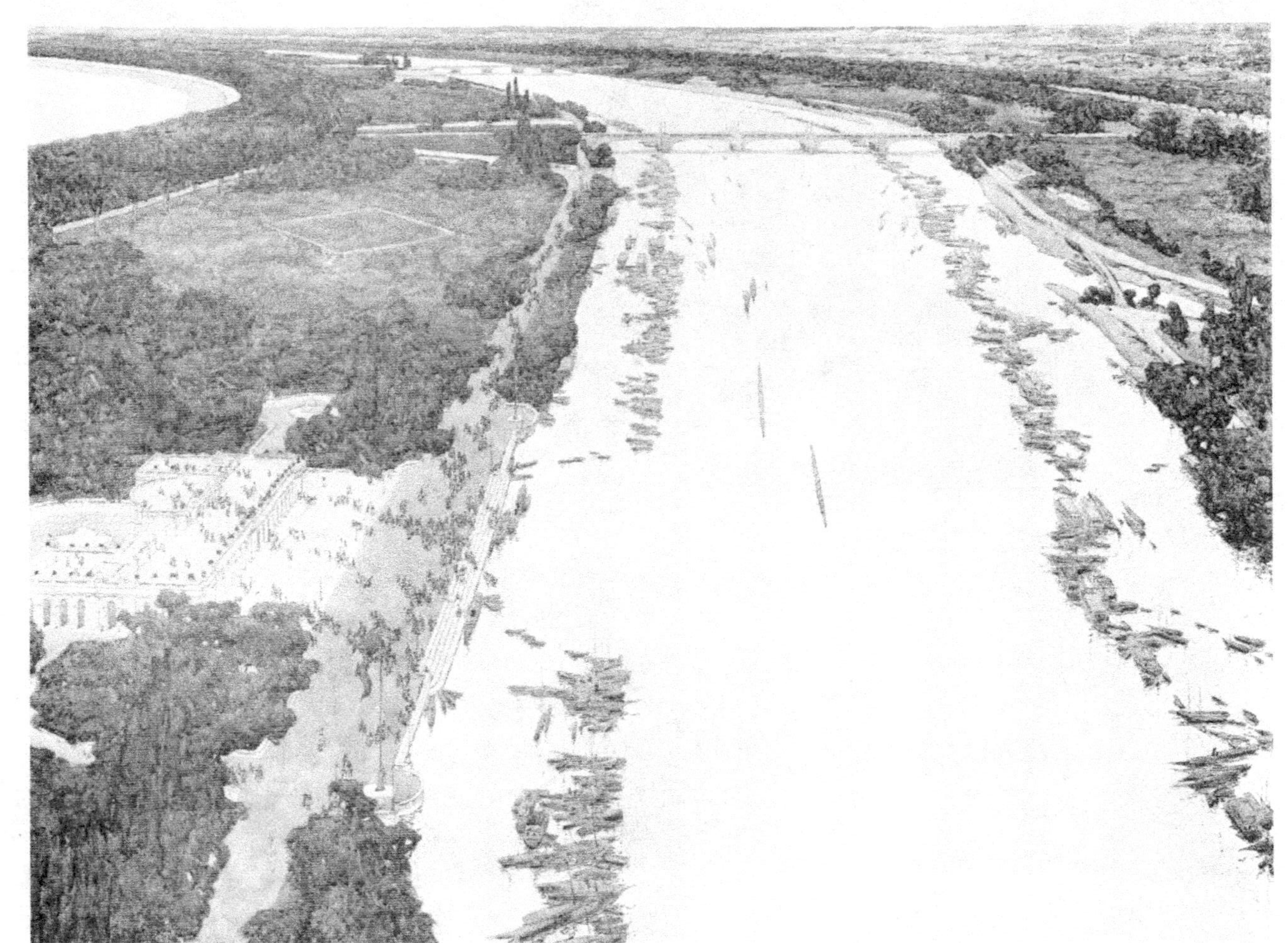

The South Shore Lake Front Improvement, Chicago.

No. 113.

Jules Guérin's drawing of Burnham and Bennet's plan.

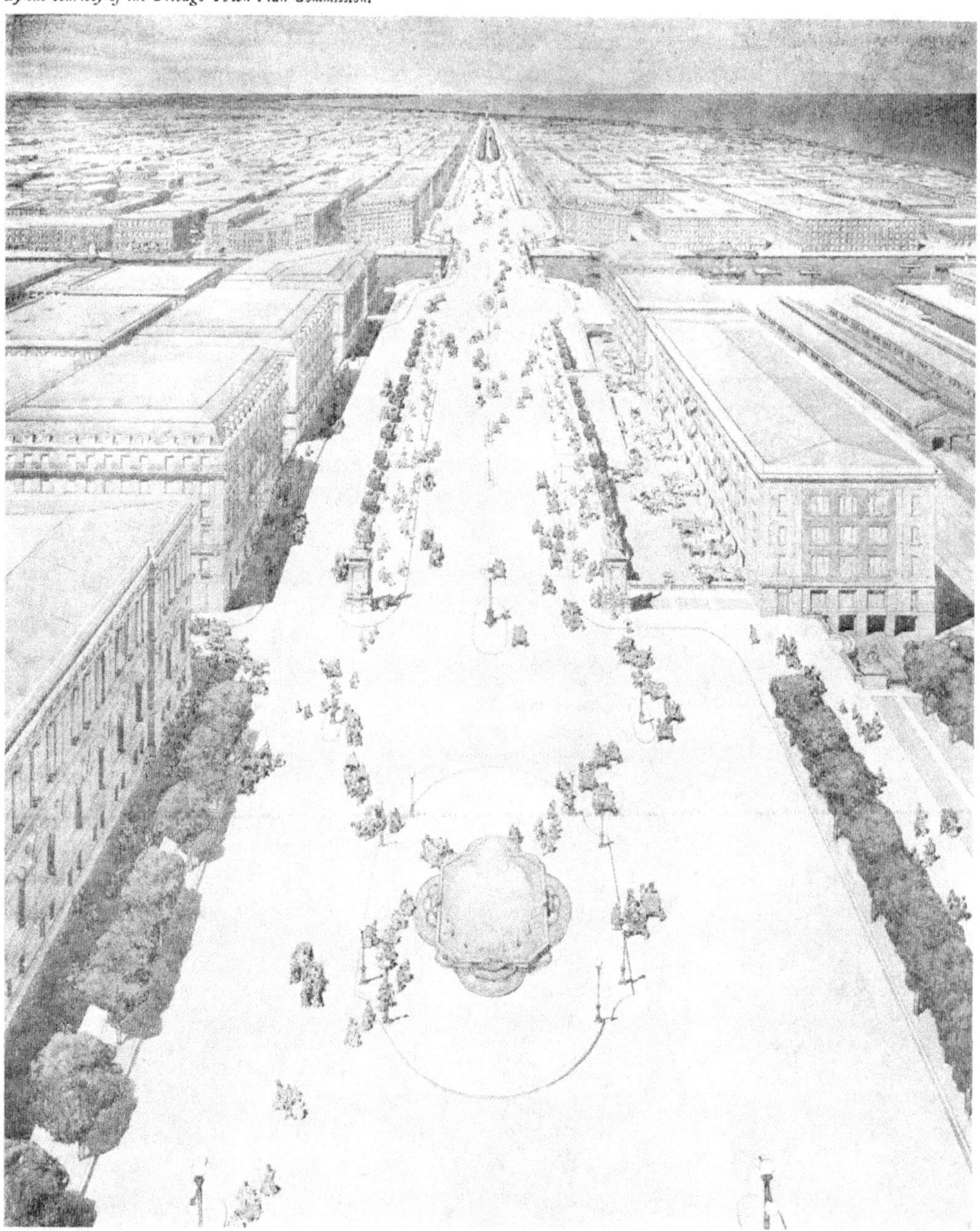

The proposed boulevard continuing Michigan Avenue northward, Chicago.   No. 114.

CHAPTER XXIX.—Simplification of Life and Public Grandeur.

The key to public grandeur is private simplicity : less personal wealth *More public beauty.* and extravagance, more corporate expenditure and enjoyment. "The great men of old," said Demosthenes, in his Third Olynthiac Oration, "built splendid edifices for the use of the State, and set up noble works of art which later ages could never match. But in private life they were severe and simple, and the dwelling of an Aristides or a Miltiades was no more sumptuous than that of an ordinary Athenian citizen."

The instinct of American Democracy is right ; the way has yet to be found. And the way so far has brought us to the Railway Station, and the University, or the Library. To sit in one of the great "depot" waiting-halls, Grand Central, or Pennsylvania New York (see No. 111), or Kansas City, or Washington, and listen to the porters intoning the trains, gives one a feeling of almost cathedral repose—the Roman rather than the Gothic. In the libraries—Boston, Columbia (see No. 112), Madison, Portland—we have the intellectual ferment, as against the business efficiency that is mastering a continent for which rapid transportation is the first essential. Life has yet to be lived, the way out through the Arts discovered.

The Chicago Town Plan is a witness to the failure of Industrialism *The Chicago Town Plan.* to find the key to the greater life ; but it is also one of its grandest day-dreams. It is over six years now since the Plan was initiated, and it is still "in procedure." Until the moral issue is understood, Chicago will never work out its Town Plan. When you ask wise men in Chicago why the Plan has not been carried out, they tell you quite simply and straightforwardly, "The business men thought it too idealistic, and the artists themselves were nervous of it." So it remains like the tomb of Aristotle, or the coffin of Mohammed in the Middle Ages, suspended in mid-air, the beautiful drawings of Jules Guérin, and the splendid Burnham enterprise (see Nos. 114, 56, 113), dreams on paper, the records of a stupendous advertisement. And why? Because the people are not yet in the mind for the permanent things. But it will come. Short-sighted men and cynics say that it will end in advertisement ; but that is because they themselves believe in advertisement rather than in reality. This living in a state of chronic advertisement comes of being too much in a hurry, of the speeding up of mechanism, and of its spawn, the cheap bargain.

135

SIMPLIFICATION OF LIFE AND PUBLIC GRANDEUR

One of the best pieces of modern civic teaching comes to us from the Chicago schools, where the author of an illustrated textbook for children has linked up the idea of public grandeur with that of private dignity and order. "We know from observation," he says to the children of the Great City, "that the wasteful household is the one in which the furniture is disarranged and in which the rooms are untidy. . . . Imagine how time and effort would be wasted in our homes if things constantly used about the stove in the kitchen should be stored in the front hall, if pianos blocked up the hall ways, ice-boxes were stored in the attics, dining-room tables in the bedrooms." * But so it is in our city. We are as a family that has hurriedly got into a new house, and an untidy family at that. That this truth is now beginning to be taught in the schools is clearer indication than any that Industrialism is finding its limitations and is settling down. And so this issue of æsthetics is a moral one. We have to prove to our rich men that there is a quality in Beauty nobler than riches, and to the poor man that he can find it by other ways than growing rich. Our search is for the new values ; our city remains soulless until we find them. We have to understand the fact as well as the need of Beauty in life.

The æsthetic issue is moral.   The black and white way of looking at life that we have inherited from our fathers still blinds us. But there is no hard and fast line between right and wrong except such as each makes for himself. The constant effort to apply the personal *morale* to the city, while at the same time ignoring the fact and the need of Beauty in life, has helped to make our cities the dreadful places they are—our historic cities, their few imperishable gems gleaming amid the burnt-out clinkers of Industrialism, our new cities sprawling litters of experiment. Moral purpose is yet to find. "It seemed to me," wrote the Reform Mayor of the American city of Toledo, of the people who saw black and white instead of Beauty, "that most of the crime in the world was the result of involuntary poverty, and the tremendous, perhaps insuperable, task, was to make involuntary poverty impossible. But in the meantime there was other work to be done. Aside from the problem of transportation, which was but one phase of the great struggle between privilege and the people, of plutocracy with democracy, there were civic centres, city halls, markets, swimming-pools, bridges to be built, parks to be improved, boulevards and parkways to be laid out, a filtration plant to be installed, improvements in all the other departments, a great mass of wonderful

* Walter D. Moody, Whacker's " Manual of the Plan of Chicago."

work for the promotion of the public amenities, the public health, and the adornment of the city ; in a word, there was a city to be built, and, strangely enough, this group of objectors of whom I have been speaking were so intensely preoccupied with moral considerations that they never had even the slightest interest in these improvements." *

Our Puritans, especially those who have themselves found great wealth, are so unpractical. They so often leave the vital things lying by the wayside. The elimination of poverty and privilege, which we considered above, is but another aspect of what we are considering now. Let us return for a moment to the plan of the Art Institute, the endowed productive Guild outlined in Chapters XXIV–XXVI. How wide an influence would it not have upon the City life ! The poor man's squalor, the rich man's vulgar extravagance, the pettiness of either, would be checked by the new sense of public grandeur that would enter into life. This re-entry into life of the Guild idea would mean moral purpose. It involves the patronage of the Arts. What is that patronage likely to be after the War ? If the War marks an era in Democracy, it will mean that the old order of the leisured class supporting its artists will give place to a new. Modern artists working for that eighteenth-century revival whose aristocratic bias we considered above may find the conditions of life changed, their patrons gone, and altogether new commodities demanded of them. But if Democracy is to be the heir to patronage it must retain also what was best in it, that fine old quality which insisted that the Arts were never commercial, and that some other payment was needed beside cash—perhaps maintenance, perhaps kind, certainly appreciation.

And the reconstruction of our Art Schools, and their devolution into Guilds, with which I dealt above, would bring with it a change in manners. We should be setting up in our city a new standard of values, the standard no longer of the plutocrat, rather that of the artist craftsman and inventor of beautiful things. His standard is bound to be simple, for his life is so, and unless he keeps it so he cannot go on labouring. His invention being free and the demand for private luxury on the decrease, we may reasonably assume that in a democratic community it would be turned to public grandeur. His actual life being based on the principle of the minimum wage, it would in itself be a challenge to the false values of plutocracy. Perhaps the change will come to us by way of some such civil conscription as " Æ " suggests for

A Guild order will bring a change of manners.

---

* Brand Whitlock, " Forty Years of it."

SIMPLIFICATION OF LIFE AND PUBLIC GRANDEUR

Ireland, the Celt's imaginative answer to the intolerable military and industrial conscription of Germany and our own Germanophobes. His is a conscription by which every young man gives two years of his life not to industrial or military power, but to the community.* We artists forecast a change in manners, and we do this from the experience of our own workshops and our study of the past. Here is no fantastic theory: it is historic fact. This simplicity of life with its sentiment for public grandeur we could have again in the modern city. They had it in the Middle Ages; it was those simple craftsmen who on their minimum wage built Amiens, Reims, and Westminster; it was the economic basis of the art of Japan, where the Samurai maintained their skilled workmen; it was an integral part of the life of Hellas. "Once a man be done with hunger," says Euripides, "rich and poor are both as one."

* "Æ," "The National Being," 1916.

CHAPTER XXX.—THE REACTION OF TOWN AND COUNTRY.

Public grandeur, then, is not possible to a community until hunger be done away with. Hunger brings us to the food supply, and the land as the first source of wealth. "The modern City," says one of the younger American writers, "marks a revolution in industry, politics, society, and life itself. Its coming has destroyed a rural society whose making has occupied mankind since the fall of Rome."* It is only recently that we have learned how the great struggle of the American Civil War was the last fierce issue between the old rural society of Europe, transplanted into the United States, and the new Industrial society we are now trying to shape. With us in England the issue remains; but it is often obscured by the many beautiful things—remnants of the old feudalism that we love and do not want to lose. "Through improved machinery," the same writer goes on to say, "three men are now able to produce from the soil food for a thousand; while the growth of large farms and the division of agricultural industry have relieved the farmer of many burdens, and at the same time rendered him dependent upon the city. The telephone and the free rural postage delivery has united the farmer with his market." That is the theory. In a new continent like America it may be operative; conditions of life are simpler. In Europe it has still to be intelligently worked out in practice.

I want in this chapter to show what this interdependence of town and country means historically, and how it is the key to much of the new life at which we aim. I want to show that we cannot have the Great City unless at the same time we rebuild the country life. Our tenth Axiom is but a modern version of the ancient legend of Antæus, who drew his strength from the soil; it has everlasting truth. *Necessary interdependence of town and country.*

"*In an industrial civilization, the reconstructed city cannot be stable without a corresponding reconstruction of the country. Town and country should be correlated and react upon one another. This correlation is a necessary consequence of the conditions of machine industry.*" *Axiom X.*

The life and the livelihood that come from marketing the country produce necessarily go together. Here (see Nos. 115, 116) are two diagrams showing the relation of the village market to the city, before and after the Industrial revolution. The black spots with

* F. C. Howe, "The City the Hope of Democracy."

139

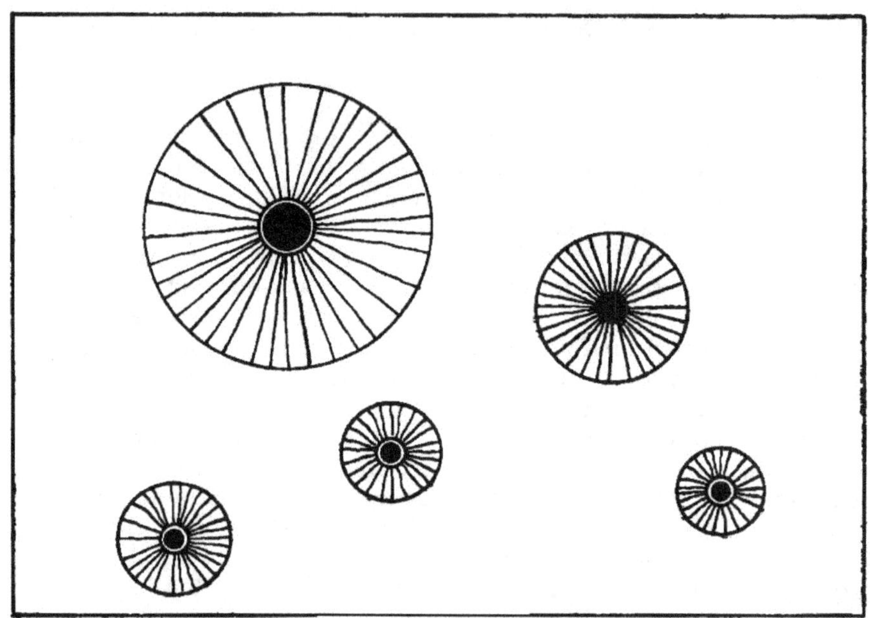

No. 115.

Relation of the Village Market to the Pre-industrial City.

their surrounding radiation represent centres of mediæval city life with their surrounding village communities from which they draw their supplies.   The coming of Industrialism, " la ville tentaculaire," with its competing railways and shipping systems, its cold storage and its factories, has brought a kaleidoscopic change.   The spots (as we see in No. 116) have now grown, the containing line of each city is broken, there is no more direct supply, but instead are long tentacles—stretching sometimes to the ends of the earth—by means of which the supplies are carried. What these diagrams show is that whereas the Pre-Industrial market was direct and at our door, the competitive market is complex and wasteful.   City and village are no longer working together.   The village life is sacrificed in the process.   The Pre-Industrial city had its surrounding villages from which it drew its foodstuffs and with which it exchanged its wares.   The modern city regards the villages merely as prospective building lots ; it draws its nourishment from a thousand such, at infinite distance, from the ends of the earth, and in the process it pits the produce of one village against another in

140

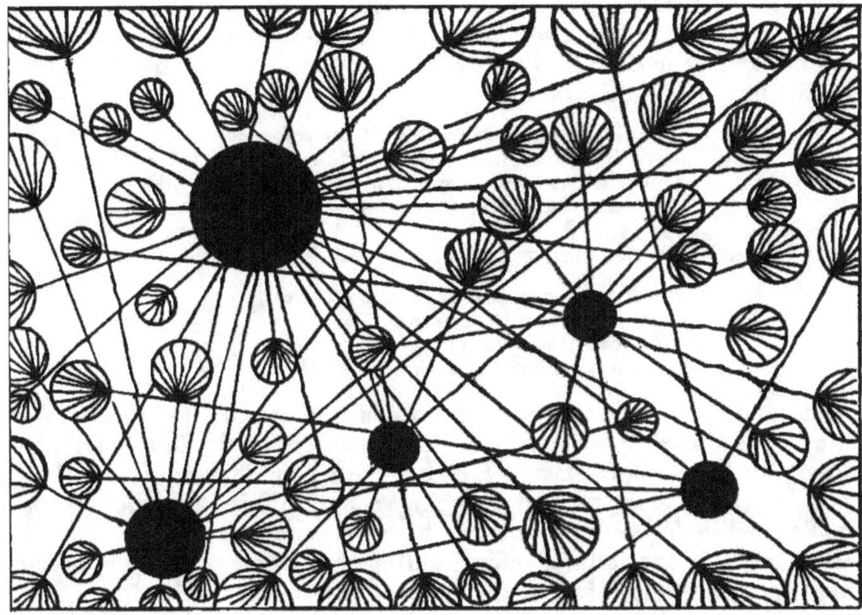

Relation of the Village Market to the Post-industrial City.   *No. 116.*

order to cheapen the townsman's food. The waste of the modern system is best gauged by comparing the length of line, and the time taken to traverse it, in the modern system with the old. But there is a deadlier waste than this, and that is in the realities of life that are dropped by the way. As a result of the complexity the village is no longer getting good value for the life blood it sends away; the exchange is no longer fair. The village gives gold, and gets tinsel in return. But it was not so of old. Few things are so interesting to study as the character of the village churches—the country architecture of Pre-Industrial Europe. Their style is indigenous, but at the same time it is drawn from the neighbouring city or cathedral. There has been a fair exchange.

The main characteristics, then, of our Industrial society, as we see it from the point of view of the village, are that country life—life in its fullness, and not merely the grinding for a living—has become unreal. It is parasitic, suburban, or impoverished of the finer things. Disintegrated by mechanism, the countryman's life has lost its unity; *Industrial society from the point of view of the village.*

141

THE REACTION OF TOWN AND COUNTRY

it is cut off from the larger life of the city. The "servingman" of our day—he is now for the most part a machine-minder—may sneer, as he did of old, but it is no longer possible for the " husbandman " to reply to his sneer. He may plead—

> The clothing that we wear is delicate and rare,
>> With our coat, lace, buckles, and band ;
> Our shirts are white as milk, our stockings they are silk—
>> That is clothing for the servingman.

The husbandman can no longer reply—

> But I value not a hair for delicate fine wear,
>> Such as gold is laced upon ;
> Give me a good great-coat, and in my purse a groat—
>> That is clothing for the husbandman.

And so it comes that when the townsman wants to escape from the city into the village he finds escape no longer possible. Divorced from the fundamental facts of country life, and having in his hands the power, he tries to remedy things ; but in his ignorance he only makes foolish legislation, soothing his own conscience. That has been the tragedy of agricultural reform during the last fifty years, and because of its unreality and injustice the husbandman leaves the land.

This unreality and injustice we can find throughout the industrial world. It ended in England in what has been called "the great strike" —the silent leaving of the land by the labourer ; and we who know the country know that it is still going on. Writing of the breakdown of the English Agricultural life in the middle of the nineteenth century, a recent historian says : " During all this period of forty years a great migration from the country went on, and men of energy and ability, instead of staying in rural England to struggle against overwhelming difficulties, drifted away to the towns and colonies; the women followed. Probably this exodus of the best people—the natural leaders—was the cause of the final disappearance of the old co-operative and social life. All that had survived of the festivals and merrymakings so characteristic of English rural life in the past was disappearing during these years, whilst the great fairs also decayed. Indeed, by the end of the period little social life remained save the harvest home, the club day of the village sick and benefit society, and such meetings of friends as occurred at the county towns on market days." *

* Montague Fordham, " A Short History of English Rural Life."

THE REACTION OF TOWN AND COUNTRY

Rural England now is at the parting of the ways. The one road Rural Eng-
leads to a suburbanized England, artificially held together by an land at the
American bastard feudalism, first invented in the eighteenth century, parting of
in which cottages and country houses are bought up by week-enders, the ways.
and artificial England, such as it was before the final debacle in 1914,
and somewhat as H. G. Wells draws it in " Matchings Easy." The
other way leads to a real country life—an England free of caste, such
as perhaps Sir Horace Plunkett, or Christopher Turnor, or a few of the
more intelligent landlords want it to become. Such men have made
the discovery that the English landed class, in allowing the real
peasantry to be destroyed, have been " putting their money on the
wrong horse." They have allowed brains, intelligence, constructive
purpose, imagination, to go by default. It is questionable now whether,
in face of the gathering storm that is soon to break upon them from
the city, they will succeed in saving themselves.

The hope lies in the silent eternity of the country-side; its dreaming among cows and pigs, and beer, and lambs, and fruit orchards;
the things that will not fit into time tables, or work to factory bells.
Above all, we who are building the Great City need the knowledge
that town and country cannot do without one another, that the city
needs the country for its own permanence and life. As for us in
England, our country gentry have yet to learn that they can only
save themselves by becoming a part of the new Industrial Democracy
in which the peasant and the dreamer, as well as the duke and the
farmer, have their part.

Much thought and intimate knowledge of the details of people's The new
lives, such as an architect has to have whose business it is to know country life.
about people's dining-rooms and kitchens, how they amuse themselves and order their conduct, and to know this in many social grades,
convinces me that what we need is an altogether new mode of life:
a mode in which the tone is no longer set by the rich country house,
but in which rich and poor—for there always must be rich and poor
—can play their part without invidious distinction. The measure
must no longer be our property qualification, but our common
citizenship, and how we live it.

When I try to apply this to the village, I find it hard to make
clear what I want to see. It is something that has to be lived—an
experience perhaps that we must pass through. Perhaps it is something like Edward Carpenter's life at Millthorpe—as many of us have
known it over a period of twenty-five years—but with the more visible

143

mark of beauty upon it. I remember once pressing this point as we walked across the moors; I compared the mechanized ugliness of the new artisan effort of Sheffield and Chesterfield—the squalid-looking allotments, their tar, tin, and cabbages—with the sturdy grace of the old Yorkshire yeoman's homestead. Yeoman's house, ducal palace, barn and cottage, all were beautiful; each had its relative place in the older scheme of life. I recall even redrawing some of the dreary modern cottages to decent pitches, and crowning them with stone finials. The philosopher perhaps dismissed all this as the irrelevant speculation of an æsthetic dreamer.

"The life is dead," said he, and this meant that for the time we must do without decent roof pitches and carven finials. Such things were trimmings fit for dukes, brewers, American millionaires, and men who were playing with the life of the past.

Since then we have had twenty-five years' workshop experience, and learned that the philosopher was right; but that we, in our search for beauty in life, were right also. We have learned that the way out is not alone through the destruction of caste, but in the creation of a new life within the existing social order—a life that must take account of the æsthetic synthesis. That way lies hope; and it is just this same hopefulness which we constructive artists, whose work has not been limited to the houses of dukes and brewers, find also growing up in the new effort in America.

Status needed for crafts-man and labourer. Status for the craftsman and status for the labourer—that is the need. The man who works with his hands, the skilled man who thinks and invents and imagines, this man has now to be considered on his own merits, and apart from the mechanism that surrounds him and that he has to dominate. The question of status, whether for the craftsman or for the agricultural labourer, is in effect the same question. The principle implied is the relation of personal skill to mechanical power.

To find this status we cannot search in the city alone. Our national economics have to be reconstructed from the point of view of the village as a unit. When I say the village, I mean any group of men and women associated together for the living of a decent life in the country, working with their hands, and with such machinery as they may need, or can use without harming other people. The village life has been destroyed by the great city, but there must be some escape from the great city (as now we understand it) with its appalling factory conditions, into a re-created village. And by the village

I do not mean the parish. This may or may not be synonymous with the village. The parish, in the old world, is the remains of the mediæval social order. I give here three plans or maps of the village in which I live. They will help to show how the reconstruction I have in mind might come about, and how the life is, and must continue to be, rooted in history. Any English village might be taken.

Plan No. 117 shows the village in its mediæval form, before *Three* enclosure, let us say in the twelfth century, and after it had been once *periods of* and for all time written down for us in the Conqueror's great Survey.* *village* There would be some five-and-twenty houses, a couple of mills, the *evolution.* Court-house and its farm buildings, the demesne of the lord of the manor. There would be the church, a priest's house, the open fields, the common pasture, and the parish bull. Up to the time of the Industrial Revolution, which is also the time of enclosure, these fundamentals remain. Their evidence is still there. For the life of over a thousand years no more was needed, and there was little change.

Plan No. 118 shows the village after enclosure. The life is now completely reconstructed. The common field system, the pasture and cow common, the bull, have gone. The latter has become a name, "Bull's hole." "The common" has "been stolen from the goose." Six or seven large farmers have taken the place of the old village life. The lord of the manor has become an absentee. The last "Court Leet" was held some eighty years ago, and the payment of twopence—it went in beer for the others—excused your non-attendance.

Plan No. 119 shows the village in process of reconstruction, at the moment when the European War cut the thread of that new social life we were trying to create. The effort, as shown in this plan, is to get it together again "democratically." There is a protest against the farmer "capitalist" entrepreneur who stands for "cheap labour," vainly competing against the Machine. A group of town craftsmen have now taken the place of one of the farmers (Farm I). The key to the situation has become the housing question—"the home"—and the wage the labourer receives to enable him to pay an economic rent for that home. The problem of the Guild of Handicraft Trust is, and for the last ten years has been, to make a decent life possible for its craftsmen and small-holders. The interest of the diagrams lies in the fact

* The Domesday entry is as follows : "The same earl holds Campdene in Witela hundred. Earl Harold held it. There are fifteen hides taxed. In demesne are six plough tillages and fifty villeins and eight bordars with twenty-one plough tillages. There are 12 servi and 2 mills of 6s. 2d. and 2 ancillae. It was worth £20. now only £20

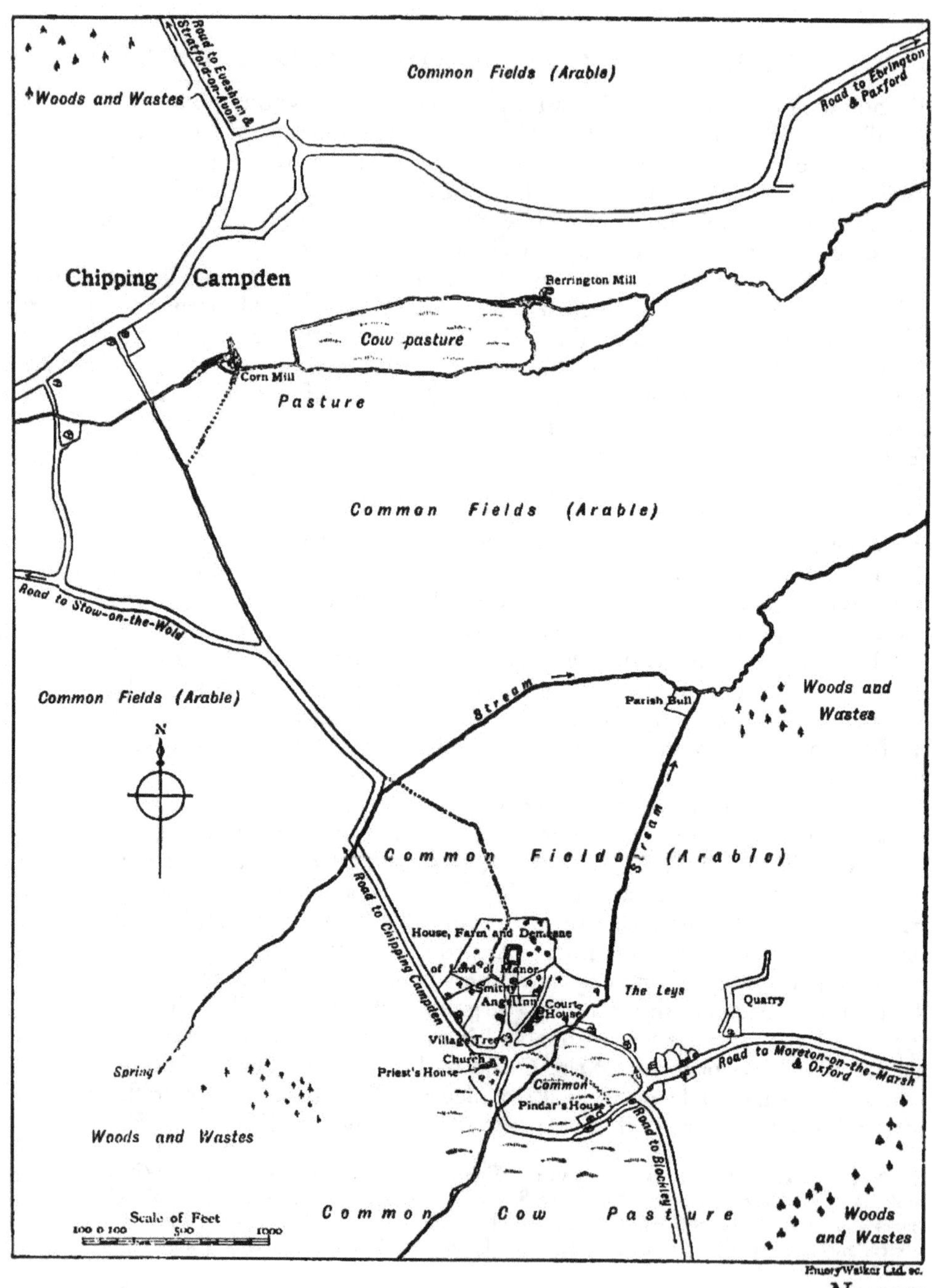

Campden in the Twelfth Century and soon after Domesday Survey.

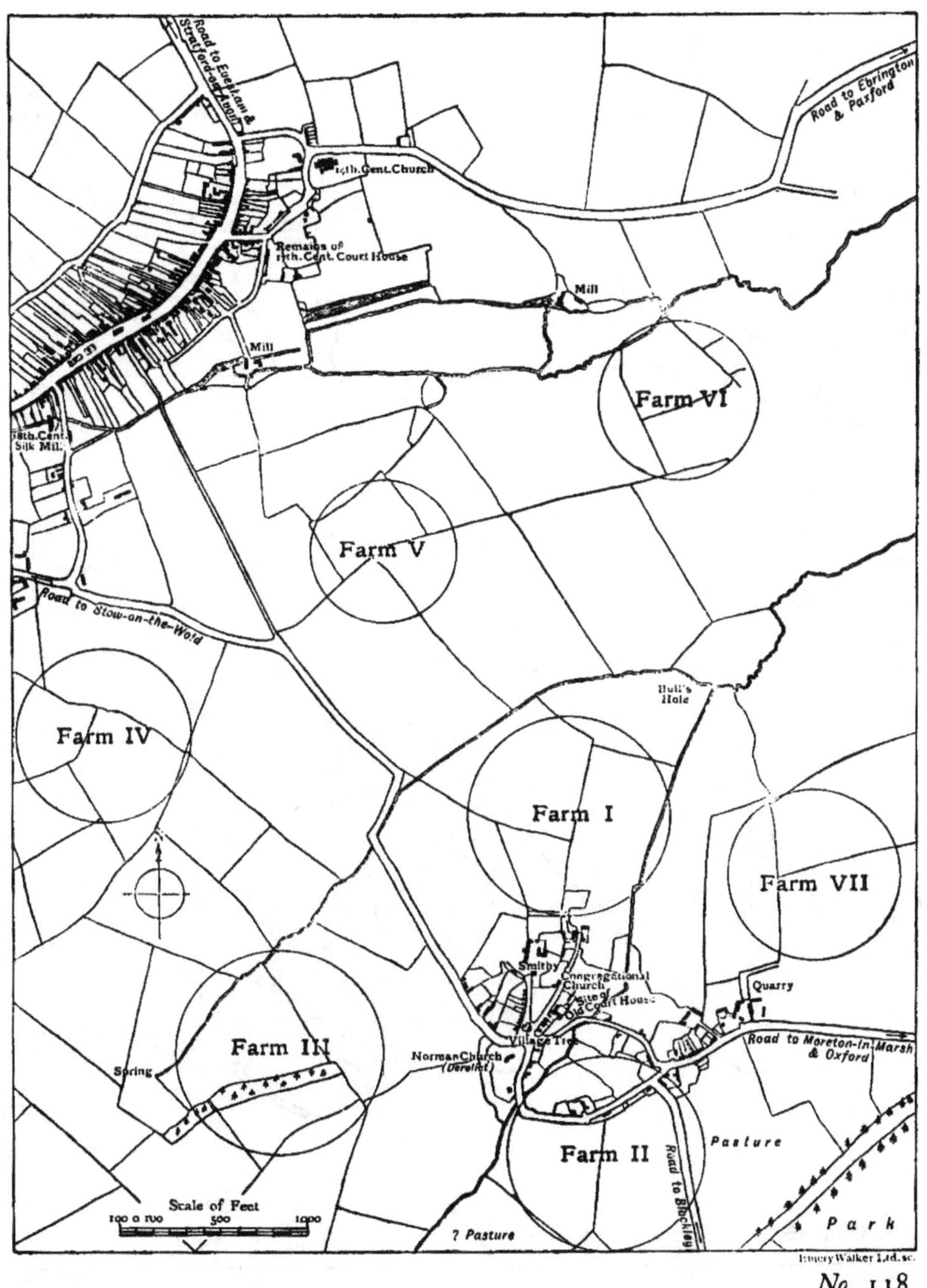

Campden in the Early Nineteenth Century, and after the enclosure of commons.

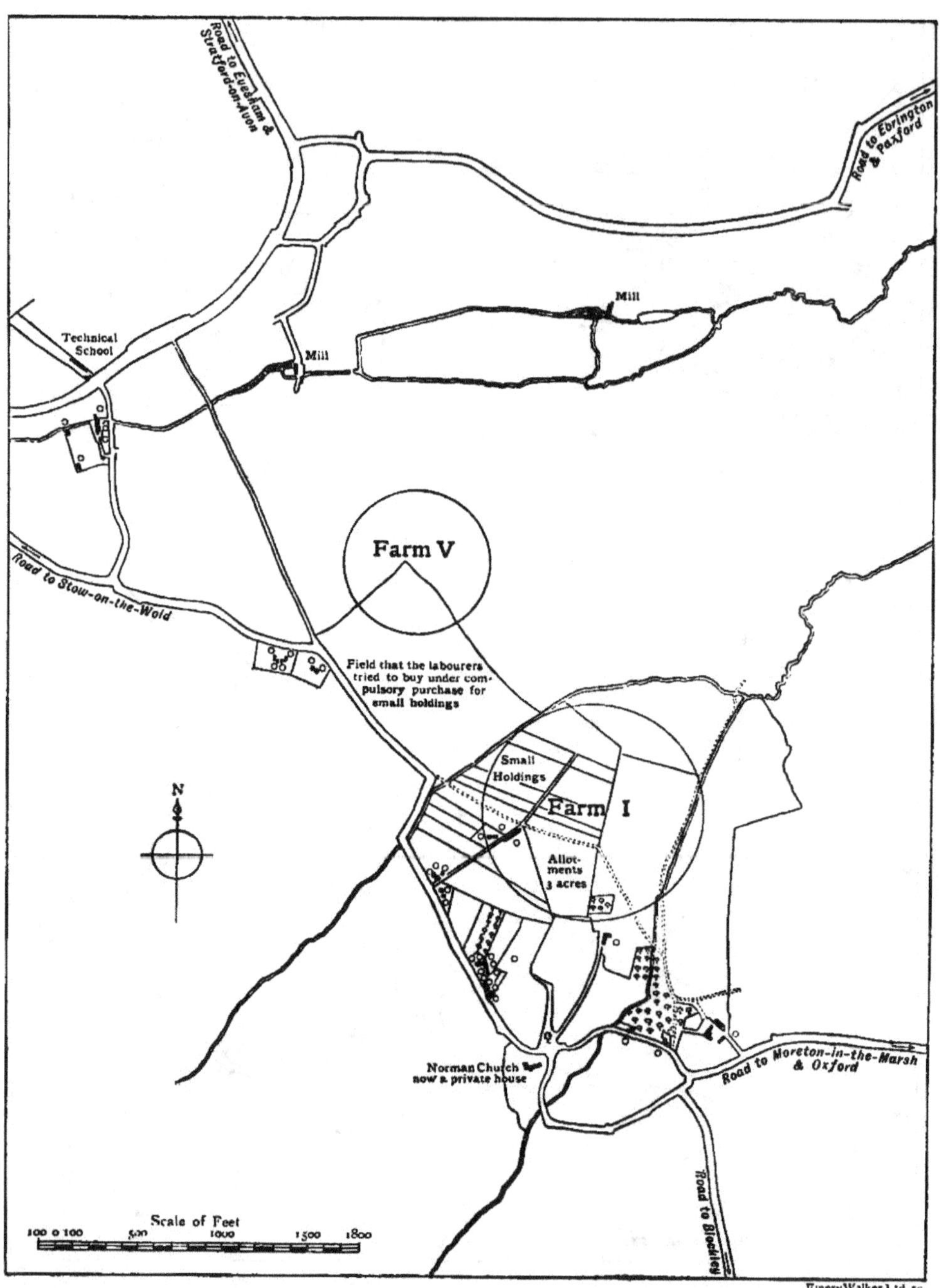

Campden, showing Farm I (the Guild estate) in process of reconstruction.

that a new attempt at grouping in houses and land is being tried, to make good the waste of life entailed in the tied cottage and the make-shift allotment, with its labourers living from hand to mouth. The protest has not in effect gone far. Circumstances have been too strong for us. But it is typical. Thus, one of the small-holders, who is also a craftsman in the workshops shown in the diagram, has to trundle his pig manure a mile before he can get it on to his land ; another has to keep his cow in a hired field a mile and a half away. A point to note, however, is that all the houses are good houses, suitable for a wage-earner of £1 a week* or over, and some of them are two adjoining labourers' cottages of the old squalid type, now made over and thrown into one. Another point to note is the placing of the common barn in the centre of the property, and adjoining the allotments. The building of this barn, together with that of some of the houses, was stopped by the War. The object, indeed, was to do better than the allotment system, a system that usually postulates wage-slave labour, and, in its sordid ugliness, is the sign of a bankrupt individualism.

These plans are only concerned with certain facts in social life and national history; other modifying facts are therefore purposely omitted, but from them we can learn better how to link up the reconstruction of the village with that of Industry as a whole. They serve to illustrate certain fundamentals which we must keep in mind. First, there is a continuity in the basic things : the plough, cattle, trees, fruit, the seasons, and the types of labour that go with them. These things do not change, or, at best, very slowly. They do not fit easily into factory conditions. Where the great city, as we saw in Diagram No. 36, has passed through many transformations, the village has remained. We learn from them next that there is a certain solidarity in the communal life of the past. By implication, anything in the nature of caste is in a modern Democracy no longer possible. The village cannot exist if divided against itself. That is its present condition in England, and that is why it is dying. Finally we are forced to the conclusion that in the interests of the Agricultural life as a whole the ordinary competitive principles, of selling wherever and as how best you can, need revision. From our newer village point of view, we are now considering Agriculture no longer as a life process carried on merely for the benefit of the capitalist farmer, but of the Community as one. It is mechanical power, in this instance railways planned for the service of the great

Reconstruction of Industry and reconstruction of the village must go hand in hand.

---

* Taken at the pre-war wage standard when the average local wage was below 15s.

THE REACTION OF TOWN AND COUNTRY

Industrial centres, that has forced the Agricultural life into a mould that will not hold it, with the result that the mould is cracking.

What, then, do we need for the new life we are trying to build up ? Some solution of the question of the labourer's wage—we must free him from his present wage-slavery ; some system by which he may himself have access to the land, and access by right, not grace ; some control of marketing by which he shall be able to reap what he has sown ; some other interests in the village—by-crafts, summer schools, the drawing of the personal and non-mechanical occupations into the country, where they are better practised than in the town ; and, above all, some control by the village as a whole, or by co-ordinated village groups, of such mechanical power as the village may need. If machinery *Axiom VIII* (see Axiom VIII) is to replace slavery it must be under control. It cannot any longer be exploited privately.

There is, as we have seen, a close tie between the Arts and Crafts, the personal avocations of the hand, and the great primal pursuits of Agriculture. In our day they stand for the same things : intelligent control of mechanical power, organization with a view to true public service, and freedom for the labourer—the little craftsman as distinct from the factory hand. If we are to develop the finer intelligence of the town, we must at the same time remake the village. Perhaps the want is best put in the words of the man whose personal experience of village life most justifies him in forecasting : "To produce for use ; that production should really take place for the benefit of the consumer ; to concentrate, not on profit to individuals, but on advantage and gain to the Community ; to drop in one inspired moment the whole mad sequence of cut-throat Rivalry, insane Waste, disgusting Fraud, and inane Uselessness, which constitute modern Industry ; all this would mean such an enormous liberation of power, such an incalculable increase in the general wealth, that the spectre of poverty would be exorcised for ever, and the numbing anxiety which weighs so heavily now on the lives of millions would be lifted away like an evil cloud. Joy would descend upon life, and the ordinary occupations would become free, spontaneous, and beautiful." *

* Edward Carpenter, "My Days and Dreams," p. 267.

CHAPTER XXXI.—Foresight and the Utopian Habit of Mind.

It is the want of imagination that has degraded our villages, and *Blind civic* that prevents our cities from being properly planned, even as it prevents our making proper provision for the planners, the craftsmen, the labourers who could do the work. This applies to 99 per cent. of the new cities that have grown up in the Industrial era. We must get rid of this reproach. We must understand what is implied in it. Its full meaning grows clearer when, as I have shown, we study the housing conditions of the Dublin of our day, and find streets of three-story houses designed for families of ten, now holding from ninety to a hundred people in each house, with one family to each room;* or when we grasp the significance of the statistical table I showed (see No. 50) of the infant mortality in the ordinary Industrial as compared with the newly planned Garden City. If we look at a well-planned modern city—planned, that is to say, after the coming of the Industrial era, and they are perilously few—Washington, Colorado Springs, Letchworth, Port Sunlight—we always discover some imaginative mind, or rather group of minds, at the back of things, men with foresight. We need more of this, and not only in the planning, but in all the affairs of the city that inevitably lead up to it. We cannot individually, in an age of Democracy, evolve a city; but two or three strong men, of the necessary imagination, can not only do that, they can do what is harder still, transform an old one. Where the group mind is thus imaginatively at work, the prayer of Saint Chrysostom is realized: "when two or three are gathered together" for the sake of something higher than the mere getting of money, they begin to find out where the Great City stands.

And the aim, as we saw in Chapters XII and XIII, is twofold. *The recast-* If it be primarily the giant city—London, Chicago, Berlin, New York *ing of old* —we have to think of, we have also to think of the wise planning *and the* of cities altogether new. The overgrown Industrial City is no longer *making of* a Syracuse, a Florence, a Nuremberg, focused within green fields or *new cities.* a one-mile radius of Charing Cross or Lake Michigan: London and Chicago are over thirty miles across. We can no longer walk as Socrates did with Phædrus to the Ilyssus, or Francis Beaumont to the Mile End to watch the London apprentices drilling on the Waste.

* Dublin Housing Inquiry Commission, 1914.

FORESIGHT AND THE UTOPIAN HABIT OF MIND

Ours are the cities of strap-hangers, and our first need is order in life, so that we find again leisure for thought and new creation. But coincidently we must experiment in the building of new cities. I know fifty cities at least that could with advantage be rebuilt, and rebuilt "to pay."

"In every age of grand scale readjustment," says the writer who was sent by President Wilson to Europe, immediately before the War, to report upon the connexion between Government and Business, "mankind pulls itself together, confounds the specialists, and tears out the partitions of life. It is perceived at such times that faith, and fine art, and civil order, and physical well-being, are really inseparable." [*]

The need for ideas.

That is what we practical Artists and Craftsmen have for the last fifteen years been trying to say in the everyday labour of our workshops. Those of us who have seen far enough ahead, have seen faith, fine art, civil order, and physical well-being as one great fact in life. But we have not been listened to, we have had our work thrown away, our workshops closed down because there was not enough return in them for financiers and exploiters, our educational ventures wrecked, and what we stood for disbelieved in. We ourselves all the time disbelieved in the system; and then came the War and justified our disbelief. The War has shattered the system. "To find a form of government that will not repress the practical arts—that is the gist of the social problem. It always has been so." [†] But it was not the cataclysm of the War that destroyed so much of what was best in English workshop enterprise and Education. Much of this was already crumbling during the ten years that preceded 1914. Without knowing what they were doing, the Post-Impressionist painters, in their incoherent formless pictures, symbolized their age. The War was merely the collapse, whether in England, Germany, or America, of an Industrial condition that was rotten, of a form of government that had neither the vision nor the power to back and save productive and educational enterprise from destruction.

The "social surplus."

We cannot have the city of our dream until we want it, and when we want it we must will it. We must master, and use for the ennoblement of the city, the "social surplus." And when we inquire where this shall be found, in "unearned increment," in "rent," "interest," "profit," "dividend," or wasting away in "graft," or "inefficient labour," or "war"; the inquiry, taking ever various forms, always comes back to one of ethics. The "social surplus" is in our-

[*] C. Fergusson, "The Great News," p. 238.
[†] Ibid. p. 156.

152

selves, a betterment from within, a clearer thinking, a cleaner living, a wider human outlook, a finer ideal of life, a greater productiveness in what is worth while. And in this shaping of the city we have to consider the three great facts of modern life—the labour movement, the organization of Industry on a national scale, the woman's movement. In each is a power without which the Great City cannot be. But if once the appeal to the imagination is made the powers now wasting or at conflict can be brought to the city's aid. When the great financier found us a new generalization for twentieth-century Industry in the phrase, "You cannot unscramble eggs," we suddenly discovered that the Trusts were a fact, and that they had given us a new definition of unearned increment, as "payment for an unnecessary service." We have yet to make sure what, in the light of our Great City, are the *necessary* services. I have in these pages touched on many of them from time to time. The Architect or city builder visualizes them somewhat as follows :—

I leave out the building of homes, and I leave out churches, *What are* for clean and beautiful homes follow as a matter of course any fine *the " City* conception of the City, and churches in the Democratic city are for *services" ?* those who need them. In Democracy all Religion that is not contained within the city ideal itself is a personal matter, an affair of the heart, over which the city can have no control. But there remain all the great, the essential civic needs: water, light, air; the theatre; the Court House; the administrative offices, clean and beautiful in themselves, with clean people inside them; an attractive public service that is in itself a ritual; swimming-pools, stadia and gymnasia for all-round physical development—the sexes apart with the beauty of the body in its nakedness, not clothed in the mediæval manner; schools; hospitals; libraries; in the more favoured cities universities; and in every city that creative centre of civic life, the Art school, gallery, or institute—the home of the endowed productive Guild, whose object shall be ethical discovery in the qualitative and quantitative processes of labour—the right and wrong of it—a constant charting of the waters of life.

For an understanding of all this we must see the City as a *We must see* whole—surveyed as every city should be, well ordered, grouped *the City as* in zones, its industrialism under control, its outlying farms, estates, or *a whole.* villages with their summer schools the necessary parts of its life, and a right balance observed between its intellectual and physical functions. We must see this life as one of healthy interchange between town and country, to keep true that balance now so unfairly and so ignorantly weighted in favour of the town.

An illustration from Portland, Oregon. This realization of the City as a whole is of the essence of our study. Yet how little is it understood! Here is another illustration: In the city of Portland, in Oregon, they have one of the finest library organizations in the United States (see No. 120); the city and the outlying country districts are linked together, and the books are carried in motor-cars by intelligent women librarians to the distant country homes of those who need them, and as they need them. This city also has one of the most magnificent sites in the world—at the junction of two rivers and looking out upon two snow-capped, cloud-veiled volcanoes. So far the citizens have shown a childlike incapacity to relate their city to its surroundings—to make it worthy. They started on a great plan, and they recently built their great new library (see No. 12). But in doing this they threw over their city plan in the interests of their library. This meant that either the plan was not properly thought out, or that the library builders showed a want of vision. The latter may have been right from their point of view; but if, as the result of their placing of the library, they set back the city plan ten or twenty years, they will probably turn out to have been wrong. The issue is one, the City is one, yet almost every modern city can tell some such story.

The City and the larger life. This sense of unity in the City's life we need in order to make actual our ethics. Conceive the City as one, and things will come alive. In the new civics there is this supreme hope. The War, if it has taught us anything, has shown us how the old national gods are dying. They cannot all be right, these tribal gods. So the City of our Utopian habit of mind will bring to man something never brought before—or perhaps only to the Hellenic or the mediæval cities in their fullest life. It will bring a new point of contact between man and the larger life. Through the City will come the new ethics. The fire of tradition, the history in us, that spirit the Greek carried from the Prytaneum, corresponds to what is now our "sentiment of nationality." Of this we shall probably always keep some in our hearts. The other quality—the personal or intimate something which the mediæval citizen perhaps found in the church or patron saint of his own rather than any other city—by which we touch God, or the origin of life, we shall always keep in our inmost hearts. But there is a third point of contact with the larger life that is neither nationality nor religion; it is where we touch our fellow men; it is there, in the enterprise of life, through the Great City, that the new faith enters.

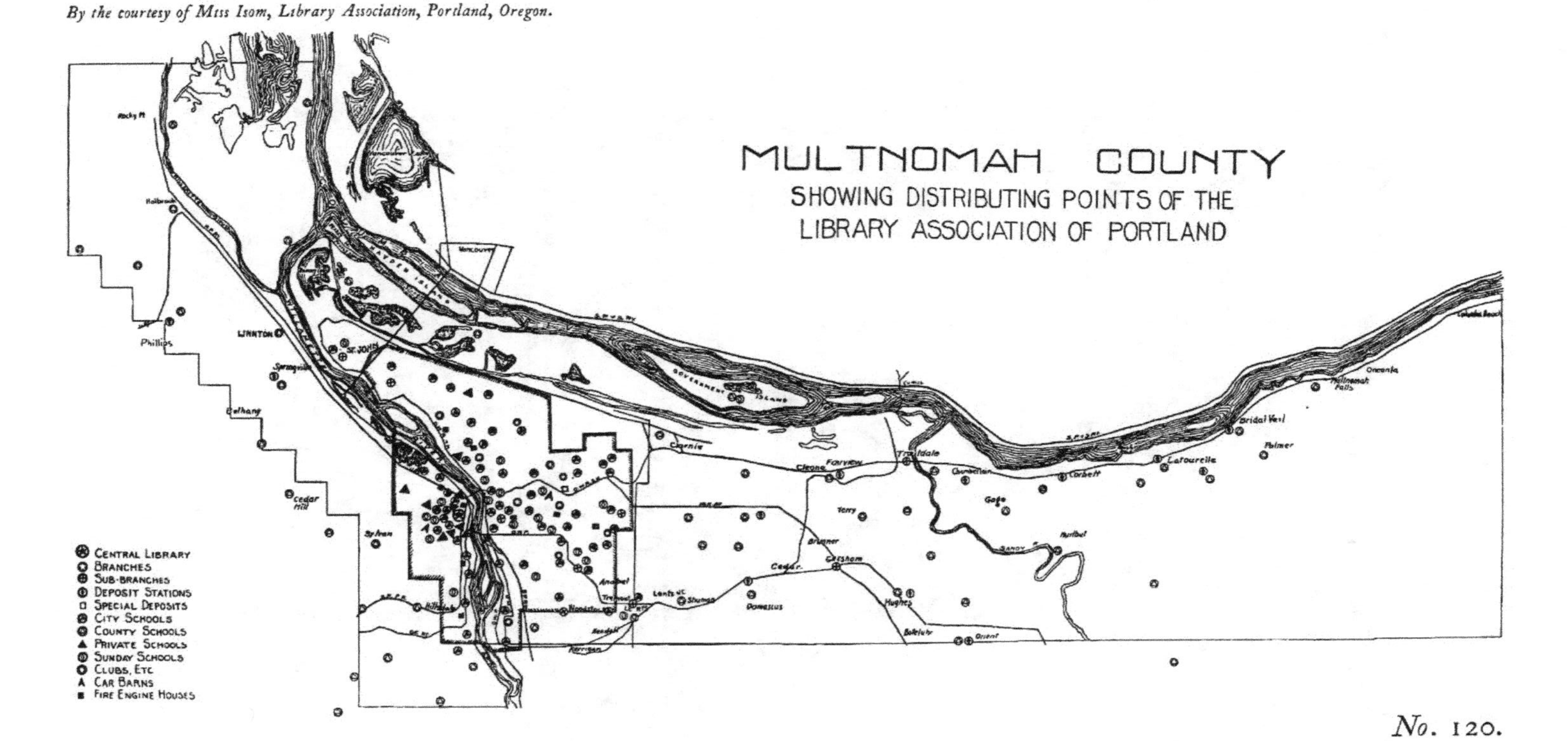

By the courtesy of Miss Isom, Library Association, Portland, Oregon.
MULTNOMAH COUNTY
SHOWING DISTRIBUTING POINTS OF THE
LIBRARY ASSOCIATION OF PORTLAND
CENTRAL LIBRARY
BRANCHES
SUB-BRANCHES
DEPOSIT STATIONS
SPECIAL DEPOSITS
CITY SCHOOLS
COUNTY SCHOOLS
PRIVATE SCHOOLS
SUNDAY SCHOOLS
CLUBS, ETC
CAR BARNS
FIRE ENGINE HOUSES
No. 120.

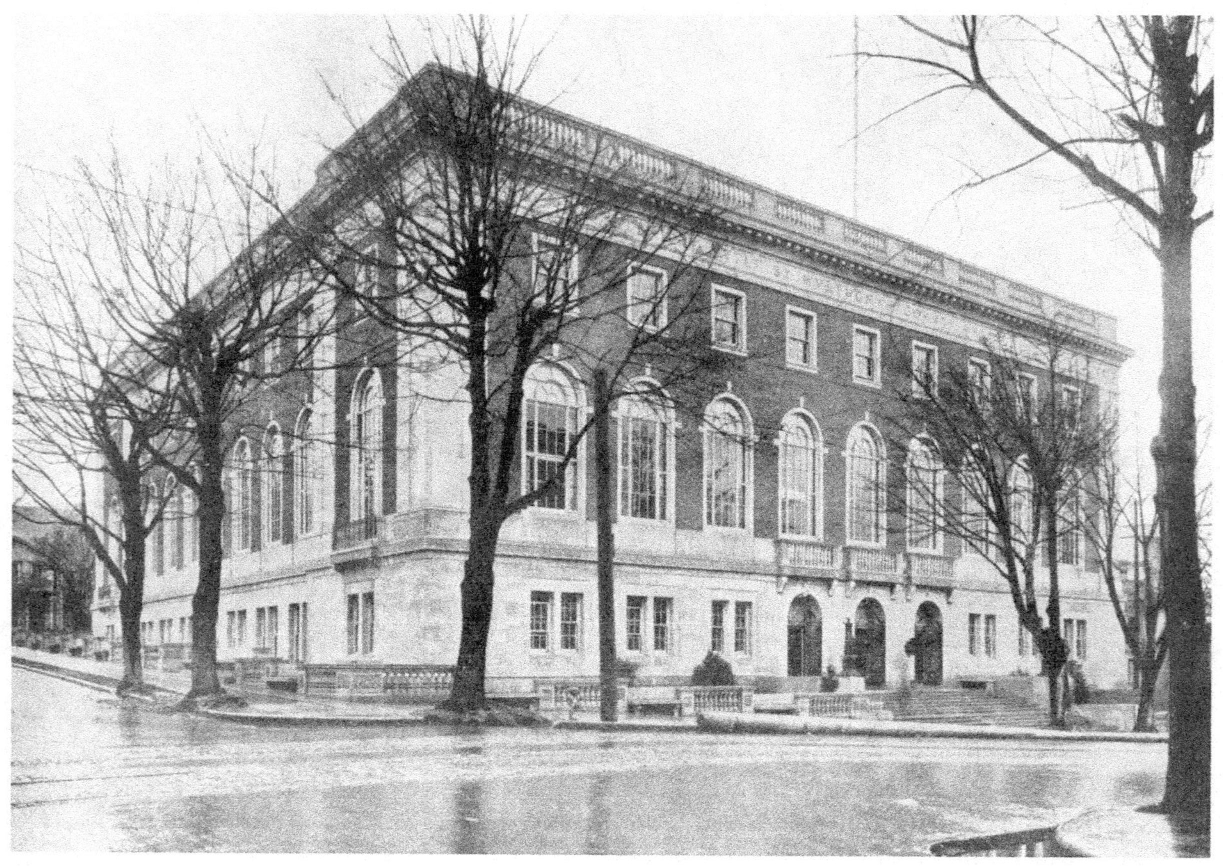

The Central Library, Portland, Oregon.

No. 121.

FORESIGHT AND THE UTOPIAN HABIT OF MIND

It is not for naught that we have rediscovered Visvakarma—the re-incarnation of the godhead in the crafts of the City.

"England will never be civilized till she has added Utopia to her other dominions," said Oscar Wilde, and it was one of the younger school of American political philosophers, I believe, who first used the phrase, "the Utopian habit of mind." For the work we have to do we need it. It is more than a phrase now: it is one of the happier accomplishments we owe to the United States. In Europe we are apt to jeer at the Americans for their superficiality and love of the rhetorical and spectacular, their happy-go-lucky, hit-or-miss altruism; it were better if we gave them credit for their power of sympathetic organization, their live desire to make things move. In that vast amorphous continent, where the peoples of Europe have been peppered out by the castor of Industrialism, the one thing that seems certain and that shows promise is the City of Democracy. There, despite all the waste, and the uncleanness, and the graft, has grown up in the last twenty-five years a civic rivalry that can only be paralleled by the Greek or mediæval cities. It is not yet a rivalry in Beauty, or in noble living, that has still to be discovered; but the motive power is there, and the civic pride. They have the Utopian habit of mind. It is this that makes so many Americans—Henry Ford and his "Peace Ark," Jane Addams with her pilgrimage of grace to the Chancelleries of Europe, Andrew Carnegie and his libraries, Joseph Fels and his land schemes—so lovable in their quixotism. To us Europeans they are such strange and yet such delightful people to meet. Their plans may be impracticable: that does not matter; something of them is in Utopia, and that much of them will live, for it is there the Great City stands.

The word "Democracy" has been often used in these pages. *The Great* It has never been used merely as a political formula, but always with *City.* some greater idea or faith behind. In all the activities of the City we have to learn what this faith means—in our methods of business, in the manner and nobility of our building, in our libraries and schools, in our way of looking at money or estimating the value of population. We must, especially we English, no longer be afraid of ideas; we must be willing to try experiments, not blind to reason, not timid of truth. We must not shrink from realities—the women's suffrage question, the labour question, the sex question—we must allow everything to be challenged by imagination. So only shall we grow civilized. It has been the privilege of Englishmen ever and again to remind Americans

FORESIGHT AND THE UTOPIAN HABIT OF MIND

of their greatest poet—what he stood for, what was the Democracy he interpreted. In closing this study of the City, it may not be out of place to recall a certain noble passage that not only sums up the best of all the wisdom of the past, but is alive with the faith of all reformers :—

The place where a great city stands is not the place of stretch'd wharves, docks,
    manufactures, deposits of produce merely,
Nor the place of ceaseless salutes of new-comers or the anchor-lifters of the departing,
Nor the place of the tallest and costliest buildings or shops selling goods from the rest
    of the earth,
Nor the place of the best libraries and schools, nor the place where money is plentiest,
Nor the place of the most numerous population.

Where the city stands with the brawniest breed of orators and bards,
Where the city stands that is belov'd by these, and loves them in return and understands
    them,
Where no monuments exist to heroes but in the common words and deeds,
Where thrift is in its place, and prudence is in its place,
Where the men and women think lightly of the laws,
Where the slave ceases, and the master of slaves ceases,
Where the populace rise at once against the never-ending audacity of elected persons,
Where fierce men and women pour forth as the sea to the whistle of death pours
    its sweeping and unripped waves,
Where outside authority enters always after the precedence of inside authority,
Where the citizen is always the head and ideal, the President, Mayor, Governor and what
    not, are agents for pay,
Where children are taught to be laws to themselves, and to depend on themselves,
Where equanimity is illustrated in affairs,
Where speculations on the soul are encouraged,
Where women walk in public processions in the streets the same as men ;
Where the city of the faithfullest friends stands,
Where the city of the cleanliness of the sexes stands,
Where the city of the healthiest fathers stands,
Where the city of the best-bodied mothers stands,
There the great city stands.

FINIS.